Social Work, Welfare and the State

Social Work, Welfare and the State

Edited by Noel Parry, Michael Rustin and Carole Satyamurti

SAGE Publications   Beverly Hills

© Edward Arnold (Publishers) Ltd 1979

First published 1979 by
Edward Arnold (Publishers) Ltd
41 Bedford Square
London WC1B 3DQ

Published in the United States of America 1980
by Sage Publications Inc.
275 South Beverly Drive
Beverly Hills California 90212

ISBN 0-8039-1415-6

Library of Congress Catalog Card No. 79-67578

Printed in Great Britain

Contents

Preface

The idea for this book grew out of conversations among sociologists at North East London Polytechnic who were involved with the teaching of sociology to social work students. We agreed that there were available too few recent and up-to-date books which applied a sociological and historical perspective to the field of social work. It was thought likely that the problems of teaching sociology to social workers would be shared by teachers in a wide range of educational institutions including polytechnics, universities and colleges of further education. As a result, a one-day conference was held in January 1977 at the North East London Polytechnic on the theme of sociology and social work and under the auspices of the organization, Sociologists in Polytechnics (SIP).

After considering the papers given at the conference and the related discussions, it was thought worthwhile to go a stage further and produce a book.

Not all the papers in this collection were presented at the conference but all have been commissioned with the aim of providing the reader with a structural and historical framework within which to situate modern social work. There has been no attempt to provide only one political viewpoint but on the contrary we aim to offer a variety of views. The editors own positions are expressed in their individual contributions and in the conclusions. While the primary orientation of the book is sociological and historical, the intention has not been only to appeal to an academic audience and to students, but also to practising social workers, administrators, voluntary workers and elected representatives, and indeed to all who are engaged in whatever way in the social work enterprise.

The editors wish most especially to acknowledge the generous assistance given by José Parry in their editorial functions. We would also like to thank the secretarial staff of North East London Polytechnic and the Polytechnic of North London who typed the manuscript under conditions where there were competing claims on their time and energy. Finally, acknowledgement should be made to library staff in several institutions whose help was invaluable.

1

State formation and social policy until 1871

Philip Corrigan and Val Corrigan

Introductory remarks

In this chapter we raise some questions about social policy in England and Wales in the period before 1871 when the creation of the Local Government Board initiates a characteristically modern state apparatus. We do not provide a detailed historical account. The note on further reading (pp. 18) indicates further resources.[1]

The chapter falls into two parts: the first examines the period from the 1530s to the 1830s, linking two stages which have both been called 'revolutions in government'. Our second section looks at the period from the 1830s to 1871.

There are, first, some general questions. What is 'social policy'? Other strategic considerations of state (such as foreign or fiscal policy) have fairly obvious objects to which they refer, but what is the object to which 'social policy' addresses itself? 'Policy' is not an easy noun, shading into matters of policing on the one hand and blurring with politics on the other.[2] This vagueness of both adjective and noun is part of the answer to our problem

1. We have drawn from a wide range of doctoral research, both in progress: V. Corrigan ('Poor law administration in Tynemouth'); R. Saville ('State and economy, c. 1680–1720s'); C. Jones ('Social work policy') and T. Novak ('Social security and the state'); and recently completed: R. Johnson, *The education department 1839–1864* (PhD, Cambridge, 1968); P. G. Richards, *The state and the working class, 1833–1841* (PhD, Birmingham, 1975).

Comparative studies are very important. For example, we stress the general applicability of Michel Foucault's work and the theoretical significance of recent American studies of 'regulating the poor' (Piven and Cloward, 1974) and 'controlling the "dangerous classes"' (Mandell, 1975) by welfare.

2. This is fully explored in P. Corrigan, *State formation and moral regulation in nineteenth-century Britain* (PhD, Durham, 1977; 1978; forthcoming 1979). A brief sketch is available within Corrigan, Ramsay and Sayer (1977). A comprehensive history of social policy has yet to be written: staging posts are Eden, Nicholls, Aschrott, the Webbs, Beales, Bruce and Fraser; note the differing views of Paul (1917) or Slater (1930) and such important appeals from below as Fish's *Supplication* (1528) or those surveyed by Christopher Hill (1972).

in that it prompts the famous question, 'Who, whom?' To whom is 'society' a problem which can be solved? Who is designated by the 'social'? Who are the agents (and who the agency) to define and attend to specifically social problems? A full answer raises questions of state power, agency, inception, and change. These questions are now asked in historical studies of state formation,[3] which must be synchronized with the development of capitalism in England.[4]

Study of all these investigations confirms Marx's general view of state formation (1867, 751), probably more generally known in Weber's famous comment (1918, 78): ' "Every state is founded on force", said Trotsky. ... That is indeed right.'[5] But, as Weber immediately notes, that force is always sanctioned by legitimacy and the state therefore deals in 'moral' matters.[6] It is the state's attempt to monopolize those definitions and actions central to social policy which is the major theme of this chapter. The agencies of state develop and change in relation to changing definitions of the situation.

The central social policy we shall examine relates to the complex formation and regulation of the labour market in England and Wales.[7] From this follows a particular problem, which we suggest is *the* 'social problem' – the consequences of a certain kind of poverty. We emphasize that it is the consequences rather than 'poverty in general'; the latter was (and is, Corrigan, 1977a) seen as not merely tolerable but inevitable. The sociology of the periodic rediscovery of poverty (or, as earlier generations called it, 'the Condition of England' question) remains to be written.

There are always two kinds of poor people – those who can be pitied and patronized (the 'impotent' or 'deserving') and those who, in truth, are to be feared (the sturdy or 'able-bodied'). The latter have to be forced or

3. Compare both older studies, such as those of Hintze or Bloch (1940, I, part 3, II, ch. 31), or recent work: Anderson (1974a, part 2, Section 1; 1974b, part 1); Tilly (1975); Strayer (1977).

4. The 'peculiarities of the English' have been charted by E. P. Thompson (1965) and resurveyed by R. Johnson (1976b) and Gray 1976, 1978). Cf. Hilton (1973); Hill (1967, 1972); Thompson (1963 onwards); Hobsbawm (1968, 1975); together with older studies: Marx (1867, part 8); Weber (1920, part 4); Mantoux (1928); and Sweezy (1938). The journal *Past and Present* (1952 onwards) is invaluable.

5. For the original statement by Trotsky see Deutscher (1954, 370). We are not suggesting either that marxism and sociology are identical, or that Weber, among practitioners of the latter, and Trotsky, of the former, are singular in this analysis. The state is the backbone of much classical sociology.

6. By 'moral' we follow the nineteenth-century use (and that of Durkheim) which equated the term with 'social'. See the discussion in Corrigan thesis, p. ii and *passim*. More generally note that both J. S. Mill (1840, 157) and S. Webb (1890, 104 – our thanks to T. Novak for this reference) speak of how the state must be made to seem a great 'benefit society'. This construction (and sustaining that appearance) is a violent story. Something of

encouraged to labour, although at different times other expedients have been used, such as coercively ('shovelling out paupers') or by inducement (as with emigration schemes) transplanting the problem.

From revolution to revolution: the pre-history of 1834

The origins of both the modern English state and social policy are to be found in the Tudor 'revolution in government'.[8] It is also in this period that the market forms of the capitalist mode of production were being established. Marx (1858, 507) relates both:

When e.g. the great English landowners dismissed their retainers, who had, together with them, consumed the surplus product of the land; when further their tenants chased off the smaller cottagers etc., then, firstly a mass of living labour powers was thereby thrown onto the *labour market*, a mass which was free in a double sense, free from the old relations of clientship, bondage and servitude, and secondly free of all belongings and possessions, and of every objective, material form of being, *free of all property*; dependent on the sale of its labour capacity or on begging, vagabondage and robbery as its only source of income. It is a matter of historic record that they tried the latter first, but were driven off this road by gallows, stocks and whippings, onto the narrow path to the labour market; owing to this fact, the *governments*, e.g. of Henry VII, VIII appear as conditions of the historic dissolution process and as makers of the conditions for the existence of capital.

Crucial to Tudor social policy was the demonic trilogy of 'rogues, vagabonds and sturdy beggars', that is, the problem of a labour force that has to be mobile but which must not be allowed to wander out of the labour market altogether. Here are the roots of those enduring categories of the poor – 'deserving' (the aged, sick, deserted or helpless) and

the overall strategy may be gleaned from the titles which the Webbs gave to their two volumes published from their minority report: *The break-up of the poor law* (1909a) and *The public organization of the labour market* (1909b). We mention the Webbs here to argue against the usual compartmentalization and 'stages-theory' of social policy. The same point is recalled when we remind readers that Beveridge's *Unemployment* also appeared in 1909 (see here Yeo, 1975, *Capitalism, leisure and voluntary organisation*. Paper to the Society for the Study of Labour History Conference, Sussex). For a discussion of the similarities between the Webbs and Fabianism and Bentham and James Mill (and the Radicals) see Corrigan thesis, ch. 5.

7. It was Marx's view, in the sketch he made for *Capital* (1858, 508), that the real accumulation of capital concerns labour: '*Capital proper does nothing but bring together the mass of hands and instruments which it finds. ... It agglomerates them under its command.* That is its *real stockpiling*; the stockpiling of workers, along with their instruments, at particular points. ... The development of exchange value ... dissolves production which is more oriented to direct use value and its corresponding forms of property ... and thus pushes forward towards the making of the labour market.' Mishra (1975) discusses Marx. The earlier analyses of Beales (1945) and Goldthorpe (1964) should not be overlooked.

8. Cf. Elton (1953a, 1953b, 1972, 1973); Hoskins (1976).

'undeserving' (those able to work). These categories were complicated by the need to permit movement for seasonal migrant workers, *bona fide* travellers, and all workers whose labour might be required in different places at differing times, but to resist the spread of vagrancy.

This Tudor revolution begins the story of how 'relieving the poor' requires increasing 'central capability' in the state:[9] more and more uniform, national (or even imperial) agencies are co-ordinated to bring about adjustment and re-creation of a certain set of social relations. In the sixteenth century, existing agencies such as the church, aristocracy and gentry, were introduced to 'policing' (related in the work of Elton); and two local institutions, the parish church and the justices of the peace were considerably strengthened. The Erastianization of the church was a turning point in a social policy directed against insurrection. The parish church was made a state agency by the introduction of compulsory registration of births, marriages and deaths in 1538. Cromwell identified the true purpose of this as to avoid disputes over age, descent and title 'and for knowledge of whether any person is our subject or no'. The problem of agencies is central to his circular of December 1538, directed to JPs, which includes an insistence on their enforcing 'the laws against vagabonds'. His 'social policy' (Elton, 1972, 260) was part of the consolidation of the 'political nation' (discussed by Loades, 1974) and responds to new capitalist problems – those in towns (Clark, 1976) and those of enclosures and 'Dearth' (Walker, 1976).[10] No less crucial were the changes in cultural norms and popular mentalities,[11] crucial because it was through notions of 'justice' and 'order', radically altered in the post-feudal period, that the state was consolidated and a *social* policy made possible.

The regulation of the labour market was central – the need to 'correctly handle' the contradiction between a policy for social tranquillity, preferring 'the common people' to know and remain in their place, and a policy for economic growth, needing a relatively mobile labour force. The legislation

9. 'Central capability' is a term used by Lee (1974); it is the largely unrecognized object of administrative history. Lafitte (1974) gives a general analysis of the 'relief function'; on which note also Piven and Cloward (1974, p. xiii).

10. It is relevant to stress, as Asa Briggs and others have done, the interconnectedness of military and social policy. Pound (1971, 5) draws attention to the development of the agency of provost marshals in London to apprehend and punish groups of discharged soldiers and sailors found begging or rioting. Flinn (1961, 1971) relates the inception of 'public works' to discharged soldiers after 1815. Similar points 'should be made about Lloyd George's 'Land fit for heroes' strategy or the sustained impact of changes during the 1939–45 war.

11. K. Thomas (1971) and C. Hill (1972) cover the major issues, but Tillyard's discussion of Elizabethan 'order' (1943) and Bossy's review essay on holiness (1977) are both important.

regarding the poor passed in the next three hundred years represents repeated efforts to balance the two.

An act of 1531 permitted 'licensed' begging by 'genuine' cases, but non-deserving beggars were to be whipped and returned whence they had come.[12] In 1536 another act outlined a system by which voluntary contributions were to be collected and distributed by parish authorities, haphazard alms-giving was to be curtailed, and the 'sturdy beggar' was to be 'whipped the first time, his right ear cropped the second time, and if he again offend, to be sent to the next gaol ... and if convicted, shall suffer execution as a felon and an enemy of the commonwealth.' A short-lived act of 1547 (repealed, because unenforceable, in 1550) went so far as to reintroduce slavery for any able-bodied person refusing to work for three days or more.

It is a feature of this social policy that vagrancy and the regulation of labour is linked with the relief of the poor unable to labour. Thus, in 1563 two related statutes were passed, one establishing the legal duty of all members of the parish to contribute to the maintenance of 'their' poor, the sanction for non-compliance being (ultimately) prison. The second, the Statute of Artificers, established entry requirements for the industrial crafts, all men not qualified being required to work as agricultural labourers; wage rates for all trades were also established. An act of 1572 repeats the punishments of the 1531 act for the demonic trilogy of 'outrageous enemies to the common weal' (rogues, vagabonds and sturdy beggars); but a small group of legitimate travellers, who were not be to be molested, is recognized.[13] The same act makes the payment of weekly contributions toward the support of 'aged and impotent' poor people compulsory for every inhabitant of 'every city, borough, town, village, hamlet or place'. There were, of course, problems in enforcing this provision. Four years later, urban authorities were empowered to provide stock-in-trade in order to 'set the poor on work' in times of unemployment. In 1597 the post of parish overseer was created (itself 'overseen' by the JPs) to administer poor relief. That year an act directed

12. Further information can be found in Pound (1971 – criticized in Beier, 1974). For charities before 1660, see Jordan (1959). Some useful insights into the family can be found in Robertson and Curtin (1977) and in a review essay by E. P. Thompson, *New Society*, 8 September 1977.
13. Regarding those whom we still call 'travellers', note the attempted genocide of gypsies: 'the wretched, wily, wandering vagabonds calling and naming themselves Egyptians' (qua Pound, 1971, 29). An act of 1530 ordered that all gypsies be imprisoned; a later act (1554) ordered their execution as felons. In 1562 anyone associating with them was to be apprehended as a felon. These travellers, as Beier (1974) and Slack (1974) show, like most 'vagrants', were simply trying to stay alive.

parish authorities to return all 'wandering persons and common labourers' to their native parish, 'there to put him or herself to labour as a true subject ought to do'. But if such persons appeared to be 'dangerous to the inferior sort of people', the ultimate sanction of banishment was provided.

All this legislation was consolidated in the '43rd Elizabeth', the act of 1601, which was the source of some elements of social policy law until the middle of the twentieth century. Note, furthermore, that one clause declares: 'The father and grandfather, the mother and grandmother, and the children of every poor, old, lame, blind, and impotent person, or other person not able to work, being of sufficient ability [must] at their own charge relieve and maintain every such poor person.' Those whose relatives were not 'of sufficient ability', or who had no relatives, were to be maintained by the parish. This emphasis on familial responsibility was made repeatedly, up to and including the Poor Law Act of 1930 (section 14 reads: 'It shall be the duty of the father, grandfather, mother, grandmother, husband or child, of a poor, old, blind, lame, or impotent person or other poor person not able to work, if possessed of sufficient means, to relieve and maintain that person.') This reiteration emphasizes the enduring nature of the problem of trying to enforce familial responsibility, as does the massive volume of litigation right into the twentieth century in which parishes engaged to force relatives to pay their contributions.

Apprenticeship and child labour were also features of the act of 1601 (usually lasting from age 7 to 24 for men or 21 for women, younger if she married). The advisability of putting children to a trade by which they could make their own living was repeated in much legislation. Since apprenticeship gave rights to 'settlement', discussed below, many overseers bound children to masters in another parish, ridding their own parish of responsibility for good; fees were often paid to 'ease' this transaction (George, 1931, 124 ff; G. Taylor, 1969, 45 ff). This practice of drafting or selling children into the workplace increased with the advent of factory production: we have the story of one such boy (Blencoe, 1832) and Marx noted cases in the 1860s (1867, 267 ff). The direction of labour is, of course, a feature of social policy in recent times: state-funded training agencies supplied servants from the 'depressed areas' to the Home Counties in the 1930s.

Questions of 'settlement' relate, once again, to the balance between tying people to their 'place' and allowing the movement of labour to find work. It had been the subject of legislation and legal precedent since at least the fourteenth century. A pauper's 'settlement' (J. S. Taylor, 1976) determined which parish would take responsibility for her or him. The Poor Relief Act of 1662, like the '43rd Elizabeth', was a statement of existing law as well as of new principles: it listed the recognized qualifications for claiming a 'settlement' in a parish 'either as a native, a householder, sojourner, apprentice or servant'. The unqualified (except those who either rented a house worth £10 a year or who had remained there for forty days) were to be removed to their own parish. Significantly, exceptions were allowed for migrant workers or workers seeking employment, who had to equip themselves with a certificate from their own parish. A statute of 1697 increased the means of qualifying to eleven (including 'annual hiring') although some fell into abeyance. More flexibility was introduced in 1795, when an act limited the overseers' rights of removal until the person became 'actually chargeable', that is applied for relief. In all this, those adjudged 'rogues, vagabonds and persons of evil repute' were excepted.

As the report of the Royal Commission on the Poor Laws recognized in 1834 (73): 'The great object of our early pauper legislation seems to have been the restraint of vagrancy.' Chamblis, in his 'sociological analysis of the law of vagrancy' (1964) has noted the steady criminalization of the vagrant in the 1530s and later. Further studies, particularly of the Elizabethan period,[14] have been made by Beier (1974), Slack (1974), who examines the period 1598–1665 and G. Taylor (1969), for 1660–1834. Christopher Hill (1972, 32) argues that these 'masterless men ... servants to nobody ... were anomalies, potential dissolvents of the society.' Not only were they without a master, they had 'no fixed abode' – still a disqualification for certain basic benefits today.

Hill (1972, 33 and 40) points to the significance of two kinds of territory for these 'servants to nobody' – London, with more casual labour, more charities and better 'prospects for earning a dishonest living' and the older 'wastes': 'Forests and woods encouraged idleness, contemporaries complained' (cf. Thompson, 1975; Beier, 1976). Hill is pointing to a significant social space and an extended struggle. What is at issue is the defining of some ways of making a living, or staying alive, as criminal. The history of social policy has to be placed into the context of recent social history of 'law and order' from the seventeenth century onwards. As Peter Linebaugh (1972, 15) has written: 'The changing nature of crime certainly related to the evolution of the industrial capitalist system.' Marx recognized, in his seminal piece of journalism about the transformation of rights to common materials into the theft of private

14. On Elizabethan law and order, see Aydellotte (1913); Hurstfield (1973); Oxley (1973). Samaha's study of Elizabethan Essex (1974) can be complemented by many published Calendars of Assize. That for Elizabethan Hertfordshire (HMSO, 1976) shows the extent of political and economic crime.

property,[15] that the expansion of the labour market to include all available labour depends on the restriction of customary and common rights, such as access to land, game or fuel, which saved some people from having to seek any or all of their income as cash from wage labour. A true history of social policy will have to encompass the attempt to transform customs into crimes, not only by force but inside people's heads; that the struggle continues is a measure of its failure. We still live in an incompletely monetized labour market today.

In the later seventeenth and eighteenth centuries[16] innovations in social policy included early recognition of certain permanent features of capitalism, such as unemployment. Houses of industry or workhouses (as compared with poorhouses, in which the impotent poor were placed) were built, and the able-bodied poor were set on work there, instead of being given raw materials to work up in their homes (J. S. Taylor, 1972). Under a statute of 1722, parishes were given the discretionary power to refuse relief except in this 'in-house' (or 'indoor') form. In many cases, however, a single institution was provided, in which deserving and undeserving, aged, sick, children and prostitutes were housed together, under a contractor, who tendered to keep them at the lowest possible price per head. Not only was unemployment recognized, but an act of 1757 specifically related destitution, *the* social problem of rural areas, to the socially 'approved' policy of enclosures; this act directed funds into the hands of enclosure commissioners 'to be applied to the relief of the poor ... where woods and pastures had been enclosed.' By then, as Mantoux shows (1928, ch. 3), engrossing as much as enclosure rendered the poor homeless, just as the new farming methods brought new forms of property relations.

By the end of the eighteenth century many elements of 'the 1834 system' had been introduced. Gilbert's act of 1782 enabled parishes to combine in administering enlarged workhouses, and the able-bodied could be found work or given doles of money ('outdoor relief'). As with so many social policies, this built on the experience of such pioneering unions as

15. Marx (1842), is explicated by Linebaugh (1976). On these areas see Beattie (1974); Linebaugh (1972); E. P. Thompson (1963, 1971, 1972, 1975); D. Hay (1975a, 1975b); D. Jones (1974, 1976, 1977); Ditton (1976). On agricultural changes, Mantoux (1928, ch. 3); Saville (1969); Hill (1972); E. P. Thompson (1977); Appleby (1975). Theoretical issues are discussed by these and the following: Mayer (1959); Hammen (1972); Lezonick (1974).

16. We have had to ignore the years of the English Revolution. Apart from Oxley (1973) and G. Taylor (1969) the extended debate about the accuracy of the 1834 Report also provides much useful data on the old poor law: Blaug (1963, 1964) is criticized by J. S. Taylor (1969, 1972); McCloskey (1972); Tucker (1975); see also Huzel (1969) and Baugh (1975). For charities after 1660, see Owen (1965).

that at Bristol in 1696. The larger workhouses were not popular (riots against their introduction are described by George, 1931, 98 ff) and comparatively few parishes adopted Gilbert's act. Bad harvests between 1794 and 1800, plus extensive purchases by the state (whose army and navy were pursuing their crusade against revolution in France), led to rapid price rises in staple foods. Local property-owners, especially in the agricultural counties of the south (most famously in Speenhamland, Berkshire, in 1795), encouraged overseers to give labourers doles to supplement low wages or to issue bread or flour at reduced prices or even free. This 'pauperization' and 'demoralization' was decried by contemporaries (and some modern historians, George, 1931, 96; cf. G. Taylor, 1969, 33 ff) and repeated gestures were made toward change, including the statutes of 1795 and 1815 which extended entitlement to relief. An enabling act of 1819 permitted the parish ratepayers to delegate the administration of the poor laws to a small committee, or 'select vestry', in each parish.

From the 1830s to the 1860s[17]

Since the source of much that animates our chapter is the writings of the state servants themselves, we can allow one to set the 1830s reforms in context for us. On 25 June 1911, George Askwith told the cabinet:

> It looks as if we were in the presence of one of those periodic upheavals in the labour world such as occurred in 1833–4, and from time to time since that date, each succeeding occurrence showing a marked advance in organization on the part of the workers and the necessity for a corresponding change in tactics on the part of the employers. [PRO CAB/37/107, 1911, no. 70; quoted Winter, 1974, 22.]

As Paul Mantoux has shown, between the 1770s and the 1830s new class organizations, and a more comprehensive 'central capability' on the part of the state, were being constructed.

To understand the differential class perception of social policy we have to recall that what Halevy (1923, 25) calls English 'counter-revolutionary terror',[18] in the 1810s and before, was one face of social policy, as the

---

17. The fifty years from the ending of the wars against Napoleon to the 1860s reforms are of crucial significance in the history of social policy. In sum, changes which would have been critically destabilizing in the early years have become the commonplace of administrative politics by the later years. In all these changes the state's donation of an appropriate 'political form', as Marx and Engels depict it, is central.

18. Apart from E. P. Thompson (1963), both White (1957) and Barrington Moore (1966) recognize, in the latter's words, such 'contributions of violence to gradualism'. Halevy's two essays (1919, 1922) remain starting points for state/labour relations; for recent attempts at a general theory see MacDonald (1976) and Ramsay (1977).

reforming 1830s was another (Richards, 1975; Finlayson, 1969; Llewellyn, 1972; Lubenow, 1971; Ward, 1970). Both demonstrate the new regulating capacity of the state, creating and sustaining the structures without which effective exchange relations would not be possible (A. J. Taylor, 1972; Corrigan thesis, ch. 1). Not only were the wars against Napoleon central to hastening changes in productive capacity, they helped form the specifically bourgeois and anti-French nationalism which is also a part of the modern English democratic nation-state (Newman, 1975). We must beware, however, the construction of a too solid, and causal, model of how ideas 'made' policy. The force of circumstances (and the great resources of flexibility within English social policy in general) is evidenced in the Poor Employment Act of 1817 (Flinn, 1961, 1971) from which the Public Works Loans Board later developed. This act of 1817 intervened directly in the labour market, facilitated a programme of 'public works', and enabled a state fiscal policy to be implemented.

There were other important transformations, above all in the conceptions of 'work' and 'non-work' and the making of factory discipline, which have been admirably surveyed (Pollard, 1963, 1965; Thompson, 1967; Reid, 1976). Many of the social policy changes of the 1830s were related to this disciplining of the workforce and regulation of the labour market. Central to local and societal changes were new conceptions of 'idleness' (Corrigan and Gillespie, 1974) as opposed to both 'useful toil' and 'rational amusements'. The theme persists: in 1872 one writer on social questions could still refer to 'idle and vicious paupers' (Stratton, 1872) and the same kind of explanation ('unstructured leisure activities') was used in relation to juvenile 'crime' in the 1960s.

The Poor Law Amendment Act of 1834 needs to be set into this context.[19] For Chadwick and Nassau Senior, the joint authors of the 1834 Report, their policy was intimately and flexibly related to regulating the labour market. Recent local studies (Digby, 1975, for example) demonstrate this clearly. The legislation of the 1830s – the Great Reform Act of 1832, the Municipal Corporations Act of 1835, the more diffuse (but no less powerful) policy initiatives on schools, factories and mines, plus the developments which were built on such foundations (Corrigan thesis, chs 4–5; Roberts, 1960) – represents an attempt to create and sustain a society-wide regulation. The establishment of this conceptual, normative and practical paradigm provided the means by which social

19. The vast literature on 1834 and beyond is mentioned in the note on further reading above; it is surveyed by the editors of the Penguin classics edition of the 1834 Report and by Fraser (1976).

policy legislation after the mid-nineteenth century could be framed in a less directly 'improving' and a more apparently neutral or 'liberal' vocabulary. This is never purely coercive (although, as the 1834 Report, p. 277, states the workhouses *were* to be 'objects of terror'), but involves moral classification and regulation. The intimate connection between the franchise, gender and poverty shows this clearly enough in poor law practice. The last paragraph of the 1834 Report shows the theoretical implications as clearly.

The architects of these reforms saw their policy leading to a gradual disappearance of coercion, as new 'kinds' of people were created by the new social forms. Throughout the nineteenth century this notion is often repeated: 34 years before T. H. Green's famous formulae in his defence of Liberal legislation, W. J. E. Bennett (1846, 43) claimed that: 'A just expenditure on education would relieve us of the overwhelming burden under which we now labour in these three evils ("poor laws, police, and prisons").' An 'educational solution' was a paradigm for social policy, as long as we recall that by 'education' far more than merely reading and writing was to be undertaken.

This legislation of the 1830s has certain general features which mark out that period as a similar 'revolution' to that of Tudor social policy. First, the 1836 Registration Act – partly a response to requests from state officials connected with both factory and poor law policies – provided for civil registration of births, deaths and marriages. This act displaced the church as a central agency in favour of the civil parish and civil servants. It was also part of a wider movement: in 1833 the first of many Statistical Societies had been founded in Manchester and G. R. Porter had been appointed to the new Department of Statistics within the Board of Trade (Cullen, 1975). The state's increasing compulsory powers of data collection are so extensive by the 1970s that we take them for granted. Secondly, there is a search for the right 'social form' which will facilitate the simplest, cheapest, yet most effective, regulation. This is starkly evident in both the published and private deliberations which have been examined. Among the 'remedial measures' of the 1834 Report is a statement of the importance of the 'agency for carrying into effect the intentions of the legislature' – the lack of such agency being considered a contributory factor to previous failure. The regulation that is central to the 1830s revolution involved many instances of a central agency (for the collection of data and the attempted standardization of provision nationally) and local agencies (applying regulations flexibly, in tune with local conditions). These were linked by a new kind of official and a new set of procedures – inspection.[20] Factories, schools, mines, poor law unions, and other institutions were all subject to 'gentle' standardization (later made more coercive through the practice of audit), which spread knowledge of the 'best' practices among similar institutions, very frequently by reference to a 'model' (officially or privately sponsored). This is part of a strategy for capitalist growth.

Thirdly, all these changes were conceptualized within a national system of improvement which involved national and local class struggles over implementation.[21] The basis of this system was the individual: improvement depended upon 'character' and thus real change was to be self-change, above all in 'habits' (R. Johnson, 1970, 1976a; Corrigan thesis, chs 4–5). Looking back in 1948, H. L. Beales (1948, 315) suggested that what Chadwick and Nassau Senior sought, 'beside economy, was a system of social police which would open up the labour market and render the labour factor of production mobile and docile, that is, disciplined and as nearly rational and predictable as may be.'[22] As we do not have the space to examine this whole 'system', we have chosen to concentrate on the central apparatus – the poor law unions after 1834.[23]

A focus on poor law administration does not, in fact, narrow our scope excessively, since this became the agency through which many social policy innovations were made. An increasing feature of poor law administration was the grafting on to it of various other functions, both formally and

20. Joseph Fletcher (a state servant himself) wrote in 1851 (33): 'The instrument of Inspection ... is of sufficient power to accomplish all that the state can desire'; Kay-Shuttleworth considered in 1853 (88) that inspection has helped to avoid 'socialist rebellion', while P. E. H. Hair (1968, 560) argues that it made possible wage reduction and labour disciplining. E. C. Tufnell (quoted Richards, 1975, 224) argued in 1837 that the poor law inspectors were an ideal means to 'indoctrinate the guardians'. On inspection see also Harris (1955) and Ball (1963).

21. State servants felt themselves to be struggling against *local* power, especially 'Jobbery' and 'Vestralization'. The class struggle is not only revealed in the anti-Poor Law Movement, but in differences over implementation of legislation (Rogers, 1971). John Foster has stressed this class dimension (1966; 1974).

22. E. P. Thompson (1963, 295 ff) and B. Inglis (1971, 372 ff). Finer (1952, 475), in his admirable study of Chadwick argues that 'The poor law administration was a machinery [sic] for enforcing competition, for creating a highly competitive labour market, and keeping it so.' Nassau Senior wrote to de Tocqueville 'The Poor Law Amendment Act was a heavier blow to the aristocracy than the Reform Act. The Reform Act principally affected the aristocracy of wealth. ... The Poor Law Act dethroned the country gentleman.' (quoted by Beales, 1931, 331, *n* 1; on Senior, see Levy, 1943.) Recent work suggests that this dethronement was far less complete than Senior argued.

23. In the period 1830–70 a number of significant developments in social policy took place. Among the most important pieces of legislation were: the Public Health Acts of 1848, 1858 and 1866 (supply of pure water and improved drainage); Burials Act of 1852 (closing choked graveyards); Nuisance Removal Acts 1848, 1855, 1860, 1863

informally. From the passing of the Civil Registration Act in 1836, it was the boards of guardians who oversaw the creation and administration of registration districts and subdistricts for their areas, and the appointment of registrars (often coinciding with poor law personnel, such as medical officers and clerks). Similarly, the Vaccination Acts of 1841 and 1867 were carried out on the basis of poor law medical districts, often using poor law officers, and special provisos were inserted that free vaccination was not to be regarded as poor relief, and thus not to carry disqualification from the franchise (as receipt of all forms of poor relief did until 1918). Valuation of property for all kinds of rating was performed by the union assessment committees, and very often poor law personnel collected county, borough, highway, sanitary, or other rates for other local authorities as well as for the union. Later in the century this trend continued, as when the guardians were automatically constituted rural sanitary authorities (forerunners of the rural district councils) under the Public Health Act of 1875, thus becoming the major local government authority for all non-urban areas.

Less formal use was also made of the poor law 'machine'. Throughout the century MPs in the House or policy-makers within the departments of state, asking questions about the national state of labourers' dwellings,[24] the value of rateable property,[25] increases in bastardy,[26] the spread of potato blight[27] or vagrancy,[28] all had their answers through the Poor Law

(excrement removal, regulation of slaughterhouses, limitation of pollution in streams and rivers); Lunatics Act 1845 (regulation and inspection of county asylums and private 'licensed' houses); Medical Act 1858 (creating the Medical Register). Further, the Factories Acts of 1833 and 1844, the Mines Act of 1842 and the Ten Hours Act of 1847, plus others, regulated child and female labour and total hours of work. Additionally much permissive legislation was important: in 1851 'the establishment of lodging-houses for the working-classes' was encouraged; by an 1866 act, loans were offered to local authorities or charities building homes for working-class tenants; and Torrens's Act of 1868 gave local authorities powers (if they wanted them) to insist that owners keep houses in repair, or made owners repay the cost of doing so. Wider aspects concerns leisure (libraries, museums, art galleries, public parks and public walks); on which see Corrigan and Corrigan (1974).

24. The following examples, drawn from the work in progress of V. Corrigan, are taken from the records of the Poor Law Commission concerning one union, that of Tynemouth, and from state papers based on data gathered from unions. For labourers' dwellings see Public Record Office (hereafter PRO) documents series MH/32/79, a return of April 1840.

25. An example of mines rateability is given in Parliamentary Papers (hereafter PP) 1887 (457) LXX.

26. Return of bastardy in the north of England, PRO MH/32/77 November 1838. Cf. Henriques (1967).

27. Report for the north of England, 9 February 1847, PRO MH/32/41/2594/47.

28. PP 1846 (391) XXXVI.

Commissioners and what became a national data-gathering network via boards of guardians, their medical officers and relieving officers. More confidential, and often a direct influence on policy, were the reports and memoranda sent in to London by inspectors, on general or specific subjects, ranging from estimates of Chartist strength,[29] to data on wage levels, rents and prices,[30] or detailed 'inside information' relevant to official correspondence or disputes over the application of regulations.[31]

Even if we restrict ourselves to considering the poor law itself as social policy, its ramifications are significant. Already by 1839, 250 new workhouse buildings dominated the social landscape. 'In 1850 the total number of unions ... had increased to 604, and of persons employed by them to 12,853' (Slater, 1930, 96, n 2). The attempt to create a new form of implementing policy – local elected bodies and central departments of state, their relations articulated by Inspectors[32] – was dogged by the fact that the guardians very generally retained more local autonomy than the framers of the act of 1834 intended. Unless the Poor Law Commissioners had funds to dispose of, as with the parliamentary grant for some officers' salaries from 1846, or to sanction, as with loans to be repaid from future rate income, their exhortations could be ignored by guardians, whose

29. PRO MH/32/77, letter of 1 January 1838; 110/126B, letter of 31 January 1838; 113/195B, letter of 6 January 1838.

30. PRO MH/32/77/121, letters of March and April 1838; MH/32/41/54429/50, reports of January 1850; MH/32/51/8589/87, report of 29 January 1887.

31. Minutes are appended to office copies of correspondence and memoranda filed throughout the MH 12 series.

32. For the sake of brevity the state servants known until 1847 as assistant commissioners have been referred to as inspectors, as they were called from that date, throughout. In 1847 the Poor Law Commission, an independent board set up under the act of 1834 to administer its provisions, was dissolved and replaced by the Poor Law Board, a normal department of state with a politician as president who was responsible to parliament and would be altered with each change of government. As Ann Digby has noted (1976, 157), the inspectors' potential was severely curtailed when their number was reduced from 21 in 1837 to 9 after 1846, administering over 600 Unions. This points to the significance of regulated and routinized procedures operating through administrative 'norms' and ultimately, fiscal measures.

33. See paragraph 2 of the note on further reading above. A series of studies have been made of Northumberland and Durham which show the extent of local variation even within a geographically related region: R. G. Barker, (Houghton-le-Spring – Newcastle Upon Tyne, MLitt, 1975); G. Cadman (Hexham Union – Newcastle Upon Tyne, MA, 1965); P. J. Dunkley (County Durham – Durham, MA, 1965); P. Mawson (South Shields – Newcastle Upon Tyne, MA, 1971).

34. 'Settlement' litigation continued to be big business right up to the twentieth century. In 1907, for example, 12,000 people were removed (cited, Bruce, 1973, 5). The emphasis tended to be upon those cases whose chargeability was likely to be long-term: orphans, deserted families, the disabled, lunatics and (supremely) illegitimate babies (cf.

priorities often centered on merely keeping rates as low as possible. Local research[33] continues to reveal antique buildings patched together, 'excessive' outdoor relief, inadequate staff, costly parish disputes over settlement[34] and the like, up to and beyond the creation of the Local Government Board in 1871.

This development points up another of the features of poor law administration in the period before 1871. The 1834 'system' was intended by its designers to effect a return to the sound principles established in legislation since 1601 – family responsibility for poverty, backed up where necessary by parish-based finance,[35] and discrimination between deserving and undeserving applicants. Thus the aged, sick and children were to be maintained, given medical attention, education, and if possible made self supporting; those able to work[36] were to be driven back to the labour market by making the conditions of relief (in these cases exclusively within the workhouse) so unpalatable that work at any price was preferable. One of the clearest intentions was the separation, or 'classification' of different categories of poor people and the development of separate treatment for them. No major changes were planned in the relief of the sick or the aged and infirm, thus tacitly approving the almost

Henriques, 1967). A major change was made by an 1846 act which prevented the removal of any migrant who had lived in a parish for five years and made the parish of her or his residence liable for maintenance. This was a real concession to rural parishes, since migrants often left them to work in towns, only to be returned when they had become a liability through unemployment, sickness or old age. The residence qualification was reduced to three years in 1861 and one year in 1865 (residence periods excluded any time in receipt of relief, or in the armed forces, in prison or in an asylum). Not until 1876 was three years' residence made a means of actual 'settlement'. The Poor Law Act of 1930 preserved this qualification.

35. Protracted efforts continued to be made to trace and prosecute relatives, to induce them to maintain, or contribute to the maintenance of, their poor relations. But the new poor law's efforts to preserve the family as the socially responsible unit did not extend to the families of 'undeserving' parents, whose children were to be protected from 'infection' by their parents' bad *habits*, by being removed from their care and brought up at the cost of the rates. The children of women living in the workhouse were housed and schooled away from their mothers' influence, and part of the policy of deterrence in workhouse relief was the rule that husband be separated from wife and sister from brother.

36. Able-bodied men were regarded as unproblematically idle; able-bodied women, however, posed a problem of classification for the poor law authorities: widowed or deserted mothers, or those with illegitimate children, might be physically fit but also have 'duties' in the home, and were never satisfactorily categorized (note that in the 1930 reiteration of familial responsibility for poor relatives, husbands but *not* wives have been added to the 1601 list). Nor was the problem solved of choosing between driving women into the labour market, only to find them making men unemployed, *or* keeping them on the rates. For a discussion of these matters see Thane, 'Women and State "Welfare" in Victorian and Edwardian England', *History Workshop*, 5, 1978.

universal practice of outdoor relief in these cases (Webbs, 1910, 17–18); this is reflected in the Commissioners' circulars and regulations, which give no clear guidance on the treatment of the sick or lunatics, until a *fait accompli* was recognized in the 1840s and makeshift arrangements for their relief in the context of the general mixed workhouse, so much criticized in the 1834 Report, were made (Webbs, 1910, 47, 52–3).

Instead of a series of different institutions, the guardians had almost universally provided a single workhouse in which children, lunatics, victims of sickness or accident, prostitutes, deserted wives, tramps and old people were all housed together (albeit separated by internal walls) and under the harsh regime intended only to deter the able-bodied. However, outdoor relief (even to the able-bodied in some unions) persisted throughout the period (its relative cheapness guaranteed its popularity with guardians), in proportions of from 2 to 1 up to 10 to 1 compared with workhouse relief; after a brief decline, poor rates continued to rise in defiance of the expected abolition of 'the problem'. In 1871 the poor law was reorganized once more, this time as a branch of a much wider state department concerned with public health and local government as well, and the conscious intention was again a return to first principles, the 'principles of 1834'.

Together with the principle of 'classification' and separate treatment of different 'grades' of pauper (strong moral judgements were made here, with great emphasis on the dangers of 'infection', for example of 'innocent girls' by 'fallen women') the Poor Law Commissioners sought to introduce a flexible but uniform system in the treatment of the poor in all parts of the country. Their orders, which had the force of law, covered the whole gamut of policy – election and working arrangements of the guardians, internal running of workhouses, medical relief and the payment and qualification of medical officers, apprenticeship of pauper children, relief of paupers belonging to other unions,[37] as well as restriction of outdoor relief to the able-bodied, which proved the object of their most concerted attention. Here significant and detailed exceptions were permitted to the indoor-relief-only rule[38] (including the capacious category 'sudden and urgent necessity') and in periods of abnormal economic depression provision was made for altogether different rules to apply.[39] Non-compulsory recommendations were also issued in the form of circulars, covering, for example, a selection of approved dietaries for inmates,

37. Cf. The General Consolidated Order, 1847. On medical provisions in general, cf. Flinn (1976).
38. Listed in the Outdoor Relief Prohibitory Order, 21 December 1844.
39. Under the Outdoor Test Order, 1842.

maximum fees payable for pauper funerals, or standards for staff, such as literacy being preferable in nurses.

One of the intentions of establishing national uniform standards was to discourage paupers from applying to unions with less stringent standards than others. Population movement was increasingly recognized as inevitable, and legal changes gradually accommodated the new position; not until 1865, however, was the pauper's settlement transferred to her or his union rather than the parish, and the qualifications for settlement were not altered until 1876 – (see note 34 above). The numbers of vagrants were still a subject of alarm and much effort was devoted by inspectors throughout the century to inducing all the guardians in a district to apply approximately uniform standards in relieving this class of pauper, so that unheated, mattress-less accommodation and enforced oakum-picking in a 'model' vagrant ward could not be simply avoided by pushing on to the next, where much laxer standards might apply.[40]

In this as in so many aspects of policy implementation, the inspectors played a major role, drafting, delivering and interpreting circulars and orders, conducting enquiries into local complaints and (rarely) public scandals, and into applications for loans from boards of guardians. They also not infrequently intervened on behalf of guardians to secure some concession in the application of regulations to take account of local conditions. In many ways they were the embodiment of state policy, to guardians and their staff seeking advice or defending their practice, to ratepayers protesting against proposals to spend their money on the 'new Bastilles', and to the poor themselves, either also agitating against the implementation of the new poor law for different reasons, or appealing against the treatment they received under it.

It is as well to conclude an essay entitled 'State formation and social policy' with that reminder. We are not talking about a 'naturally evolving' social policy, nor yet the human response of patrician governors to signs of

---

40. The lack of a clear policy for vagrants in 1834 was reproduced in a series of contradictory orders and circulars from the centre. From about 1842, however, a general tendency can be seen to distinguish between 'professional tramps' and the 'honest unemployed in search of work' (Webbs, 1910, 95) and to make conditions in casual wards even less pleasant than those in the rest of the house, imposing a severe task of work, and taking powers to forcibly detain vagrants for several hours in order that they perform such tasks. The cost of relief to vagrants in London was made a common charge on all metropolitan unions in 1864; this was the first of many moves towards 'rates equalization' and the rate support grant, resulting eventually in the final abandonment of the principle of locally funded poor relief. But the 'vagrancy problem' was not resolved by the end of the century and was the subject of a Home Office inquiry which drew attention to how vagrants were treated more harshly than felons. The north of England data can be found in PRO MH/32/51/103439/90, 1 December 1890.

distress when these are brought to their attention, although both are also involved. The 'condition of England' question is multifaceted. The question is posed differently for different classes, and their favoured solutions will also differ.[41] The long history we have sketched here obscures the history of diverted, distorted, or suppressed alternative policies. It should not be read as the story of unproblematic progress. We have, after all, been examining attempts not so much to solve the problem of poverty, as to regulate its effects. One part of the problem for the majority is state formation itself.

In 1871, the year of the inauguration of the Local Government Board, Karl Marx (writing in English in a pamphlet that had a wide circulation in London) made a sociologically illuminating comparison.[42] He contrasts the Paris Commune with both the classical bourgeois government of France and the 'peculiarities' of England – 'corrupt vestries, jobbing councillors, and ferocious poor law guardians' (1871, 70). 'From the members of the Commune downwards, the public service had to be done at workmen's wages ... Public functions ceased to be the private property of the tools of the central government' (1871, 68). But it was not only that the social form, albeit crucially, differed, it was that the Commune addressed itself to the real problem.

> The Commune made that catchword of bourgeois revolutions, cheap government, a reality by destroying the two greatest sources of expenditure – the standing army and state functionarism. ... Its true secret was this. It was essentially a working-class government ... the political form at last discovered to work out the economic emancipation of labour. [1871, 71, 72.]

Further reading

The fundamental primary sources for any study of English social policy

41. That is, the social policy 'embodied in the new poor law, mitigated as it was by the goodwill of many individuals including devoted guardians and assistant commissioners, was part of a body of class legislation' (Henriques, 1968, 371). 'In a sense', Michael Rose (1970, 79) argues, 'there was continuous agitation against the new poor law from its creation in 1834 until the demise of the boards of guardians in 1929.' This ignores the contemporary agitation concerning social security related to the National Assistance Board/ Supplementary Benefits Commission, itself a final nationalization of the previous – and extremely transitional – public assistance committees in the local areas. Although in 1948 only 3 per cent of the total population of Great Britain was dependent on national assistance, by 1968 the comparable figures was 7·4 per cent and by 1975, 8·1 per cent (written DHSS answer, Hansard, 21 April 1977).
42. It is not until we compare social policy and state formation in different capitalist developments that we can see the general regulatory features. Explicit 'learning from abroad' has been insufficiently emphasized in the aetiology and concrete achievement of social policy. Cf. Corrigan 'State formation', thesis and book.

remain in two kinds of state papers: the unpublished material held in the Public Record Office and that published in the series of Parliamentary Papers. To these must be added the complementary unpublished local records (for example, for each poor law union) and important sources of information in local and national newspapers, in private papers in the locality or in London (such as the Chadwick collection at University College, London). Great assistance in understanding social policy organizationally can be obtained from the series, Office-Holders in Modern Britain, by J. C. Sainty.

There is much recent research in the area. A useful guide to literature on the 1834 poor law is given in Fraser (1976), which also contains a list of theses on the poor law. Peter Bell's *Social reform and social structure in Victorian England* (1972, Victorian Studies Handlists, 5), also a list of theses, remains of use, and may be updated by the annual list no. 36 of the Institute of Historical Research, London. Most of these university theses (Cambridge is an important exception) may be borrowed through any library. Each year a number of journals publish bibliographies of work in their respective areas; three valuable examples are the *Bulletin* of the Society for the Study of Labour History, *Victorian Studies*, and *Northern History*.

Aside from general introductions (e.g. the Webbs, Oxley, 1973; Fraser, 1973) and the sets of documents mentioned below, social policy questions feature in several introductory historical series, for example: Studies in Economic and Social History (Macmillan) and Seminar Studies in History (Longman). In the latter, the titles by Pound, G. Taylor, Midwinter, and R. C. Birch are important, and P. Thane's volume on Social policy, 1870–1945, is forthcoming; in the former series the significant studies include Rose (1972) and J. R. Hay, while A. J. Taylor (1972) discusses more general issues of state formation. Taylor has also (1975) edited a volume in Methuen's Debates in Economic History which usefully gathers contributions to the debate on the 'standard of living' in nineteenth-century England, a debate given context by Inglis (1972) and added to by Flinn (1974) and the work of E. H. Hunt. Penguin's Topics in History has a number of relevant volumes (e.g. Martin, 1971) and has the advantage of pictorial information, a feature also of Norman Longmate's *The workhouse* (1974).

The books in the Seminar Series (Longman) have excellent bibliographies, together with a useful sample of documents. Other collections of documents include Bruce, 1973, Rose, 1971, and Watkin, 1975. Guidance on using documents can be obtained from a variety of sources; useful starting points are Richardson's *Local Historian's Encyclopedia* (1974, especially section G) and Coulson's essay in the

Open University volume 'Sources and Historiography' *Great Britain 1750–1950* (A 401 I 1–2, 1974). Since the short version of the 1834 Report is now available as a Penguin classic (1974, edited by the Checklands) there is no excuse for not studying the letter as well as the spirit of the 'principles of 1834'.

Statistics of poverty are a notorious *lacuna* in social policy until comparatively recently; some attempts at generalization are indicated in Table IV, of Appendix II to Corrigan's PhD thesis (which draws on Aschrott, 1902, Appendix XII and Rose, 1972, Appendix A). Pre-1800 figures are imaginative guesses: see the discussion of Gregory King's calculations for the year 1688 and Patrick Colquhoun's reworking of the census of 1801 and the pauper returns of 1803 in Dorothy George, *England in transition* (1931, her Appendix reproduces both sets of figures). For the old poor law see PP 1818 XIX; 1830/31 (83) XI; 1835 (444) XLV II. For the new poor law see the annual reports of the Poor Law Commission/Poor Law Board, whose appendices give statistical information from every union. Some returns (e.g. PP 1840 (147) XVIII; 1871 (441) LIX) go beyond the poor law unions and provide township data.

Finally we apologize for absorbing Wales without specifying its particular qualities; the full SSRC Report (HR 2970, 1975) of Alan Bainbridge, and David Jones's work has some crucial illumination on the latter. Scotland was entirely different as Loch, 1898, Mitchison, 1974, and Lindsay, 1975, all show. For background on Scotland see Johnston, 1946 and Smout, 1969 and issues of the *Journal* of the Scottish Society of Labour History.

2

Social work, professionalism and the state
Noel Parry and José Parry

Nineteenth-century preconditions: the developing relationships between voluntary charity and government

The nineteenth century was the age of private enterprise. Few would deny the drive and vigour of Victorian capitalism in the economic sphere (Hobsbawn, 1968). What is less often remarked upon is the connection between enterprise in the realm of production and that of voluntary charitable activity (Owen, 1965). The phenomenal growth of philanthropic effort matched that in production and both were bound together by the transfer of resources through the flow of voluntary gifts by individuals or charitable associations. Charity was largely organized and legitimated through Christian religious bodies. Traditionally, Christianity had always been concerned with the poor; Christ had taught his followers, 'love thy neighbour as thyself,' and had told them, 'the poor you always have with you.' The problem for Christians in the nineteenth century was how to put this general principle into practice in the context of a market economy.

There was much controversy over the nature and origins of poverty and over the extent to which those in poverty had brought this condition upon themselves by their own moral failings. The distinction between the 'deserving' and the 'undeserving' poor was enshrined in the Poor Law Amendment Act of 1834 which urged that the undeserving should be treated punitively.[1] The government and the local poor law unions were the backstop of the system of charitable endeavour. Official schemes for the relief of poverty were concerned with keeping down the poor rates and leaving voluntary charitable effort to support the wider ideals of Christian family life among the 'deserving'. Influenced by Malthusian doctrine which theorized that the growth of population would always tend to outstrip the resources necessary to support it, the poor law system practised the splitting up of families and the segregation of the sexes. Hence, outdoor relief was officially discouraged and the workhouse policy had a punitive effect; whereas voluntary charity, by contrast, typically

1. See chapter 1 above.

aimed to keep families intact. The poor law was concerned with those at the economic margin of subsistence who were either unable or unwilling to support themselves (Rose, 1971).

Given the nature of the poor law, voluntary charitable effort gradually came to focus more specifically upon the 'deserving poor' and began to leave the 'undeserving' to the poor law system. With the exception of the poor law, government at this stage left to organized religion matters concerned with family life. The traditional division of function between church and state regarded the family as a private domain under the general moral guidance of the church (and the dissenting sects). Despite some straws in the wind such as the introduction in the late 1830s of civil marriage and of civil registration of births, marriages and deaths, the legal system continued to uphold Christian beliefs on family life and sexual conduct. The institutions of the family and marriage were still regarded as very much part of the religious domain. Government – despite the considerable power exercised by Britain overseas – was not regarded, at least by Hegel, as constituting a 'state' in the modern sense (Sabine, 1951, 556). The localized nature of British government did not compare with the centralized French or Prussian state systems.

The character of early nineteenth-century Britain is well summarized by Norman McCord (1976, 87):

> The society which created the 1834 Poor Law Amendment Act ... was essentially a decentralized rural society, with very limited resources and techniques in the fields of government and official administration. The energies and achievements of that society were not primarily exercised in official forms, and it is scarcely surprising then that the response to social problems came for the most part, not from the state, but from private and local energies which lay at the heart of Britain's development in the age of the Industrial Revolution.

McCord goes on to argue that although during the industrial revolution the nature of philanthropic activity was changing, strong continuities could also be traced. The landed aristocracy and gentry continued to play a leading role but they were joined by successful industrial entrepreneurs. The period was characterized by a sustained burst of growth among organized philanthropic societies and an expansion in individual charitable benefactions. In addition, local communities exerted themselves to meet any temporary problems or disasters, or to celebrate particular notable events. Local autonomy generated widespread hostility to the supervisory functions entrusted to government under the poor law and there was a certain attraction in handling local problems through unofficial agencies immune from bureaucratic influence.

It would be incorrect, however, to picture the official poor law machinery as being quite distinct from unofficial philanthropy. Generally both were controlled by much the same kind of people (McCord, 1976, 100). Those who were poor law guardians were frequently also on the committees of voluntary hospitals, schools and dispensaries and were likely to be involved in a variety of other charitable activities. Nevertheless, in the nineteenth century, voluntary charity and government provided officially distinct systems of philanthropic endeavour and poor relief. The scale of voluntary fund-raising was enormous. As late as the 1860s philanthropic funds raised in London alone amounted to more than was available to the poor law system in the whole of England and Wales (Owen, 1965, 218; McCord, 1976, 97). Yet the comparison is not wholly just because the expenditure of government – both central and local – upon elementary education is discounted in this calculation.

This last point draws attention to the variety of relationships which developed between government and voluntary charity. The formal division between the official poor law and voluntary philanthropy can be contrasted with the field of elementary education where government and the religious societies formed a partnership. From 1833 a small grant was paid by way of subsidy to the two principal religious societies. The societies approached the government because it was increasingly difficult to raise enough charitable finance from voluntary sources to cover expenditure. For its part, the government took the view that it was better to subsidize rather than to see the societies go into decline because this might lead, in the long run, to the government having to bear the whole cost of education for the working class. During the nineteenth century government was not directly involved in secondary education except in a minimal sense through royal commissions, debates in parliament and through the establishment of the Charity Commissioners seeking the rationalization and regulation of endowments (Hurt, 1972; Owen, 1965; Parry, 1974).

The formal partnership between the religious societies and government which laid the foundations for the development of state education and of the modern teaching profession was not matched in the field of poor relief. Yet the evangelical revival which stimulated the growth of church educational provision also created the conditions for the emergence of social work. The revival was a reaction by movements within the Church of England to the attacks upon it during the years before and after the reform of parliament in 1832. The church was regarded by many, at that time, as a moribund part of the old landed order. The growing strength of dissent, particularly among sections of the urban-based artisan and middle classes, fuelled a struggle between Anglicanism and its opponents which was partly a regional, partly a class and partly a party-political conflict (Gilbert, 1976). The first sign of modern social work appeared during the 1850s with the introduction of paid welfare work activities associated with the church and directed mainly at the moral welfare of women and girls (Walton, 1975, 41). The priest adapted his role not only to organize voluntary workers, which had long been his task, but also to managing full-time paid workers, like the elementary school teacher and the new moral welfare workers. The latter were employed by the clergy and worked under clerical control but, unlike the teachers, they had no connection with government. The introduction of full-time moral welfare work was an important step in the rise of modern professional social work, although the predominant characteristic looked for was still religious vocation rather than any notion of specialist knowledge or training. Moral welfare workers were largely employed in residential care, especially in the running of homes which were designed to remove fallen women and girls from their old haunts. They aimed to inculcate religious and moral values and give training for employment. Some moral welfare work was undertaken by nuns in religious houses but in any case the new paid workers were invariably lay women. It was but a short step from voluntary work to paid work for impecunious but religious women.

The settlement movement

The reforming evangelical trend in the Church of England which led to the emergence of the full-time moral welfare worker also contributed another important element in the formation of social work as an institution and an occupation: this was the settlement movement. The pressure for reform within and without the church applied also in the hitherto exclusive Anglican universities of Oxford and Cambridge. The colleges were largely staffed by clergymen and had an important function in the recruitment, training and placement in 'livings' of young priests. The universities thus had an ecclesiastical ethos and were subject to a ferment of religious ideas and enthusiasms. The reform of Oxford and Cambridge in the mid-nineteenth century opened them first to non-Anglicans and subsequently to women. This marked the shift away from ecclesiastical control towards the idea of the liberal university dominated neither by church nor state. The revitalization of the church generally, and within the university in particular, provided the conditions for the evangelical social mission which found its expression in the pioneering work of the settlement movement.

Canon Barnett may be regarded as the founder of the movement which was started at Toynbee Hall in 1884. He not only had university connections and experience as a parish priest in the impoverished East End of London, but also close relationships with a network of other social reformers. Indeed he married one of Octavia Hill's assistants in 1873, and Mrs Barnett thereafter played a key role in the foundation of women's settlements. Like several other contemporary social reformers and intellectuals, Barnett came to believe that 'scientific' charity was inadequate to solve the problem of poverty. He diagnosed the key problem of the day as the failure to bridge the widening gap between social classes in the urban context. His central idea was that the universities should share their cultural riches with the poor through members living and teaching in poor areas, befriending local people, running extension classes and engaging in related cultural activities. The university settlements were intended in the long run to go deeper than philanthropy by making knowledge the common property of all classes (Harris, 1977, 43–63; Walton, 1975, 50–56; Seed, 1973, 29–36).

With his Oxford connections, Barnett saw the settlements as being led by graduates who would be paid a salary by a college. University volunteers would live in a settlement to undertake voluntary work. During the same years, women began to enter universities and the settlement idea was extended to them (aided by the considerable influence of Mrs Barnett). The established practice of separate university colleges for men and women was replicated in the settlements. Within the movement there emerged a significant difference in the character and function of settlements for women compared with those for men. Men who became residents typically regarded the settlement as offering a short but broadening life experience which could be used as a basis for subsequent careers in the church, the professions, business or politics. The men's settlements exerted their influence on many future statesmen and civil servants, including Clement Attlee and Beveridge who were to play such important roles in the formation of the welfare state. Women faced restricted career opportunities so that settlement work came to offer a training for social work, whether in a voluntary or a paid capacity. As a result the women's settlements began to collaborate with the Charity Organization Society (COS) in the setting up of professional training courses for social work. In 1903, E. J. Urwick noted that the ideals of the settlement proper were being substituted by the function of a training college (Walton, 1975, 63). Women thus led the way in the development of professional social work training, as they did in the training of secondary school teachers. The reasons were similar in each case: middle-class women were marginal in the male-dominated public world of occupations. For them a professional qualification was a badge of competence, a symbol of their right to follow paid professional work. For men such work was merely a phase in life, not a career in itself. The identity of the male derived from his role as clergyman, or from his prospects in business or the major professions. Men from 'good social backgrounds' who engaged in social work for any length of time tended to participate in an organizing or managing capacity. It was the women's settlements, then, which developed training for social work as a career. This was done from the early years of the twentieth century in conjunction with the newly formed social studies departments of the younger universities and the local offices of the COS. The high proportion of women entering both voluntary and paid social work established its image from the outset as a women's profession.

The Charity Organization Society

The development of social work, as a nascent profession, grew out of the activities of the COS, which was founded prior to the settlements in 1869. Although the voluntary charitable and philanthropic movement had proved its capacity to survive and expand in the new urban conditions, it was criticized as ineffective because it was disorganized and divided into a bewildering variety of religious and charitable organizations. The COS represented an attempt to cope with this particular problem and reflected the view that further state intervention should be contained by applying rational and scientific principles to private philanthropy. It diagnosed the problem of the charitable relationship in terms of the break-down of the tight-knit community in which donor and recipient had knowledge of each other. A new urban industrial setting and the massive growth and movement of population had produced a segregation of classes, physically and morally, and destroyed contact and communication between them. In this situation the Society asserted that disorganized and random benefactions simply produced a class of dependent mendicants without the will to stand on their own feet and the emergence of widespread and morally reprehensible abuse of the charitable system. In short, it was claimed that, paradoxically, charity itself could produce pauperism. The Society proposed to take over the coordination and application of all existing charitable work so as to channel funds in a rational and scientific manner. Moreover, members of the COS argued that giving money was not itself enough; it was essential to make contact with individuals and families on the basis of systematic visiting. This involved the ethic of personal service which indicated that 'the greatest gift is to give yourself.'

The founders and leaders of the COS were drawn largely from the middle and upper class and the organization had aristocratic patronage. Some of the most assiduous members were men who had already retired from a career in business or the professions and adopted the work of the Society almost as a second occupation to which they gave their services free. A large number of COS social workers were well-off middle-class women who had the opportunity to devote time and resources to the work.

Thus the Society depended upon voluntary effort whether in committee work, administration, fund-raising, or in social work visiting. The method used by the Society was casework conducted through district offices which, it hoped, would become the single agency of contact between charitable sources and the poor. By this means it was intended to prevent multiple approaches by the poor to charity which were regarded as a major source of abuse. Clearly the achievement of this objective required careful and systematic record-keeping.

The COS was not opposed to the poor law, or to the principle of deterrence as such, but regarded the current administration of the system as insufficiently firm or efficient. Its aim was to assist the 'deserving' poor while also collaborating with the poor law by referring 'undeserving' cases to it. It was concerned to prevent pauperization by strengthening and supporting deserving individuals and families who, through no fault of their own, had fallen upon hard times. The casework method introduced by the COS involved both contact and friendship with the poor, but equally a marked degree of surveillance and control over the lives of beneficiaries. There is no doubt that the attempt of the COS to become the single channel of charitable contact with the poor weakened the religious character of social work. The more secular and 'professional' approach was enhanced by the introduction of full-time salaried social workers who were recruited in the early days from among the 'superior sort' of working men. There was an insistence on training for both salaried and voluntary workers. The modern pattern of training which combines practical fieldwork and academic tuition began in the collaboration between the district office of the COS, the social studies department of the adjacent university and the settlement.[2]

The almoner

It was Loch, the secretary of the COS, who conceived the idea of putting some of his caseworkers into the hospital setting where they could implement the philosophy of the Society by functioning as gatekeepers to free medical treatment (Loch, 1892). The medical structure which the caseworkers were entering was quite different from that either in education or poor relief. In education, the government had formed a partnership with the voluntary religious societies for the provision of elementary education. The arrangements for the relief of the poor were formally divided between the government's poor law system and voluntary charitable effort. In the

2. Education is a central issue in the formation of professionalism but owing to lack of space is only partially developed in this chapter. For further details, see chapter 4 below.

medical field a predominant partnership had grown up between the medical profession and voluntary charity. This partnership was institutionalized chiefly in the voluntary hospitals. Unlike teaching or social work, the medical profession was, from 1858, already unified and self-governing. It approximated most closely to the ideal type of free professionalism. The relationship of doctors to government was limited mainly to contractual work for the poor law service. The base of the profession was in the private market. This conferred a degree of economic independence and power which, through doctors associations, could be applied in the interests of the small proportion of doctors who were directly employed by the poor law, the mental hospitals, the army, the friendly societies or the commercial companies (Parry, 1976).

In the voluntary hospitals and dispensaries the question of how to separate those who could afford to pay for treatment from those who could not was regarded as a chronic and fundamental problem. The caseworker, now called the almoner, brought skills from her experience with the COS in sorting out the 'deserving' from the 'undeserving'. She was trained to ensure that patients were followed up in the community so that the benefits of treatment would not be lost. In the early days almoners worked almost entirely with provident medical associations and COS committees. After the first appointment of an almoner to the Royal Free Hospital in 1895, other hospitals gradually followed suit as they came to realize that almoners might save hospital funds and conserve beds by excluding people who were judged not to need free treatment. There was, however, little enthusiasm among hospital doctors for the wider social work function which pioneers of medical social work, like Miss Cummins and others, wanted to see as the main task of the almoner. In 1903 a Hospital Almoners Association was established. This began by offering opportunities for the exchange of information and for sociability but was not concerned with trade union functions such as pay, hours or conditions of work. In 1907 a Hospital Almoners Council was created which became responsible for the selection, training and appointment of almoners. Originally the Council consisted of leading members of the COS together with three doctors and two almoners but, as the years went by, doctors and almoners became more strongly represented. In the early days, training was carried on in conjunction with the COS. This comprised practical work which was undertaken for six months in a COS office, plus an equal amount of time in an almoner's office. A certificate was awarded to successful probationers. Almoning was exclusively a female social work occupation with a high recruitment from the middle and upper classes. By contrast with some other areas of social work, which relied upon a large proportion of untrained or voluntary personnel, almoning became an élite social work occupation involving only salaried and fully trained workers with a considerable social standing (Walton, 1975, 43–7).

Probation

Probation, unlike almoning, had its origins in the religious revival of the Church of England. It shared common roots with moral welfare work. The Church of England Temperance Society, which was part of the wider temperance movement, appointed the first police court missionary in London, in 1876 (Harrison, 1971). Others were soon to follow in provincial towns and cities. Earlier experiments anticipating probation had been known since the 1820s but had faded away. The new missionaries were drawn mainly from the respectable working class and were male. Soon afterwards, women workers were recruited to deal with female offenders. Probation is significant not only because of its different recruitment pattern but also because of its relationship to the state through the legal system. Influenced by experience in the United States, statutory responsibilities of a limited kind were imposed by parliament in 1887. Thus began the long road by which modern social workers have acquired a wide range of statutory duties. The courts also came to rely on the missionaries for reports in individual cases and after an act of 1895 concerning maintenance and separation orders, involvement in matrimonial work established the links between social work, the family and the state. From the probation officer's position as the servant of the court emerged the principal aspects of the role, which were supervision of offenders, especially young offenders, and matrimonial and family matters. The probation officer, if he had not been created in the voluntary sector, would probably have had to be invented in some form by the state in order to ensure that legislative intentions were implemented. These required something different from the existing roles of the policeman or the prison officer. An important early example is the Probation of First Offenders Act (1887) which gave the probation officer the basis in legal machinery for the enforcement of the new probation orders. These statutory duties made little immediate difference to the work of the probation officer whose role tended to be isolated and even rather lonely. There was little or no central guidance except that given by the particular mission to which the officer was attached. A departmental committee was set up to examine the working of the act and reported at the end of 1909. It recommended the formation of a society of probation officers, managed by themselves, as a theatre for discussion and a means of disseminating information. The underpaid and scattered probation officers, most of whom had a prior loyalty to their employing missionary organizations, were unlikely to take the initiative. Sidney Edridge, clerk to the justices of Croydon and a former mayor, called a first meeting in 1912 at which it was agreed to set up a National Association of Probation Officers. The Association moved gradually away from its prime concerns of improving the work and knowledge of the officers and securing public recognition for the service, to taking on trade union functions such as bargaining over salaries and conditions of service. Gradually, and without any sharp break, the Association became a democratic autonomous body. From the beginning, however, the Association sought to develop a relationship with the Home Office such that it was accepted as a representative body, competent to speak for the probation service and to advise on legislative proposals.

The most important development in the creation of a professional probation service was the ending of the 'dual control' system between the Home Office and the Church of England Temperance Society. In 1926 the Criminal Justice Act had provided for a probation service covering the whole country. This set the scene for the recommendation by the Social Services Committee in Courts of Summary Jurisdiction (1936) to place probation on a completely public and entirely full-time basis (Bochel, 1976, 149). Acting on the Committee's advice, government excluded the voluntary societies from probation proper and relegated their duties to those of the residential care of offenders. The agents of the missions serving as probation officers were from 1938 transferred to the direct employ of the Home Office. Improvements in recruitment, training and the adoption of case-work method resulted from the new structure for probation which laid down the main lines of development for a period of some twenty-five years.

Sexual and class divisions in the formation of social work

Almoning and probation, although both forms of social work, yield some general points of comparison and contrast. As we have seen, almoning operated entirely as an élite, paid occupation exclusively recruited from among middle-class women. Like nursing after the reforms of Miss Nightingale and also like teaching in the girls' public and grammar schools, women worked together in the development of occupations which excluded men. In nursing only the less prestigious field of mental nursing was open to males. The formation of these women's occupations was inspired by the leadership of an élite group of women who urged an altruistic vocational commitment deriving from Christian and familial values. They were deeply committed to systematic professional training and in their attempts to achieve some degree of self-government and occupational control they modelled themselves on the values of professionalism which they shared with the men of their own social class. The difference was that men were chiefly engaged in the commercial consulting professions which could normally command a price sufficient to make the sale of a service profitable. Women, during the nineteenth century, were generally excluded from these 'market-based' professions. Even where after a struggle they gained entry, they achieved little more than token representation. In limited instances, such as in the commercially more profitable areas of teaching, there was sometimes created a special corner of the market where women provided a service to their own sex. Typically, middle-class women carved out areas of work which involved public service. Such a service was either publicly or privately funded and functioned as an extension into the occupational world of domestic, familial and religious duties which conventionally defined women's role in society.

There were increasing pressures for the moderation and reform of the poor law coming both from sections in the labour movement and from middle-class radicals. Part of this arose from the contact of middle-class voluntary workers, particularly women, with conditions in the workhouse. There was also the entry of women, after 1869, into the civil service and their appointment to the inspectorate of several public services, including the poor law. The first woman guardian was elected in 1869 and others were to follow. Professionals, including doctors and Nightingale-trained nurses were employed in increasing numbers in the poor law service and were generally a force for change. The class line was of fundamental importance in recruitment of personnel. Whether among elementary teachers, poor law officials or other minor servants of the state or local government, the tendency was to recruit working-class people to provide services for their own class. Only among the higher levels of administration were middle-class people recruited to 'officer' the services. In social work, and other professional or aspirant professional occupations, the notion of personal service brought middle-class people into direct contact with working-class clients. In the poor law service, for example, they found themselves at least partly under the authority of officials, such as the relieving officers whom they regarded as their social inferiors, and hence worked to achieve professional autonomy and some reform of the system. Doctors who belonged to a unified all-graduate profession gave their services personally. In social work there was typically a mixture of personal service by lady voluntary workers and the deputing of social work to specially recruited paid workers, usually male, from working-class or lower middle-class backgrounds. Examples of this include the first paid caseworkers of the COS and early police court missionaries. Thus, within what was admittedly a fragmented field of social work occupations, there were striking class divisions in recruitment and status which were closely related to sexual divisions.

At the end of the nineteenth century the clear division between the poor law system and voluntary charity was strongly institutionalized. Social work had grown out of private philanthropy and had penetrated the poor law service only marginally. The COS had specifically aimed to limit state intervention in the relief of the poor. By the turn of the century social work as a group of several related yet organizationally distinct occupations was already well established, but the intellectual pace on questions of social policy was no longer being made by the COS. The initiative was passing to those who believed that the state both could and should evolve a social policy aimed at improving standards of living for all its citizens (Evans, 1978, 213). Legislation concerned with old age pensions, health insurance and labour exchanges is but an example from a spate of interventionist acts of parliament which were passed in the first decade of the twentieth century. It might have seemed, on the face of it, that social work could quickly become engaged in a partnership with the state. In fact only in the case of probation did rapid movement in this direction occur. Generally, the new interventionists defined their task in economic terms. An important effect was to separate the element of 'scientific administration', which had been a central part of the COS tradition, from 'social work'. Scientific administration passed into the hands of men like Beveridge who rejected social casework. It became part of the developing movement in social and political life which was eventually to produce the welfare state. Within this framework of state intervention there was no conception of a place for social work: on the contrary, there was some hostility to it. As early as 1905 Beveridge had 'condemned proposals from the COS for converting the poor law into a gigantic system of casework, in which relief would be given only when accompanied by "advice, encouragement or moral exhortation" from trained almoners and charitable volunteers'. Such a system, Beveridge conceded, might achieve the objective of promoting contact between different social classes; but it totally ignored the economic causes of poverty and 'simply stereotyped an unhealthy relationship of patron and dependant' between rich and poor, (Harris, 1977, 97).

The effective separation of the strategy of social reform via state intervention and social administration from the social work tradition was to have important consequences. On the one hand, the Fabian/Labour Party connection was to move towards a decisive rejection of the class-based particularist values of the poor law towards a universalist model of welfare provision for all citizens under the state. Such a programme would require reforms of the poor law and local government, the most important of which, in the inter-war years, took place in 1929 under the reforming Conservative, Chamberlain. On the other hand, the social work enterprise in its most vigorous development remained a phenomenon flourishing outside the state sector. The First World War encouraged and indeed necessitated the expansion of state machinery. It generated massive disruption of family life which caused the state to set up agencies to deal with family matters outside the poor law. This necessarily drew social work into a closer engagement with the state. Another effect of the war was the official take-up of psychology and psychiatry; this was in part due to problems of mental illness, particularly 'shell shock', but, also, to the requirements of the armed forces for selection techniques and industry for improved methods of management and production.

Psychiatric social work, scientific legitimacy and professionalism

Following the influence of wartime developments, psychology and psychiatry had a profound impact on policy in several areas, such as education, mental illness and the treatment of offenders. Psychology had already deeply influenced American social work theory and practice. In Britain the main impact on social work was to come through the development of a new occupation – psychiatric social work. The formation of this occupation was important because of its strong assertion of professionalism as a mode of occupational organization and control, and its commitment to scientific psychology as a legitimating knowledge base which could, for the first time, provide a theoretical underpinning for casework practice. It is true that the COS had claimed inspiration from science but it was a notion of science without much substantive content, being in fact little more than an adherence to the principle of bureaucratic rationality. By contrast, psychiatric theory in the 1920s was conceived to be a science directly applicable to social casework. It could serve to replace religious legitimation, functioning instead as a secular ideology.

Another difference between psychiatric social work and the COS tradition was organizational. Whereas the COS was based on the neighbourhood office, psychiatric social work had a functional mode of organization without specific neighbourhood commitment. Psychiatric social work had originated in the United States and was imported into Britain by those who had been impressed by seeing it at work in America. It emerged as an auxiliary medical service and may be compared with almoning which had penetrated the hospital from outside. In 1926 an approach was made, by what was regarded as a highly representative

British group, to the Commonwealth Fund of America. The intention was to set up in England a child guidance clinic for training, service and research, and there was a specific aim to increase the impact and spread of psychiatric theory in social work. The Fund responded favourably and a group of social workers were sent to America for training. In 1927 the Child Guidance Council was established in London and within two years the first clinic had been opened in Islington. After 1930 it became an independent organization with its own governing body, including both medical and lay representatives. Joint training was established with the social sciences department at the London School of Economics and such was the speed of development that in 1930 the Association of Psychiatric Social Workers was founded. The American connection was typical of the way in which the funds of the great American foundations were tapped in Britain during the inter-war years for the fulfilment of educational and welfare objectives. British observers noted that in America the professional social worker was already more established and accepted, and that the mental hygiene movement was penetrating the field of family casework through the attachment of psychiatric consultants to district charity. However, in Britain by the end of the 1930s there were already over forty clinics, most of which were voluntary, although significantly for the involvement of social work with the state, some were funded by the London County Council and by certain other local authorities. Some psychiatric social workers after training began to find posts in the hospital service, thus expanding the scope of the new occupation. Like the almoners, they were very much dependent on the recruiting initiatives of individual hospitals.

The glamour of psychiatry and the special relationship of psychiatric social workers to psychiatrists was an important element in the rapid emergence of psychiatric social work as a profession. Proximity to a successful independent profession – like medicine – generated problems but tended also to establish and reinforce strong aspirations to professionalism. Psychology offered the promise of transcending and escaping the limitations of Victorian social work, and yielded the possibility of 'generalizing the client' by focusing on universalized conception of the human individual, rather than on class categories. Fruedian psychology gave the wider opportunity of universalizing the familial relationship between father, mother and child and, theoretically, offered the possibility of dealing with problems arising at any social level, or in any social group or society. Moreover, psychological theory claimed to penetrate beyond 'superficial social characteristics', such as those of class or culture, to absolutely fundamental problems of personality. These aspects, hidden in the unconscious beyond the knowledge of the client, offered the chance of developing a specialized 'mystery' and a warrant for professional authority rooted in science.

The growth of psychiatric social work and the use of psychological theory as a basis for casework strengthened the movement towards professionalism in social work. There had already been one attempt soon after the First World War to organize social workers into a single professional association. In 1936 the British Federation of Social Workers (BFSW) was launched and continued for some years to be the only representative association bringing together under its umbrella a range of social work bodies. These were twelve in number and included family caseworkers, moral welfare workers, probation officers, psychiatric social workers and almoners. The Federation found it difficult to develop a coherent policy because of the continued functional division between the social work occupations. It was, in any case, short of money but it did not lack in the enthusiasm and dedication of its leading council members. Its council was predominantly female, and psychiatric social workers – with their strong orientation to professionalism – were particularly active. Almoners and psychiatric social workers were the only social work occupations whose associations had developed sufficient collective professional control to admit only trained and certificated workers to membership. They held up the model of professionalism as an example to other social workers, but in no branch of social work was professional control strong enough to prevent employers appointing untrained people. Although almoners and psychiatric social workers were a small proportion of those employed in social work, they

> formed a quasi-professional élite of middle- and upper-class women, insisting on high intellectual and moral standards, the greater number of them still single, and with a broad social purpose realized in a particular form of social work. Probation officers with a preponderance of men had driven quickly for the establishment of a universal service and decent salaries ... [but] the creation of a national network of court social workers did not carry automatically the establishment of a high level of training. [Walton, 1975, 156.]

The state and social work – the process of convergence

Leadership in the development of professional social work, in the inter-war years, remained outside the ambit of the state. Yet the clear-cut division which characterized the Victorian origins of social work – namely, between voluntary charity and the poor law – was being eroded. The reform of the poor law in 1930, and the takeover of some of its functions by the local authorities, was an important factor. The imposition by government of new statutory duties encouraged the appointment of social workers in state-funded agencies at both national and local government level. This amounted to a growing convergence and engagement between social work and the state which, unlike the fields of education or health, as yet lacked any major legislative framework. Mess drew attention to the way in which the salariat of the voluntary organizations had increased very much in numbers, in status, and in efficiency. He noted that there had been a striking transformation of voluntary social service which operated on a larger scale, 'with more science and less sentimentality than formerly'. Much of the administrative work was carried out by professional social workers who tended more and more to be staffs analogous to the staffs of government departments or of local authorities. They continued to work under the direction of committees of unpaid persons, representing subscribers and others, but the social workers had become 'so skilled that their advice, like that of high permanent officials of the civil service or heads of departments of a local authority, counts for a great deal, and they have a considerable voice in shaping policy' (Mess, 1948, 204). As a result, voluntary workers were gradually relegated to the simpler and subordinate tasks. Convergence was demonstrated by the increasing similarity both of professional training and orientation in statutory and voluntary agencies alike. Also, statutory agencies were becoming less rigid, more humane and more ready to experiment. Mess concluded (1948, 205) that 'the contrast between the spirit and the methods of voluntary agencies and of statutory agencies is less sharp than it used to be.' This encouraged more contact between the professional social worker in the voluntary sector and statutory officials. Equally, the newer statutory agencies began to make much more use of voluntary workers and voluntary agencies.

The characterization of social work by Mess gives us in part a description of changes in social work and its relationship with the state during the inter-war years. But it also contains tacitly his approbation of the professional aspirations of social work. As a counterweight to his enthusiasms we may refer to the conclusions of a report on the re- cruitment and training of social workers to the National Council of Social Service, which was published in 1939 just prior to the outbreak of the Second World War. It recognized the rather chaotic variety of occupations existing under the general label 'social work' and the attendant problems of variety in methods of working, recruitment, training and conditions of service. This situation was thought to confuse potential recruits – a problem which was made worse by low salaries paid to some social workers, and by the absence of recognized professional standards which militated against the growth of an established status such as existed in other professions and in the civil service.

The Second World War brought an even greater disruption of family life than the First. This was due to the threat from German bombing and the consequent programme of evacuation. The state put the nation on a total war footing and extended its control over economic and social life to an unprecedented degree. Voluntary social work responded quickly to the needs of the community, but the war pinpointed the very small scale of professional and statutory services which, as a result also of inadequate staffing, found difficulty coping with the magnitude of the social problems thrust upon them. The women's voluntary associations played a major part in plugging the gap and pioneered new ventures, such as the Citizen's Advice Bureau. Evacuation focused attention on class distinctions in the quality of family life as children were moved from the slums to the countryside. The needs of children became a central concern because of increases in juvenile delinquency and disturbed behaviour. The authorities responded with schemes for fostering, advisory facilities and hostel services. Nursery care was provided because of the rapid increase in the employment of women in support of the war effort. Among the voluntary associations the Charity Organization Society proved valuable in meeting social distress. In line with the national emphasis on family welfare its name was changed, in 1942, to the Family Welfare Association. Conscientious objectors formed the Pacificists Service Units, later called Family Service Units, with the aim of giving practical help to poor families. From this developed the post-war concentration on the question of 'problem families' (Philp *et al.*, 1957).

The effects of war on the professional social work occupations were various, but all were drawn more closely into the ambit of the state. To some extent the divisions between the social work occupations began to break down. For example, psychiatric social workers who had already begun to be recruited into probation before the war now moved also into borstal training and children's services. Significantly their employment by local authorities formed the basis for the post-war development of community work (Mayo, 1975). A conference called by the BFSW at Caxton Hall in 1942 underlined the extent to which a community of sentiment and fellow feeling among different branches of social work was emerging. This heightened the aspiration to create one unified profession. From the conference came a measure of agreement on the desirability of a common training for all intending social workers. This was envisaged as a step towards professional unification. The leadership of the profession urged that the dominant method should be family casework in the community rather than residential or institutional care, and this reflected the power and status hierarchy within the social work occupations.

The experience of the war underlined the gulf between legislative aspirations and the reality of minimal administrative provision. Social workers proved themselves useful in implementing government intentions and rose in official esteem so that the scene was apparently set for the incorporation of professional social work within the post-war welfare state. The war produced a strong sense of national unity and a heightening of the consciousness of citizenship, while class conflict was to some extent muffled and overlaid with sentiments of inter-class reconciliation. The National Government produced the Education Act of 1944 which was based on the principle of equality of opportunity and offered secondary education to all. It also set up machinery to consider questions of postwar national reconstruction which most notably gave Beveridge the opportunity to produce his celebrated report (1942). The Labour government, elected in 1945, set out to use the apparatus of state to provide welfare, largely on the insurance principle, to cover the citizen against the major exigencies of life. Nowhere, however, among the official conceptions of the welfare state was a place envisaged for social work. The foundations of the welfare state were conceived as the control of poverty, unemployment and sickness by rational planning of economic production and distribution. If social work had historically been concerned with poverty, then it would wither away with poverty. If it now dealt with psycho-social needs, then these were not perceived as having anything to do with the fundamentally economic strategy of the welfare state.

The integration of social work with the state

But in practice, if not in theory, social work was already deeply embedded in the state machinery, and when, in 1948, the National Assistance Act repealed the poor law the last and major stumbling block to the integration of social work with the new state welfare system was removed. The act was intended to abolish the stigma attached to the old poor law system by affording the poor financial assistance as of right. The disappearance of the poor law, however, did not cause its functions – particularly in residential care – to vanish. On the contrary, its legacy in the form of workhouses, hospitals and other buildings and their staffs was transferred to the local authorities and to the National Health Service. The character and traditions of these staffs and the patterns of recruitment and training (or lack of it) had a tendency to persist. Local authorities now had to carry out some of the old functions, such as the care of children and the aged, in a new legislative context. For this task the employment of trained social workers seemed clearly necessary.

During the same period the wartime concern with families and children was taken up as an issue by the social work élite (supported by the foundations), which led to the appointment of the Curtis Committee. Its terms of reference made it possible to focus on children irrespective of social class, income or specific problem and thus reflected in its own way the universalism of the welfare state. It gave the opportunity to challenge the functional divisions existing in the organization of social work which historically had created a fragmented set of occupations. Because child welfare could not be contained under the work of any one ministry, such as health or education, the logic of the situation suggested that a local authority agency might be established whose primary function would be social work. Here, for the first time, was the opportunity to recommend to government the establishment of a distinctive sphere of social work upon the foundations of which a unified profession might be built (Walton, 1975, 197).

The recommendations of the Curtis Committee (1946) led to the Children Act of 1948 which set up a new local government department in each area under the overall responsibility of the Home Office. It was specifically a social work department and involved the appointment of children's officers with supporting boarding-out visitors. The new children's departments gave opportunities to women in the management of social work, not of a temporary kind as in wartime, but in a permanent, paid and professional form. The new child care service was quickly judged to have gone further than probation in respect of both standards of recruitment and training, and in the level of responsibilities given to the social workers. It brought social workers with professional aspirations into the local authorities, alongside already established departments employing professionals, such as education. The paradox of the child care service was that it was both a new social work occupation added to those already in existence, while at the same time representing a model of social work professionals managing their own local government department.[3] The Children Act, therefore, was an important landmark in the formation of a partnership between social work and the state.

The struggle for professional unification

To achieve a unified profession the divisions between social workers in their several distinct occupations would have to be overcome. In order to encourage a sense of unity the BFSW altered its constitution to permit individual membership by qualified social workers and thus breached the

3. The impression should not be taken that, in the early days, all recruits to the child care service were fully trained or that professional coherence sprang into existence from the moment of inception.

federal principle. This brought about a further change when, in 1951, BFSW was replaced with a new organization, the Association of Social Workers (ASW). It was created out of the former individual members of BFSW plus new recruits. Though ASW was a small organization, its influence was considerable. For example, it recruited qualified teachers of social work, some of whom had not been eligible for the specialist associations, and they were naturally influential in the profession. Also, there was a growing body of workers who were very active both in their specialist associations and in the ASW and who had the express intention of moving towards a unified social work profession. The foundation of the monthly journal, *Case Conference*, first published in 1954, supported the policy of creating one association of social workers. *Case Conference* readers were treated as if they were already a unified professional group. These years also represented a period when there was little effective challenge to, although some intellectual criticism of, the growing dominance of casework which was regarded as the distinctive theoretical core of professional social work practice (Wootton, 1959b). The social work élite had espoused and developed the application of psychology to casework and the influence of these ideas was spread through the increasing number of social work courses. Casework could thus be used as a unifying ideology in an attempt to establish a professional mode of occupational control. In line with this thinking, generic training was urged. In Britain, the first generic course for social workers was started at the London School of Economics in 1954. Those who experienced generic courses themselves came to question the division of social work into specialisms and some of them formed a generic social workers' group. Many rejected membership of the specialist associations, choosing to make ASW their only professional association.

The new generic courses in the universities could not cope by themselves with the increasing pressure of demand. Following the Younghusband Report (1959) a new form of training outside the universities was instituted. The Council for Training in Social Work was established in 1962 and offered the certificate in social work as a national qualification for those completing a two-year approved course of study and supervised fieldwork, usually at a polytechnic or a college of further education. Students emerging from such courses were going principally into the health and welfare side of local authority social work. Significantly, many untrained staff from local authority departments were seconded by their employers for professional training. Counter-pressure from new areas of specialization, which demanded their own training courses, delayed the spread of the generic principle which was embodied in the certificate in social work. There was concern in the profession about the confused structure of training. Whereas in 1955 the future of training for social work seemed agreed and ASW had set up a committee to give consideration to a register of trained social workers, four years later ASW sponsored a Joint Training Council for Social Work comprised of representatives of nine organizations.

As a way out of the confusion in patterns of training the council began to consider, as a possible solution, the formation of a unified profession. From the discussion, and under the leadership of a probation officer, came the Standing Conference of Organizations of Social Workers (1963). Despite protracted negotiations, no decision had been reached by 1966. Some of the constituent associations were restless and with its membership beginning to rise ASW could see the chance that it could itself, with some reorganization, become the unified professional association. Standing Conference published a discussion paper on professional unification which was circulated to all individual members of constituent organizations. It had already set up working parties concerning organization, finance, membership, training, salaries and working conditions. Finally, after lengthy deliberations the British Association of Social Workers (BASW) replaced ASW in 1970 and was intended to be the single professional association of social workers. Standing Conference had been strongly supported in this development by women in the profession. Walton notes that in matters concerning the employment situation, for example, in the working party on salaries and service, men outnumbered women; whereas in the committee dealing with professional standards the balance was in favour of women, thus continuing a tradition which was strong from the earliest days of social work.[4]

The probation officers had long been in the forefront in seeking professional unification, but the National Association of Probation Officers (NAPO) did not, in the end, join BASW because of fears about the possible consequences of reorganization of social services. The Home Office paper, *The Child, the Family and the Young Offender* (1965) seemed likely to undermine the responsibilities of both the courts and the probation service with a transfer of some of these powers to the local authorities, especially to the children's departments. Probation officers became suspicious about generic developments and their fears were heightened when the reorganization of the Scottish services were seen actually to involve the abolition of a separate probation service and the absorption of probation officers into the new Scottish social work departments. It soon became clear that in England probation officers were

---

4. It has been possible to outline only the major features concerning the progress of social work and professionalism in this period.

determined to remain a central government service and hence they rejected incorporation within BASW. Thus, the goal of a unified profession still eluded social workers. It is ironic that, despite the professional aims in its constitution, BASW represented in one sense a retreat. Both almoning and medical social work had well-established exclusive professional registers which were finally terminated when the two associations handed over their assets and merged within BASW. It was disappointing for the supporters of professionalism that BASW, from its inception, was too weak to institute such a degree of professional control. In any case, officially the certificate of qualification in social work was by now awarded through a quasi-autonomous body, the Central Council for Education and Training in Social Work (CCETSW, 1977). The unified bureau-professional structure in social work was strengthened in 1971 when the Central Council for Education and Training in Social Work was established by statutory instrument. By 1974, it had incorporated the Council for Training in Social Work and the Training Council for Teachers of the Mentally Handicapped as well as the Central Training Council in Child Care. Also, it took over the training functions of the Institute of Medical Social Workers, the Association of Psychiatric Social Workers and the Training Committee of the Advisory Council for Probation and Aftercare. Thus, CCETSW unified the process of professional certification in social work, including probation which had stood out successfully from incorporation into the social services and from BASW. Although CCETSW was established as an independent body, appointments to it were largely in the gift of the secretary of state for the social services within the Department of Health and Social Security (DHSS), which had been created in 1968 to bring under a single umbrella, social security, health and personal social services.

The divisions among the various social work occupations paralleled and reflected the administrative divisions in the provision of services and this was a particular problem in the local authority child care and welfare departments. Here, it was not the imperatives of professionalism and of uniformity of training which weighed so heavily, but rather the fragmentation and duplication of services (or gaps in services) as they were provided to the client. This was an organizational and managerial problem, and in 1968, the establishment of the Seebohm Committee signalled the intention to face up to both the professional and management problems of the social services. Although the discussions about the formation of a unified social work profession long preceded Seebohm, yet the climate of opinion was such that social services reorganization and professional unification came up together. Because the two processes went along side by side they were often elided and people were generally either for or against both (McDougall, 1972, 104). The Seebohm report also followed through the logic of organizational managerialism by urging the creation of unified local authority personal social services departments. At the same time Seebohm affirmed the claims of social work to professionalism. It stressed the necessity for patterns of recruitment, training, career opportunities, status and remuneration fully comparable with the other major departments already established in local government (Seebohm, 1968).

In 1970 the new social services departments came into being; they represented the culmination of post-war developments in social work involving, as they did, a blending of elements of professionalism and bureaucratic organization. Neither autonomous professionalism nor purely bureaucratic hierarchies emerged from the reorganization. Instead, the new departments were a conflation of both elements, manifesting something of the strains and complexities which such a mixture involves. This mode of organization which had already developed in other important departments of state provision – such as education and health – is a hybrid, which we shall refer to as bureau-professionalism (Parry, 1977). In so far as the reorganization was a success for the social work élite, it involved a negotiated partnership between social work, attempting to organize as a profession on the one hand, and the managerial and organizational approach of the state and the local authorities on the other. Autonomous professionalism could never be a serious possibility in social work, at least on any scale, because opportunities to sell social work skills on the private market are few especially when compared with the imput of resources coming to social work from the state as well as from voluntary associations (Turner, 1977, 357–8). Bureau-professionalism has thus offered a chance to create a unified social work profession but within a 'humanized' bureaucratic structure. By this method the social work élite hoped to establish a position of definite, if limited, professional control which could in the long run incorporate, through professional training, the large army of untrained social workers in the employ of local authorities, whether in field work or residential care services.

The reorganization of local government in 1974 involved an attempt to rationalize the provision of social services and the administration of social work on managerial principles. Medical functions, coming under the former medical officer of health, were passed over to the National Health Service. Conversely, medical social workers were transferred from the control of the National Heath Service and put under local authority personal social services – this despite considerable protests from among many medical social workers themselves. Social workers employed in the public sector, with the exception of probation, were brought under one administrative authority. Within this new system the thrust towards professionalism in social work was countered by the rise of unionism. The National Association of Local Government Officers (NALGO) quickly became the most important and powerful representative association for social workers, unlike BASW which concerned itself chiefly with professional functions. NALGO in 1978 had 710,000 members across the range of local government employees of whom only 25,000 were social workers. While many social workers belong both to BASW and to NALGO, the evidence suggests that BASW has been losing ground, particularly with younger social workers. In any case, the more radical element share in the contemporary ethos which regards the professional aims of BASW as élitist. Whereas in 1968 professionalism seemed about to triumph, today, despite the fact that social work has become established within the apparatus of state on bureau-professional lines, there is a sense of retreat and even rejection of the professional ideal. In practice the creation of the bureau-professional structures has assisted the thrust towards unionism among social workers like that of other government employees. This trend has been a response not only to bureaucracy, but to the cuts in welfare expenditure which have resulted from the economic crisis of the early 1970s. The state has increasingly been drawn into health and welfare and personal social services over a long period precisely because, through taxation, it has access to greater resources than voluntary charitable effort. But in a low growth situation disillusionment has set in. This is especially so in the personal social services because, very soon after reorganization, the economic recession brought a curtailment of resources. Although since the nineteenth century the relative positions of voluntary and state funding have been reversed, this new situation has brought the state to a reconsideration of the role of voluntary effort (Wolfenden, 1978). Towards the end of his life Beveridge, who had rejected social work in his youth, came to accept it, though he feared that the altruism of the Christian voluntary tradition would be lost in large-scale bureaucratic welfare provision. Today, with social workers intermittently taking strike action, the questions raised by the paradox of altruist caring provided through paid employment in bureau-professional structures poses Beveridge's questions, but with a new urgency and acuteness (Harris, 1977, 548–9; Beveridge, 1948).

For social work as an aspirant profession the problem is that the inheritance of the poor law and the traditions of local government service, expressed in the dominance of NALGO as an occupational association, have tended to militate against the success of BASW. This is true particularly of the residential care setting with its predominance of untrained social workers mainly of working-class or overseas origin, and largely uninterested in or even hostile to professionalism. Management, too, has introduced its own certificate in social service, as a lower level qualification than the CQSW, based on in-service training and day-release – a model far different from the older-style professionalism (CCETSW, 1975 and 1976). The directors of social services have come to view the current graduate products as including radicals who subvert the system. Equally, the flow of graduates has included a greater proportion with working-class backgrounds. Even among the probation officers, who retained their independent association NAPO, there have been bitter controversies over the contemporary role of the probation officer. The London branch was expelled in 1977 because of its support for the Grunwick strike owing to the appearance of probation officers on the picket line (*The Times*, 22 May 1978, 3).

Those committed to professionalism feel that these changes threaten not merely the advance of their cause, but mark a positive regression. In this they share common ground with other professional or quasi-professional groups in Britain today. Under conflicting pressures many social workers have become disillusioned with NALGO. The annual meeting of BASW in September 1978 resolved to form a new trade union because, as one delegate, himself a NALGO member, put it: 'a conglomerate union has shown it could frustrate the wishes of social workers and their employers alike. Social workers must be masters of their own fate. I am not against industrial action but want to make the decision myself as a member of a professional group.' It should be noted that BASW is itself precluded by its constitution from becoming a union. But such was the strength of feeling in the conference that it was decided to set up a working party to establish a new social work union within six months. Even more significant was the conference resolution to open full membership of BASW – hitherto exclusively an organization of the qualified – to unqualified members. This change was urged because the strength of BASW had been declining and because it had acquired an image as an élitist, middle management organization. Only 30 per cent of those currently eligible are members of the Association. As one delegate put it, 'we can decline into exclusiveness or we can move on to create a British association of all social workers' (*The Times*, 16 September 1978, 4).

Conclusion

The modern occupation of social work emerged from religious, church-sponsored charitable enterprise in an age when private voluntary charity and the statutory poor law represented in their shared conception of the 'deserving' and the 'undeserving' poor a profound ideological and institutional division. The division centred on the issue of class relations and the proper degree of state intervention in society. The question of poverty focused and symbolized issues about class relations in Victorian society in such a vivid and powerful way that the subject has continued to exercise a high degree of fascination and partisanship for scholars even in our own day.

The Church of England under political and social attack and threatened with the possibility of disestablishment experienced a profound religious revival which issued in an attempt to come to grips with the new urban-industrial society. The moral welfare and settlement movements were important elements of the response to urban poverty. Equally the Charity Organization Society attempted to cope with the breakdown of traditional communal relations between classes and end the consequent abuse of the disorganized charitable system through systematic and scientific casework methods. Also, it aimed to pre-empt the necessity for the expansion of state charity beyond its limited role under the poor law.

Those who were employed to operate the poor law were minor functionaries working to a bureaucratic routine and recruited mainly from elements of the working class itself. The ethos of the poor law and the attitudes of its servants militated against the adoption of professionalism as an ideology and occupational practice. Such influence as professionalism had in the poor law − and it was always limited − was carried there by middle-class men and women such as doctors and nurses, and much later by social workers. At the level of the political process, professionals and intellectuals played a growing part in pressing for the reform of the service.

It was chiefly from among middle-class women seeking to create occupational opportunities that the impetus came for the adoption of professionalism as a form of occupational development and control in social work, nursing and teaching. These women shared the ideology of professionalism with the men of their own class, such as doctors and lawyers. They adapted it and combined it with the caring ideology of familialism which conventionally defined the role of woman in society. Professionalism in social work was strengthened by the influence of psychiatric theory with its scientific roots which issued in the creation of a new social work occupation, psychiatric social work, in the late 1920s.

There was a separation in the early twentieth century of social administration from social work in dealing with the problem of poverty. The neo-liberal and Fabian Socialist approach was through state action on the basis of the insurance principle and the management of unemployment via employment exchanges. Social work was regarded by the proponents of such policies as patronizing and irrelevant. Yet, the disruption of war − particularly to family life − and the weakening of the deterrent principle of the poor law and the moderation of its practices by the penetration of middle-class professionals, especially women, led to a convergence during the inter-war years between the practices of voluntary agencies and state agencies.

The repeal of the poor law in 1948 and the take over of its responsibilities by the National Health Service and the local authorities created the opportunity for the employment of social workers by the local authorities, particularly in the new occupation of child care. The disappearance of the poor law removed the long-standing division which had blocked the integration of social work into the state welfare system.

The struggle for professional unification among the several social work occupations had begun between the wars, but in the post-war period the movement towards an integrated managerial structure of state welfare services was deeply influenced by the professional interests of social workers. Managerial integration could reduce functional divisions among the social work occupations and lead to professional unification. There was a thrust towards a single professional association controlling the process of recruitment, entry and educational qualification.

Autonomous professionalism was never a serious possibility for social workers, partly because of the drive towards state managerialism, but also because of limited market opportunities. What in fact emerged was a hybrid form of organization for social services which was reflected in the Seebohm report and incorporated in the reform of local government in 1974. This form we have called bureau-professionalism. In practice Scotland achieved such a unified structure for social work; in England the probation service baulked both at incorporation within the administrative structure of the social services and at the proposed unified professional association of social workers (BASW).

Bureau-professionalism engenders a conflict between alternative forms of occupational association, namely, professional association and trade unionism which, arising from the nineteenth-century inheritance, remains as a contentious issue in social work today.

3

Working-class association, private capital, welfare and the state in the late-nineteenth and twentieth centuries:
'Spade deep in order to gain some idea of the under-soil throughout'

Stephen Yeo

> We all of us in England still fancy, at least, that we believe in the blessings of freedom, yet, to quote an expression which has become proverbial, 'today we are all of us socialists.' The confusion reaches much deeper than a mere opposition between the beliefs of different classes. Let each man, according to the advice of the preachers, look within. He will find that inconsistent social theories are battling in his own mind for victory.
> A. V. Dicey (1914)

> I do not believe the Friendly Society people knew what they were doing. They all had a very good lunch (with wine) and got very convivial. ... No further effort was ever made to secure real self-government. The power, however, is there, latent to be awakened one day.
> W. J. Braithwaite (1911)

I

Bernard Shaw would have been the best person to write this chapter. H. G. Wells tried imaginative discussion of our themes in a novel *The New Machiavelli* (1911), but drama would be the best form to embody the anxious personal and social struggles which characterized the 'social politics' of the late nineteenth and early twentieth centuries.

Persons became symbols, carrying the weight of opposed social directions with labels like 'collectivism' or 'individualism'. Such 'isms' now appear blurred and inaccurate, but to participants in the struggles they felt distinct. They confronted each other across royal commissions such as the strategic Royal Commission on the Poor Laws 1905–9. They manipulated and laughed at each other at breakfast tables such as Lloyd George's or dinner tables such as the Webbs' – the joke being richer for recent reading of *The New Machiavelli* by participants, with its acid caricature of the Webbs as 'the Baileys' (Braithwaite, 1957, 116).

The struggles were accompanied by the feeling that a new epoch was being made, by ambiguous forces called 'the people', 'the Coming Race', 'the masses', or 'bureaucrats' (Kirkman Gray, 1908 *passim*). There was promise and expectation that political power and minimum living standards would in some sense be diffused or generalized. But on whose terms? It was not yet determined that 'the vote' and 'the benefit' would be the predominant forms of mass consumption of 'politics' and 'welfare'. Nor indeed that passive, individuated, alienated, centralized, *consumption* rather than active, associated, accessible, controlled *production* by and for the majority would colour these areas of social life so strongly during the twentieth century.

Drama could also best convey the 'inconsistencies' referred to by A. V. Dicey in the 1914 quotation above and the sense of defeated but not destroyed power and possibility, the unfinished business in the back of W. J. Braithwaite's mind in 1911. Which 'social theories' were to live with and which were to suppress others? Which were progressive – the ones which won, or parts of the ones which lost? Which would have carried, perhaps could still carry a different, more ambitiously democratic day?

Reactions to social politics during the years 1908–14 were certainly as theatrical and shrill as they had been to franchise politics in the equally climatic years 1866–7. A. V. Dicey took part in both. In 1867 he was quite sanguine (Dicey, 1867). By 1914 his worry at the statist, unconstitutional directions Liberal social policy had taken in his new long introduction to his *Lectures* was as 'extreme' as Carlyle's worry about suffrage reform had been in his 'Shooting Niagara' (1867). Acts like the Education (Provision of Meals) Act 1906, the Trades Disputes Act (1906), National Insurance (1911), Acts fixing minimum rates of wages in particular trades, the Finance (1909–10) Act, and the Mental Deficiency Act (1913), together constituted, for Dicey, a revolution. They constituted 'socialism' but not 'democracy'.

How are we to understand his outrage? What can it tell us about what was going on? Was it merely the 'reaction' of a quaint Liberal Unionist who could seriously suggest that old age pensioners (after the Pensions Act of 1908) should be disenfranchised? They were, thought Dicey, in receipt of 'a new form of outdoor relief for the poor'.

It is tempting to pass by on the other side of such resistance to an act which modern welfare historians claim 'enormously eased the financial burden of old age' (Hennock, 1968). After all, old age pensions were part of a series of measures usually seen as 'the foundations of the welfare state'. They get written about as milestones in books with titles like *England's Road to Social Security* (de Schweinitz, 1947) and are seen as part of a whole period from the Education Act of 1870 to National Health in 1948, during which benevolent social reform was added to political reform.

Perhaps, however, we should stop and look. To see, for instance, that Section 3, sub-section I(b) of the Pensions Act (1908) did indeed state that a person is not entitled to a pension if before he becomes so entitled 'he has habitually failed to work according to his ability, opportunity and need, for the maintenance or benefit of himself and those legally dependent upon him'. Or to see the scales of pensionability. One of the Charity Organization Society's criticisms of the act was that the sums involved were so small. They started at 70 years of age with 5s. a week (the cost of a cabinet minister's cigar, Ben Tillett pointed out at the 1908 TUC) if the recipient's means did not exceed about 8s. a week. The 'enormous easement' of the financial burdens of old age then went gradually down, to 1s. a week pension if income did not exceed about 12s. a week, and then to nothing. Readers who wish to penetrate behind the systematic exaggeration of the material benefits conferred by Liberal social legislation in these years or to see behind the pictures and newspaper hymns about the first Pension Day, should place such sums of money beside any contemporary surveys of the lives of the poor, for example, Mrs Pember Reeves's *Round About a Pound a Week* (1913).

As worried as Dicey, but from a different point of view and class position, were the Friendly Societies. Although their offices can still be seen from most inner-city bus routes in Britain, it is safe to say that what goes on inside them is unknown to most social workers, socialists and social historians. They were enormous, but not universal, mutual associations of working men, the theory of whose practice was collective self-help. In their most developed forms they practised and believed in federal, associated self-government and in the connections between social goods like recreation, drink, helping others, hospital care, proper funerals, and the maintenance of an adequate life when sick, old or unemployed. They were autonomous working-class products in which the state and respectable opinion showed an obsessive and shaping interest through the nineteenth century (Supple, 1974). Their 'failure' to become universal, and the 'failure' of their most advanced forms to fulfil their highest ambitions must not be attributed to their intentions or lack of intentions, and thus be moralized rather than explained. It has, rather, to be attached to the material constraints of majority working-class life – the absolute deprivation of spare time, money and cultural resources for all but a minority stratum of workers.

There was competition within and between different forms of Friendly Society. This was between those which assimilated to the principles and modes of organization of private businesses with their wage-workers/consumer mode, as opposed to those with greater commitment to mutuality, and associated production of insurance through mutual social relations. 'The state' materially aided the former types as well as the latter, through legal recognition under Industrial and Provident Society legislation. There was a continual effort to 'license' and 'register' both into acceptable forms. Business forms were also encouraged into being through the effects of competition from private capitalist firms active in the same field, registered under the Companies Acts. As with retailing, from the 1860s onwards private capitalist forms of insurance were preparing to reap where working-class forms had sown. Through the second half of the nineteenth century, however, the vast Affiliated Orders – the Ancient Order of Foresters (1899, 666,000 members) and the Manchester Unity of Oddfellows (1899, 713,000 members) – had greatly expanded. Considering their size they have not been greatly studied (except by Gosden, 1961 and 1973). Their history may be read – against current orthodoxies – as attempts (albeit cribbed, cabined and confined) to universalize the whole range of Friendly Society benefits – mutuality as well as insurance – but on Friendly Society or for-labour terms rather than on private company, for-capital, terms. Their internal history as well as the history of their relations with other forms like the Collecting Societies, may then be read as a terrain upon which active and explicit struggle took place – as active and explicit as in China over the past twenty years – over whether 'economics' was to triumph over 'politics', rationalization over *democratic* centralism, 'actuarial science' over fraternal social relations, state subordination over public subsidy. Through the second half of the nineteenth century the Affiliated Orders and parallel smaller associations struggled on in times which were increasingly difficult ones for the latter emphases.

For example, they were keen on combining the contradictory goods of democratic branch autonomy with centralized scale and administrative/financial back-up. They were keen on 'irrationally' diffused office-holding. From each according to his ability meant *resistance* to the actuarial common sense of contributions graded according to age. They were *affiliated* orders: affiliation and federation being quintessentially working-class or mass democratic devices, as opposed to the vertically organized business, political and cultural machines which private capital favours and which have penetrated working-class forms during the twentieth century.

How, then, are we to understand their worries? Because their politics – which must be seen as such however unfamiliar the term – were anti-state, and because 'progressive' politics during the twentieth century (including Marxist/socialist politics) have been statist, Friendly Society fears and resistance to welfare changes have been made to appear archaic. They have been understood as mere institutional conservatism, labour aristocratic self-interest – as 'reactionary' like Dicey.

When they are allowed to speak, and still less when their own associations are examined in the detail which cannot be provided here, it cannot now, in the late 1970s, seem so simple. Their own time witnessed

many explicit statist critiques of working-class forms, and proposals for
their replacement by national compulsion, for instance by H. S.
Tremenheere in the 1870s and 1880s (Corrigan, 1977b, 333–4). Our
own time has been too full of bloated states masquerading as socialisms for
us to pass by on the other side of any such large-scale working-class
creativity. The Grand High Chief Ranger of the Foresters (Bro. Radley)
described the offer of government subsidy for pensions in 1891 as

> a mess of pottage which does not exist in reality. ... Care must be taken that the
> rising generations are not enticed by bribes drawn from the pockets of those
> who esteem their freedom or forced by legislative compulsion to exchange the
> stimulating atmosphere of independence and work for an enervating system of
> mechanical obedience to State management and control – the certain sequel to
> State subsidy. [quoted in Treble, 1970, 274.]

In a clever speech in Birmingham Town Hall in 1894 Joseph Chamberlain
tried to allay such fears. After all, he urged, 'the nation and the Friendly
Societies have a common interest and a common object, and our effort
should be to bring them into cooperation.' 'It is evident that a great deal
too much has been made of this question of State interference which is not
so important as many of my critics suppose. ... The honest man does not
fear the policeman, and it is only the thief that thinks each bush an officer.'
One of his critics – evidently with thieving tendencies – was J. Lister
Stead, assistant secretary of the Foresters. Chamberlain's pension scheme,
thought Stead, 'is considered a very alluring bait to obtain the support of
Friendly Societies; but concealed under the bait, to use an angler's
illustration, is an insidious hook, which would drag us out of the free
waters of self-dependence, and land us on the enervating bank of State
control. ... It may be depended upon as a solid truth that the State will not
grant us special privileges without wanting to have a finger in our pie'
(quoted in Chamberlain, 1895). The history of the succeeding fifteen
years, let alone the next fifty, might well suggest that such 'reactionaries'
were at least half right and their 'progressive' foes three quarters sinister.

2

It can be liberating for people with an interest in changing any situation, to
try to understand its place in *time* and in *struggle*. This is particularly so in
a situation such as 'the welfare state' which can seem so hugely present,
progressive, for the good of all and for always. It is particularly difficult for
my generation (born 1939) to get behind welfare's baroque facade. We
have been the direct beneficiaries of one of its most creative periods, from
1941 to 1948. We literally have it in our bones. Fairer shares for all *were*
fought for and achieved during this time under the pressure of war and its

associated radical populism. There *was* a (temporary) thrust towards universal public provision of (some) minimum rights, even towards universalizing the best of some social goods away from the market place, as in the National Health Service. Late, but large steps have been taken in our time. In 1948 not only was 'one person, one vote' achieved in the Representation of the People Act, but the poor law was repealed in the National Assistance Act.

Never particularly popular among working people, the welfare state has produced and been produced by national experts in 'social administration' (that is running the way we live), who then explain it to further professionals (including social workers) who try to distribute its benefits to consumers or clients.

The 'welfare state' was a term first used late in the 1930s and not generally current until the mid-1940s. 'It' was not, any more than 'democracy', a known destination deliberately reached through routes carefully chosen by far-sighted reformers or statesmen. Improvisation in response to immediately felt pressures was Lloyd George's method during the passage of National Insurance in 1911. But it has also been the way with much welfare legislation.

Nevertheless, with hindsight we can pick out broad directions of development between the end of the period dealt with in chapter 1 above (1871) and the 1940s.

First, elected *ad hoc* bodies (like school boards, or boards of guardians) with access to public finance and potentially beyond the control of central government or even of local middle-class leadership, were finally abolished when the guardians' functions were taken over by public assistance committees of county boroughs/councils, in 1929. The Local Government Act of that year was part of an aggressive central tightening-up of control over relatively autonomous local, and sometimes working-class, practices which followed the defeat of the General Strike. Secondly, national 'services', whether of local government (block grants 1929) or of unemployment relief (Unemployment Assistance Board, 1934) or of hospitals (Public Health Act, 1936), became visible as rationalizing edges cutting through overlapping local responsibilities. There were, and still are, resistances – formidable and partly successful in the case of the UAB. But such services were eventually to be centrally financed and controlled, often by appointment rather than election. The absorption of the Local Government Board (1871), alongside the Insurance Commission (1911) into the Ministry of Health in 1919 was another step towards rationalization of welfare. Thirdly, the adoption of the contributory 'insurance' principle as the main mode of British welfare provision, with the triad of state, employer and worker each paying notionally fair (but highly regressive) contributions towards 'benefits', also characterized this period. Richard Titmuss saw the 1911 National Insurance Act as 'the birth of the "insurance principle" as a public institution in Britain'. There always remained a stratum to be dealt with away from contributions, through the poor law and its successors down to the modern 'SS'. Pensions had been financed out of taxation in 1908 but moved towards insurance in 1925. The same triad of state, employer and worker at the same time became, with the same degree of dignified 'fairness', parties to the mainstream conduct of industrial relations, in an almost 'constitutional' manner. Fourth, there was also a decisive switch during this period away from working-class associations – the 'English Associations of Working Men' which were so celebrated by serious liberals from about 1850 to 1900 – as creative *producers* of welfare, with the real subordination of Friendly Societies as 'Approved Societies' in 1911. Then there was a switch away from such associations even as *distributors* of welfare, with the 1937 'Black-Coated Workers' Pensions Act and the 1948 National Health Insurance measures pushing even Approved Societies off the stage. By then an ironic bit of incorporation had been achieved. A working-class association – the Co-operative Insurance Society – having found a place in the sun to grow as an Approved Society after 1911 – came to act as a major lobbyist against one of the recommendations of the Beveridge Report, the nationalization of the industrial insurance industry. Fifth, administrative changes in welfare often concealed – or were undertaken in order to ensure – underlying continuities of attitude. Arrangements for 'Deposit Contributors' in 1911 recalled the ideas behind 1834. The Poor Law Act of 1930 restated poor law principles for the guidance of public assistance committees just after the abolition of the guardians; and poor law attitudes have survived all of the thirty years beyond 1948, as anyone on social security will know.

But large, contextual, philosophical changes also defined the period. On the one hand, after 1934 it was no longer possible to insist – even in theory – that relief could only be given to an able-bodied man in an institution, or to keep formal deterrent tests. Universal rights and dignities did not inform the realities of welfare provision, but they had increasingly to be taken into account as ideas and as material possibilities. On the other hand, competitive business nationalism became pervasive as the main context for welfare reform. Between the 1880s and the 1920s – to be safe and vague about dating – a general ruling recognition broke through, that a discontinuously large amount of state activity/expenditure was, first, possible; and then that it was, however much disliked in the back of the mind, an essential concomitant of national efficiency, health, security, prosperity ... vis à vis 'competitors', whether the competition came from domestic working-class forces and potentials, or from other national economies/empires. War was the most obvious but not the only spur to this development.

Rather than chronicling the major acts of people or acts of parliament in order to give flesh to these trends – they are now accessible in many brief histories listed in the references to chapter 1 above – it may be more helpful to lift the eyes away from the separate trees towards the whole wood, before lowering them again to a single tree. The important thing to notice about the whole wood is precisely its accumulated size: twenty acts of parliament on unemployment between 1920 and the Unemployment Act of 1934; 15 million claims for various kinds of benefit in England and Wales in one 'normal' year (1956) – about one for every three inhabitants; discontinuous public spending proportions which have become part of the daily rhetoric of politics, for and against. All these acts and consolidated acts were important as a total phenomenon almost regardless of their specific content. Such a volume of centrally made 'machinery' – as with machinery in its more conventional realm of material production – necessarily limits and shapes (even 'determines') the freedom of manoeuvre of subsequent actors wishing to compete on the same stage, whatever their social or ideological position. It accumulates capital for capital in a process sometimes known as 'stabilization', and constrains the accumulation of labour's own future capital. The other side of the reactionary label for all this state activity, as 'demoralization' of the individual and family, is that it is indeed de-skilling of the working class in spheres other than the 'economic'.

Once there, such a large and rising national, state, bureaucratic or public composition of 'capital' in this 'social policy' sphere has material consequences comparable to those of the more familiar rising technical or organic composition of 'economic' capital. As the simplest, it has to be taken account of: it has to be gone through rather than ignored, in order to come out on the other side. The 'welfare state' is, as it were, a state: it will not and cannot wither, without positive and creative activity which has to risk, all the time, the danger of incorporation if ever, in Beveridge's vision, 'human society may become a friendly society'. W. H. Beveridge's contradictory, inconsistent central belief, against all his statist contributions, was that 'the making of a good society depends not on the state but on the citizens, acting individually or in free association with one another.' He had a dream, a deeply troubled one by the 1940s, of how society as a friendly society might be 'an affiliated order of branches, some large and many small, each with its own life in freedom, each linked to the rest by common purpose and by bonds to serve that purpose. So the night's insane dream of power over other men, without limit and without

mercy, shall fade. So mankind in brotherhood shall bring back the day'
(Beveridge, 1948, 320, 324).

3

Certain opponents of the statist tendency of Liberal pre-1914 social
legislation, writing in a study of and by Devon fishermen but one which
had much wider implications, maintained in 1911: 'The alternative lies,
not between knowing a few people and knowing all to an equal degree, but
between scratching the surface of the whole of a field, and digging a
portion of it spade-deep in order to gain some idea of the under-soil
throughout' (Reynolds and Woolley, 1911, xv). The same could not be
said of the acts and attitudes they reacted to in their work *Seems So!*
Rather than attempting a wide survey therefore, the focus of the rest of this
chapter will shift to a single act or part of an act – the health sections of
National Insurance, 1911.

Lloyd George chose to call it 'health' rather than 'sickness' because, as
a recent historian has put it, 'in the rapidly expanding area where politics
and advertising overlap', it sounded better. The measure brought
beneficiary-contributed health insurance to five-sixths of the families of the
nation. It imposed by law novel duties on some 15 million individuals –
workers, employers, officials, doctors. It was presented with new razz-
matazz, 'the Great Insurance Act', in *Tit Bits* (23 May 1911) and
elsewhere. And it was *experienced* as something discontinuous, however
subsequent historians may try to insist on continuities. Everyone reacted to
it, in a manner reminiscent of 1866–7. 'It was, I believe', wrote an
insurance civil servant Sir Henry Bunbury, 'the first time that civil servants
had to explain novel and complex matters to the unlettered masses in plain
and simple English.' 'It is no use', replied Stephen Reynolds on behalf of
some distinctly lettered masses who hated the term, 'offering them
freedom from destitution if, as a condition, they must knuckle under to a
scheme of industrial conscription like the Webb Minority Report; or
offering them national insurance if the result is to make the master more
powerfully a master, and the man more impotently a workman than ever'
(Reynolds and Woolley, 1911, xxv).

In other words, there is some digging to do, to gain some idea of the
under-soil throughout. There is some digging to do in order to see that
what is large or small, recessive or dominant in our social relations today –
for example the relative and shifting weight of private (for profit) as against
mutual (for fraternity) as against state or 'social'[1] (for what?) insurance in

1. For W. H. Beveridge in his famous report, *Social Insurance and Allied Services*
(1942), 'the term "social insurance" implies both that it is compulsory and that men stand
together with their fellows.'

the welfare field – is an *achieved* result. It is the consequence of by-passing, suppressing or concealing alternatives, through struggle. Such struggle may best be understood (from the point of view of achieving change) in class terms. This is not to say that it may best be understood as a straight fight between proletarians in the red corner and bosses in the blue. Class is an historical and theoretical category which may help us precisely to see behind such crude simplicities, and to explain their non-appearance. It may help us to get at Dicey's 'inconsistencies' mentioned above. Each latent alternative in the welfare field, as well as the temporarily manifest present, has its own mix of distinct material possibilities and constraints and is carried by its own mix of social relations or class forces.

W. J. Braithwaite was the civil servant at the heart of the struggles over the National Insurance Bill 1911. He was a liberal and a Liberal, liked to see himself as a 'socialist' but staunchly anti-Fabian. His father had been a Friendly Society stalwart. He moved from the Inland Revenue to being Lloyd George's principal Treasury assistant on insurance, and was then unceremoniously pushed back to Inland Revenue, after the defeat of his, and the mutual Friendly Societies' hopes for the Act.

By contrast to many people who have talked about the withering away of the State, Braithwaite fought for practicable plans towards such an end, near to the centres of power. He wanted the whole national insurance machine constructed on mutual, local, autonomous, self-governing lines in such a way that it 'could be run from a third floor office in the Strand' with the Government interfering minimally. He wanted to exclude private capitals from administering the Act as 'Approved Societies', unless they allowed consumers to be *members* in a Friendly Society sense. He also wanted to exclude Friendly Societies whose only relationship to their 'members' was through collectors, by inserting clauses in the act which required first, that there should be democratic 'local management committees' for each 250 members of an Approved Society who lived more than three miles from the nearest branch office. This became Clause 18 of the Bill introduced on 4 May 1911. Secondly, he wanted to insist that Approved Societies should be precluded from distributing any of their funds except by way of benefits and that they should provide in their constitutions for the election of all their committees, representatives and officers by members (Clause 21).

We are fortunate in having a ringside seat from which to observe what happened. Braithwaite's memoirs of these years were published, partly in diary form, as *Lloyd George's Ambulance Wagon*. Bentley Gilbert (1965) has also produced an outstandingly honest modern account, based upon these and other personal, state and printed papers. At stake were large human needs and the social relations through which they were predominantly to be met in twentieth-century Britain: such basics as the need to provide a decent funeral for one's own dead, or the need to be able to live with dignity when old, sick, left alone or out of work. Just as with other human needs during precisely the same years, like the need to eat and be clothed, or to wash with a helpful substance such as soap; or the need to entertain and be entertained, or to drink stimulating/refreshing liquids or to acquire shelter, there was open conflict between large combines of private capital as forms for irritating or exploiting such needs through competition and for profit, and working-class forms for meeting them in ways which showed the immanent possibility of alternative, co-operative, associated, social relations. This conflict was class conflict in the fullest sense, whether obvious, even though as yet largely undescribed, as between the Prudential and the Ancient Order of Foresters, Unilever and the Co-ops, big brewers and Working Men's Clubs, or more subtle, as in the conflicts *within* mutual or potentially mutual forms themselves, for example Building Societies or Friendly Societies. More and more of these conflicts, as in the case of national insurance, were necessarily taking place early in the twentieth century in and through the public area of social/ political relations known as 'the state'.

The industrial insurance industry was a very powerful, concentrated and, after 1901, well-organized branch of capital. The Prudential was the nation's largest holder of railway stock, the largest private owner of ground rents and freehold properties, the biggest source of local government borrowing and the largest holder of Bank of England stocks. In 1901 the 24 largest companies formed an association, known as the 'Combine'. They had voices such as the *Insurance Mail*, and lobbyists such as a young solicitor later to become powerful in Conservative and National politics as an active antagonist of labour's forms on behalf of private property, Kingsley Wood. But their most powerful weapon was their army of agents. 70,000 collecting agents were employed (20,000 of them by the Prudential) to collect 40 million funeral policies (20 million with the Prudential). These men sold benefits door to door – $1^1/_2$ pence a week drew a £10 death benefit – and thus had direct access to most working-class homes. They were also the owners of commodities, their 'books', which gave them semi self-employed livelihoods they could not afford to lose. As canvassers they were the fear and envy of other machines beginning to operate with the door-to-door, 'consumer' mode (rather than with the branch-meeting, membership, processional or 'mutual' mode) such as the orthodox political parties. These agents may not have liked their companies. There is some evidence that they did not (*Clarion*, 14 July 1911) but they had a direct interest in seeing their business grow.

When the companies were under pressure, the agents were presented as 'philosophers', guides and friends of the people, as social workers not salesmen. The 'man from the Pru' was said to be 'looked upon as a member of the family consulted on many matters quite apart from his business' (Gilbert, 1965, 143). The whole operation was paradigmatic of the kind of private social relations twentieth century private capital has favoured, and diametrically opposite to the most developed labour aristocratic and liberal public visions of the second half of the nineteenth century.

The industry made a lot of money – each month the Prudential's investment portfolio grew by an additional half million pounds. In that sense, and in that sense alone, was it 'efficient'. To read the semi-automatic description of Friendly Societies by modern historians as 'inefficient' or 'out of date' leaves one aghast at the biased measure being used. Scarcely one third of the total amount collected in private industrial insurance contributions was ever paid in benefits. Efficiency lies in the class eye of the beholder. The Independent Labour Party had long been after the Prudential in particular, before the formation of the Combine, as a sweated employer. Throughout the period there were signs of pressure from 'modern office methods' on clerks and agents, and of resistance to such pressure (*Labour Leader*, 10 September 1898 through to 15 April 1899). Indeed, the insurance industry has been in the van of twentieth-century private capital's power and concentrated presence. Liberals like Braithwaite and even Lloyd George always assumed that eventually it would be displaced from its perch by an assertion through nationalization of public social responsibility.

When the Combine got wind of the possible democratic shapes of a major state innovation – national insurance – a formidable campaign was launched. It was up to then the most aggressive parliamentary lobby mounted by capital. The fascinating details cannot be rehearsed here. Through the summer of 1910 and into the late-autumn of 1911 the Combine managed to secure, first, the dropping of widows and orphans pensions from the plan. These were not to be reintroduced until 1925. They were thought to threaten the death benefit business by the Friendly Societies as much as by the industry. Then they got Clauses 18 and 21 removed from the bill, thus allowing themselves in as Approved Societies to register the insured, conduct the day-to-day business of health insurance, examine claims, help to determine benefits and so on. Then, alongside the British Medical Association, they encouraged the doctors to get out from under the control of Approved Societies and to assert their professional status. At one stage of the battle, Braithwaite recalled Kingsley Wood leaning over to him and whispering, 'we have got Lloyd George there (putting his thumb on the desk) and shall get our own terms.' They thus became the most important administrative agency of National Health insurance. In Gilbert's words (1965, 128, 148, since it is to his researches that all of the above is owed):

> The insurance companies sought not to keep government insurance out of their field of operation, but rather to take over the government programme and run it themselves. Their enemy was not the state, but the originally designated operators of the national insurance plan, the British Friendly Societies. It was private, not government competition they sought to destroy. ... During the passage of the National Insurance Act, the Societies were pushed aside by the insurance industry. While destroying the position of the old Friendly Societies, the insurance men reconstructed the entire Act. The measure had contemplated a simple extension of the fraternal Friendly Society principle to those elements of the population hitherto not covered. It became instead a form of national compulsory savings, administered awkwardly and expensively by private insurance firms, most of which saw the programme only as an avenue to the extension of their private business. ... The result was to destroy the fraternal aspects of even the strongest friendly societies and to turn them into semi-official agencies whose only reason for existence was the administration of health insurance.

Braithwaite was sent back to the Inland Revenue after the bill thus mauled became statute. Robert Morant, the favourite civil servant of the Webbs, who had master-minded the destruction of the school boards in 1902, took over. The Webbs breathed a sigh of relief.

They had been unhappy with the act, even in its final form. To be fair to them, this was partly because of its real subordination of independent working-class forms. For these they had always had, particularly Beatrice, great respect. It puts the fears of the Friendly Societies about pensions, quoted earlier, in a firm and rational context to reinforce Gilbert by quoting what the Webbs wrote in 1911 (169–70) on the implications of the form of national insurance:

> And when we consider the question of self-government, we can hardly recognize as independence the condition of the 'Approved Friendly Societies' under the chancellor of the exchequer's scheme of 1911 – a condition in which the hitherto autonomous society has to accept a government scheme of benefits in lieu of its own, performs none of the work of collection, exercises no control over the accumulating funds, has no responsibility for their investment, is compelled every three years to vary its benefits as it may, on valuation, peremptorily be required to do, and is even subject to governmental regulation and control in respect of the formation of branches, and the appointment and payment of the medical men on whose skill and honourable dealing the whole efficiency, and indeed, the actuarial solvency, of the organization depends. In fact the 'Approved Friendly Societies' in this scheme become merely canvassing agents and benefit-paying cashiers to the great new government department

which will control the taxation on employers and wage-earners of some five-and-twenty million pounds annually and which will manage the investment of a fund presently running into a hundred millions.

What price Joseph Chamberlain's bland reassurances in 1894 now? By 1926 a minority report of the Royal Commission on Health Insurance found the lack of control of Approved Societies by their members scandalous. There were other reasons for the Webb's dissatisfaction, smacking of the 'inconsistencies' warring within individuals' attitudes noticed by Dicey. Adequate *control* was also lacking, for them, in the scheme, as well as autonomy. Indeed they admired the Friendly Societies partly because of the moral control exercised by branches over members. 'A most unscientific state aid', commented Beatrice in her diaries. 'The unconditionality of all payments under insurance schemes constitutes a grave defect. The state gets nothing for its money in the way of conduct, it may even encourage malingerers.' In its draft stages she thought the Bill was 'communist' (Webb, 1948, 468, 430, 473-4). However, Sydney minded the act less, and reassurance came. 'Years afterwards I was told', wrote Braithwaite (1957, 47), 'that Webb had said that things would be "alright after all" as Morant was appointed to administer the Act.'

4

The word 'administer' conceals a much more creative process 'not a classical ... a gothic building' as Lucy Masterman put it (1939, 342). Unlike the other Liberal reforms of this period, this one could not slot into a pre-existing government department. A vast new machine had to be brought into being. The act became law on December 16th 1911: collections began to be made on 15 July 1912, and it was not until 15 January 1913 that medical benefits began to take effect. For those involved, like Morant or C. F. G. Masterman, it was touch-and-go whether the act would ever get off the ground. They genuinely feared that contributors might not pay. In a violent campaign which Braithwaite found 'entirely undemocratic' the *Daily Mail* was agitating that they should not.

Some features of this process of 'administration' need to be highlighted, before further reactions to it can make sense. First, as with pensions, the material consequences for beneficiaries must not be exaggerated or pre-dated. 'Security' did not 'happen' with each step along 'England's Road' to it. The health provisions were more comprehensive than pensions had been in 1908. They applied to all wage-earners below £160 per annum. In return for 4*d.* a week from the workers, 3*d.* from his employer and 2*d.* from the Treasury ('9*d.* for 4*d.*' was Lloyd George's advertising slogan), beneficiaries were to get sickness benefit of 10*s.* a week for 13 weeks, 5*s.*

for the next 13 weeks, plus free medical services and some other grants. All in all, E. P. Hennock has suggested, for the younger worker in good health 'this was not very much more than he would have obtained previously from a well-run [Friendly] Society.' The description in the socialist press was 'the great insurance fraud'. There was also restriction, maternity grants being the only benefit not depending on the sickness or liability of the wage-earner rather than others in the family.

Second, the material consequences *were* exaggerated and systematically so. In the process it became clear that this was because they were not just financial, but had to do with novel social relations. The act was complicated, necessitating four dense pages of even *Tit-Bits* ('we have been able to secure an early copy of the bill ...') in their special supplement of 23 May 1911. In this supplement it was the 'Great' National Insurance Bill. Like something else alleged to be 'Great' which began three years later, it was important to explain 'how it will affect nearly 15 million workers'. It had to be *sold*, it was a form of conscription or national mobilization. 'No More Doctors' Bills', ran the *Tit-Bits* headline. 'No More Medicine Accounts!! Wages When Out-O'-Work! Baby Grants Paid to Mothers!!' Meanwhile Lloyd George was busy appearing on the plates, tiles, china bits of all kinds, as well as in the national and provincial press, which were the then means of bringing politicians into the nation's front rooms. Lecturers were recruited to expound the act up and down the land. More than a million people attended. Columns of the local press were syndicated. In March 1912 the joint committee in charge of operations ordered the printing of 25 million circulars, explaining the act in the simplest possible terms. Market-research and opinion-testing techniques were used, while the *Daily Mail* was screaming 'It [the Act] Must Not Happen'. 'In the early days of 1912', recalled R.W. Harris (1946, 17) the author of the mass-circular, with biblical solemnity, 'it was decreed that there should be delivered by post at every home, cottage and tenement in the land, a paper which should tell every inhabitant of these islands what his position was under the new scheme. It was the first such wholesale delivery that had even been undertaken. It fell to my lot to draw up this leaflet. I put it through a series of ten proofs and tried twenty copies of each on all sorts of people, including maidservants'.

Third, in the hurry, corners were cut. These were corners with large constitutional consequences for a 'democracy' which in certain quarters took itself seriously as such. Lloyd George can be watched cutting them, as he told warring Friendly Society and insurance representatives in October 1911 at a secret meeting that 'at the present moment we are making law' (Gilbert, 1965, 147). So where was parliament, where the courts? The best witnesses to such incisions in dignified bourgeois democratic theory were honest and worried contemporary liberals. Even those doing the cutting themselves, such as C. F. G. Masterman (1939, 223), confessed: 'We were asked to complete a ... difficult scheme in six months. ... Half the clauses were highly technical; many contradicted each other, *some rendered necessary action obviously illegal*' (my emphasis). What was sauce for the state gander was not for the voluntary associational goose – remember that these were years of considerable preoccupation with the *ultra vires* actions of working-class forms like trade unions. A correspondent in *Clarion* made an explicit connection between the bill and the Osborne Judgement calling it 'the second move of the employing classes to smash the trade unions' (*Clarion*, 28 July 1911). Sir Ernest Gowers served a thoughtful apprenticeship for *Plain Words* on the Insurance Commission. He recognized the dangers of illegality on the state's part which 'officials' had to be careful not to abet. He was particularly concerned about the interpretative role of the modern official and the consequent 'need of the official to adhere scrupulously to the words of an act at a time when he finds it more and more difficult to be helpful otherwise than by departure from them'. He placed all his hopes for the protection of the citizens from officialdom not in the courts, where redress was too expensive for the ordinary person, but in local committees of taxpayers and contributors who could, he thought, act as juries and mediators. He and C. F. G. Masterman invested great hope in the less than autonomous local committees which accompanied pre-1914 Liberal social legislation, such as the insurance committees (Gowers, 1948, 12–13; Masterman, 1939, 385). A. V. Dicey was more shrill. He thought the National Insurance Act had introduced a large dose of the French *droit administratif* into the British polity. Government and its officials had acquired judicial authority: parliament and the courts had had their powers momentously impaired by the power of the Insurance Commissioners for Part I of the Act (Health) and insurance officers and courts of referees in the case of Part II (Unemployment), without anyone realizing what had happened. 'The power to make regulations is probably the widest power of subordinate legislation ever conferred by parliament upon any body of officials.'

This perception of the quality of what was going on explained Dicey's whole tone in his 1914 introduction. He wanted to make it clear that there was a difference in ideals between 'an English socialist' and 'an English democrat' – 'in the attitude they respectively take up towards scientific experts. The socialist's ideal is a state ruled by officials or experts who are socialists. The democrat's ideal is a state governed by the people in conformity with the broad common sense he attributes to ordinary citizens.' This concern was not his alone. Braithwaite was obviously bitter after his defeat, but in more than a personal way. About Morant he wrote, in 1912:

> Officially he was my very opposite in every way – distrustful, suspicious, a bureaucrat who really and truly thought bureaucracy a good thing in itself and for itself, who really believed that officials could and should do things for people; whereas I was so constituted that I regarded the humble efforts of small people to do their best for themselves and their neighbours as productive and praiseworthy and the frantic struggle of bureaucrats and bureaucracies for power, position and privilege and the right to control other people as demoralizing and disgusting.

5

'Disgusting' is a strong word. But it may be an important one to hear if we are to avoid seeing the history of these years in terms of unimpeachably 'good things', such as adding 'welfare' and 'social security' to an achieved 'democracy', or 'founding' sociology, or 'professionalizing' case work, or reconciling 'old' and 'new' liberalism in calm work like L. T. Hobhouse's classic *Liberalism* (1911).

'Disgusting' may help us to listen for uglier sounds – such as those picked up by Stedman Jones in his *Outcast London* (1971) when he pointed to the surgical, authoritarian, labour camp (in those days 'colony') prescriptions behind late-nineteenth century 'progressive', 'limited socialist' ways of dealing with 'the social problem'. It may help to place national insurance – and ourselves in relation to it – and indeed welfare legislation throughout this period if, in the rest of this chapter we follow the scent laid by Braithwaite's strong language.

Ben Keeling (1886–1916) was, according to H. G. Wells, 'as complete and expressive a specimen of the educated youth of the first decade of this century as perhaps we are likely to get'. His mind was full of inconsistent social theories, battling for victory. Fortunately we can trace the dominant directions it was taking through his letters (1918). After a conventional élite education ending at Cambridge, he became a Fabian, a 'socialist', a social worker, a would-be 'sociologist', at a time when all these categories were cohering and, like cement, 'going off'. By the time of the 1911 National Insurance, Keeling had begun to define himself as a Liberal. He was a rank-and-file Webbian – if such a thing is possible – naming one of his children Bernard Sydney after his two heroes. By about 1908 he had 'seen enough of "democratic" politics to sicken me of them for life', by which he meant his flirtations with working-class and socialist associations such as SDF open-air meetings and ILP branch membership in south London.

His importance lies in the fact that he was self-conscious about characteristic twentieth-century replacements for such 'democratic politics'. He articulated these replacements, because he came to believe in them, shockingly well and in a manner which may make sense of words like 'disgusting'. In 1908 he explained to a correspondent how shocked some of his friends 'used to be when I explained how obvious it is that one must always sacrifice individuals whatever their general position or relation to one self, to the general good'. He had children, but left their mother alone to look after them because, after all, there was social reform to be achieved. 'My whole philosophy of the business of life centres round the State', he wrote, even though 'on the whole it is a damned interesting thing to breed about the earth.' 'I have noticed several times that my entire disregard of any individual feelings when I am aiming at what I conceive to be a social end strikes many people as simply horrible.'

Through his work and opinions as chief administrator of the Leeds Labour Exchange (the product of the Trade Boards Act of 1909, and of Beveridge's earliest influential intervention) Keeling can serve as an essential reminder that statism of an authentically disgusting kind constituted material relations between the 'new class' and workers, rather than mere study reveries or multi-volume histories. Furthermore, such statism seized some of the spaces for anti-capitalism, even socialism, and occupied them. When in Leeds in 1910, Keeling joined the Leeds Club,

> the exclusive snobbish club of the place – for the purpose of observing the habits
> of employers more closely. The only way of defeating a man is to be able to beat
> him at his own game. We have got to be better capitalists than the capitalists are.
> When we – that is, the administrative classes – have more will, more
> relentlessness, more austerity, more organizing ability, more class consciousness
> than they have, we shall crumple them in our hands. ... From day to day my
> dream shall be of a new model army, of vigilant administrators supplanting
> property inch by inch, steadily and slowly – with a jovial carouse to loosen the
> muscles now and again. And to hell with the snufflers and pimps alike. They
> shall go in pairs one of each to a hurdle after the precedent set by Henry VIII.

The state won his mind, and 'social reforms' like child health, school care committees, re-employment, industrial regulation, juvenile labour became his daily bread and the vehicle for his ambitions. Like many intellectuals at the time, he reached for a science and a practice which could put them together. Kirkman Gray felt 'the want of a word which will express the relation of the State and individual corresponding to that which is indicated between the town community and individual in the word *citizen*'.

Eugenics appealed to Keeling, as did the army and 'turning the whole mass of unskilled boy workers into a corps' (1912). 'If only the State can make itself sufficiently loved – if only people feel that they owe a considerable part at least of the good things of life to it, that will be the real beginning of the end of *aberglaube*.' Trade unions were, for Keeling, good, and working men in general were admirable. But there was a danger that they may 'fail to see ... the crying need for a strong State' (1909). It was in the context of this kind of thought that Keeling found national insurance acceptable enough for him to get closer to Liberalism at that time. But he regretted that there had to be any *contributory* element in it at all. Contributions might weaken a general sense of debt and subordination to the state, a sense which Keeling observed to be much weaker in Britain than, say, in Australia or Germany. By 1913 he cared 'less and less about the shibboleths of socialism, and I think I like the socialist element in the Labour movement (except for a very few intellectuals) less than other parts of it. All we want is an infinite willingness to use the State or the municipality ... for any practical ends in the direction of increasing the security, wealth and civilization of the masses. ... Probably a much greater increase of conscious socialism would not really help practical socialist methods. It would tend to throw up dogmatists to the front – and they are a pernicious race on the whole.'

Such language and opinions smell worse than they were in the context of their own time, because they come through to us now with the stench of their twentieth-century extrapolations in Stalinism and fascism in our nostrils. Against them, what can be set by way of contemporary argument and opposition, as a different colour on the canvas upon which twentieth century social policy in Britian was to be drawn? After all, Keeling would still not feel in Britain and in the late-1970s that *aberglaube* of a potentially dangerous kind had been eliminated. And that is somebodies' or somethings' achievement, because it has been more nearly eliminated in other capitalisms and in other socialisms. Furthermore, Braithwaite's sense of 'power ... there latent, to be awakened one day' still does not read as wholly ridiculous. Why not?

The resistance of Braithwaite's own brand of liberalism, so near to the centres of power in Britain at times, must provide part of the answer. But that too was tainted, and limited, and should not be allowed to make its exit as the hero of this chapter. Braithwaite thought within eugenic categories. He too, like any sound 1834 man, was terrified of 'preferential' treatment of the inefficient (Braithwaite, 1957, 217–18). And his reaction to working-class people when they presented themselves as critics of his whole universe was patronizing in the extreme. In June 1911 there was a Social Democratic Party deputation to Lloyd George on national insurance. In Braithwaite's diary (180–81) it became:

> One of the most amusing deputations from the SDF, the theoretical workmen. One of them, Mr Knee, ought really to have come out of a picture book. A little man with a large forehead and specs, going bald, very glib with the catch words

of socialism, palpably genuine and honest, entirely unpractical, and unrepresentative of the British working man, asking the most impossible things, in a manner which at once became inconsistent under the Chancellor's cross examination, boldly sticking to his guns, and showing himself really a very decent little fellow; I could see that the Chancellor was very much amused at him, and at the same time quite liked and admired the little fellow. As a practical man of course, he could not go with him and had to show his proposals up to the press ... but he did it very kindly, and there was a good deal of good-natured chaff, and the whole thing was a great success from everybody's point of view.

Fortunately this 'very decent little fellow' Fred Knee, thanks to the work of David Englander and the Society for the Study of Labour History, can now speak for himself (Englander, 1977).

He and others in the organized labour and socialist movements spoke where they could at the time. The Social Democratic Party (formerly Federation) had 'always advocated a universal system of free national insurance' (*Justice*, 1 July 1911). They strongly opposed the contributory element. They were, on the whole, antagonistic to or disinterested in, the Friendly Societies. 'With the rival demands of the doctors and friendly societies we have no concern, save for the hope their quarrel gives us that the Bill may be doomed not to pass at all, or not to work if passed' (*Justice*, 21 October 1911). The Parliamentary Labour Party and Independent Labour Party were less definite. There were disagreements, for example between Snowden and Keir Hardie, which Lloyd George could exploit. Parliamentary Labour opposition was weak, 'they don't seem to know really what they want' (Braithwaite, 1957, 188). They were bought off in October 1911 by a Lloyd George promise to introduce a bill for the payment of MPs and by a favourable actuary's report (for which Lloyd George paid) on the effect of the bill on trade union finances (Braithwaite, 1957, 196, 206; *Justice*, 21 October 1911).

Such organizational self-interest at the highest levels of the labour movement constituted something less than rising to the occasion. Hopefully it is clear by now that the occasion was of some moment, both to working people and to twentieth-century socialism. What was going on, way beyond Keeling, during the late nineteenth and early twentieth centuries was a scramble for socialism – as imperialistic as the contemporary scramble for Africa. An attempt was being made to take its (socialism's) germs away from working-class hosts and to vaccinate the body politic, seen *as* 'corporate', with them in harmless, even health-giving, forms. There was an attempt, partly successful, to de-class the idea of socialism, or to nationalize it; to suggest loudly and often that it was a 'good thing' as an idea, even a *necessary*, idea but not attached to working-class interests or associations. One measure of the success of this imperialism has been the extent to which modern British socialists – particularly Fabians and Marxists – have come to regard working-class creativity and its fate (expressed in the situation of enormous associations like Friendly Societies or Co-operative Societies between, say, 1850 and 1950) as irrelevant for the socialist project.

Nor is this view of the portent of early twentieth-century welfare history mere historian's hindsight. The signals were there at the time. They were there, for example, in Chamberlain's 1894 Birmingham speech quoted earlier. A perceived 'danger to social order', fears of 'a speedy and possibly a dangerous reaction' if a response other than the poor law was not made to old age 'in the bitter competition to which everyone is subjected', was the setting of this speech. It was *because* 'I regard it as a serious thing that there should be growing up, as I believe there is among the working classes, a sentiment that they are being treated with injustice and neglect' that Chamberlain felt that the Friendly Societies and 'the nation' must be brought 'into co-operation'. He was most surprised to be regarded as 'an intruder on their private domain and a poacher on their preserves', although Friendly Society figures were not the only people to see in Joseph Chamberlain a would-be populist 'despot' (Webb, Beatrice, 1926, diary entry 12 January 1884).

Thinkers like Durkheim or, closer to the home of this chapter, A. V. Dicey, were very frank about the merits of national socialism over against articulate working-class interest. 'We must assume, we must indeed hope', Dicey whistled in the 1914 dark, 'that the socialists of England will accept the profoundly true dictum of Gabrielle Tarde that "a socialist party can, but a working man's party cannot, be in the great current of progress". For a party of socialists may aim at the benefit of a whole state, a labour party seeks the benefit of a class.' There was a chorus of thought and action at this time to *make* people think, in spite of recalcitrant experience, that "the government" is no entity outside of ourselves', and to regard 'the state as a vast benefit society of which the whole body of citizens are necessarily members' (Webb, 1890). As L. T. Hobhouse told his readers in his strategic restatement of *Liberalism* in the year of national insurance: 'The British nation is not a mysterious entity over and above the 40-odd millions of living souls who dwell together under a common law. Its life is their life, its well-being or ill-fortune their well-being or ill-fortune.' What better material expression of this than a national, compulsory, accumulating (as opposed to dividing-out) insurance scheme?

A significant but small area of working-class thought, action, and association for which 'syndicalism' is a convenient label sensed the high stakes being played for from a class point of view. Bob Holton has begun to uncover the meanings and extent of an active reassertion of socialism as *working-class* industrial and political activity from below which characterized the years before 1914, and which focused explicitly, among other things, on responding to the statist implications of Liberal welfare reforms. Hilaire Belloc's *The Servile State* (1912) is the best known articulation of a much wider cultural movement. For Belloc, National Insurance (particularly the employment sections of the act) had been designed 'to capture organized labour and to cut its claws' (Holton, 1976). The largest circulation socialist paper agreed (*Clarion*, 16 June 1911; 23 July 1911).

Harder to catch but probably of more subsequent staying power in preventing Keeling's dreams becoming mainstream realities of twentieth-century British social history, was a much wider working-class 'mentality'. This was a term used in Reynolds and Woolley's *Seems So!* (1911), whose views on national insurance have already been quoted. Their work makes it possible to hypothesize a collective, primarily defensive refusal to be incorporated, by important strands of twentieth-century working-class opinion in Britain.

Since the creative, public, associational voluntary life of so many English working people during the second half of the nineteenth century – for example in Friendly Societies – has been subordinated, rendered less ambitious, or assimilated to rational capitalist or bureaucratic models during the twentieth century, there has arguably been a turning away, a privatization, a refusal to be attached in any deeply-felt way to 'the state' or to most other benevolent-seeming associations. There has been a closing of the door, with a 'not today thank you', and many decisions, for example, to go fishing, alone. State 'benefits' and 'consumer' goods have been taken, but not always and not often with enthusiasm or gratitude. There has been a certain resigned submission to being defined, from the outside, as 'apathetic', or as 'masses' for a 'mass market', but a refusal to accept such definitions as self-definitions. There has been a turning inwards towards, for example, the family as a defence and towards doing-it-yourself. Areas of private, crabbed, deformed autonomy have been carved out, for such creative self-production and introspection as can be channelled through private zones such as the home, the allotment, dog ownership and so on (Berger, 1967, 99). When an adequate twentieth-century social history is written from labour's point of view, it will have to pay close attention to meanings for working people (as well as for capital) of these zones, including, of course, the often lamented 'failure' of those 'most in need' to 'take up' welfare benefits. It is to the other side, or other sides, of 'apathy', 'privatization', 'mass consumption' and so on, that we shall have to turn for 'a working-class view of politics' in the spaces left by the social policies of the enlarged twentieth-century state.

This last paragraph is speculative, but rests on a text of the times which answered the likes of Keeling point by point – Stephen Reynolds and Bob and Tom Woolley's book published in 1911, *Seems So! A Working-Class View of Politics*. This remarkable work was written by two Devon fishermen and Reynolds, a 'settler'/novelist/writer/anthropologist of great acumen. It was a local study, but with universal ambition.

> States of mind, changes and trends of opinion, among large masses of people are notoriously difficult to ascertain – to catch on the wing, as it were, and to fasten down in plain statements – additionally so among working people whose only form of publicity is talk. The whole of the evidence can never be gathered together and against that which can be brought, contrary examples are nearly always obtainable. Opinion is fluid. Feeling is mostly subconscious. To try and arrest either is like scooping up water in a net. One *feels* the change: the change in direction and speed; and one *feels* the change in feeling [my italics].

Aware of the difficulties, Reynolds and the Woolley brothers got much nearer than their modesty implies to articulation. In attacking Fabian and New Liberal attitudes and acts of parliament (national insurance as making 'the master more powerfully a master and the man more impotently a workman than ever') through the words and thoughts of working people, they made clear how central struggle – class struggle – was and is in the social history of welfare and social policy. Different conceptions of the world were at stake, different views of what ought to be. A full reading of the text should be required for social workers, socialists and social historians alike. All that can be said here, by way of ending this chapter with it, is that it is a text partly written by working people which is, first, fully aware of the opacity of the world they are writing about. Next, the text is also fully and explicitly aware of the cultural imperialism which buries that world – including modern socialisms. The text is also fully aware of the growing gap between private and public expression, and the obtuse angle between 'political', 'party' organization and 'mass' political opinion. 'Evidently there's a link broken somewhere between politics and people.' 'Class antagonism is a very powerful force, growing rather than diminishing, acting in all sorts of unsuspected ways, cropping up in all sorts of unexpected places. Let things go wrong, make a false step, and in a moment it flashes out. ... It was there, beneath, all the time.' Social policy, social reform, is explicitly seen in *Seems So!* as reformation of one class by another. Resistance to 'inspection' and to 'progressive' intellectuals is articulated in rare detail. 'It is possible to honour the socialists on account of their good intentions, but at the same time the worst tyranny to beware of is that of intellectuals ordering other people's lives. They are so well intentioned, so merely logical, so cruel.' All this from one man who was 'an enthusiastic Tariff Reformer, another a Free Trader, and the third a political dark horse whose way of voting nobody knows'.

We wants more money and they gives us more laws. ... An' when we ask for more rivets [money] they pass laws how us shall behave, so's our want of rivets shan't show, an' how to keep our health, so's us shall work better to their profit. What we wants is proper pay, the rivets to work out our own life according to our own ideas, not their's. But they is trying to make it heaven on the cheap. T'isn't to be done, I tell 'ee, an' so they'll find. ...

New Acts, with new penalties attached, come tumbling upon his [the working man's] head from on high. After being left to fend for himself – with a success much greater in reality than in appearance – he suddenly finds himself regarded as incapable of taking care of himself in any respect whatever. He sees, dimly perhaps, that his democratic leaders flatter him and hold him in contempt at the same time. He is treated like a child badly brought up by its parents, a child very wronged and very naughty. If he could, and if he would, express his own private opinion with a frankness which he has found to be inexpedient, and with a particularity for which elections afford no scope, his well-wishers would be more than surprised. 'Why', they would ask, 'should he still be so ungrateful and resentful? See what we have done for him. See what we have given him'.

4

Social work education, 1900–1977
Chris Jones

In 1903 the Charity Organization Society (COS) established the School of Sociology in London for the purposes of training and educating social workers. The opening of this school marked the first formal training programme for social workers in this country. By 1975 there were 130 social work courses which issued 2,650 qualifying certificates in social work in that year. Despite the many common features which these contemporary courses share with that of the COS, social work education like social work itself has not enjoyed an untroubled or smooth evolutionary development from the beginning of this century. In fact, social work stands out as a 'profession' which has had an extremely arduous time in establishing itself and gaining recognition as a discrete and 'expert' activity. If we take the formation of the COS in 1869 as marking the origins of modern social work, then its subsequent development is characterized by a period of influence followed by a period of relative quiescence between 1914 and 1945, before experiencing a gradual but increasing ascendancy in the post–1945 period.

An historically informed analysis of social work education can provide us with an exceptionally fruitful standpoint from which to examine the character of social work and its development in this country. There are certain heuristic advantages in that social work courses were broadly similar for all the specialized branches of social work, both prior to the Seebohm unification in 1970 and after; but above all it provides a standpoint of explanatory strength in that social work education has traditionally been one of the key places where the social work world view has been explicated for the purposes of transmission to students and neophyte professionals. Thus, social work education is no mere appendage of the social work profession and in many ways it could be considered as one of its centres: in pursuit of the objectives of socializing students into the mores and methods of social work, social work courses have exercised important regulatory and unifying functions within the profession, and are regarded by social work leaders themselves as one of the crucial places where the social work perspective is established and sustained. The emergence of generic courses in the mid-1950s at a time of considerable administrative fragmentation within social work is but one of the more obvious indices of this role of social work education as an integrating institution.

Inevitably in a chapter of this length there are severe limits to the range and extent of discussion of what is an exceptionally rich and interesting field. What I am attempting to do is to provide the bare bones of an analytical framework, pinpointing what I consider to be some of the most important features of social work education and its development[1]. Despite the gaps and the all too brief discussion of important points, I hope the reader will concur with my concern to provide a brief and critical overview, in order to advance our understanding of this now important part of the modern state apparatus, and to counter the immense weight of literature produced by the social work establishment, which Gettleman (1974, 153) succinctly described as 'inspirational pap ... about the glorious tradition of social work'.

Max Weber (1972, 226) provided an exceptionally fruitful starting point for our analysis of social work education when he wrote:

> When we hear from all sides the demand for an introduction of regular curricula and special examinations, the reason behind it is, of course, not a suddenly 'awakened thirst for education' but the desire for restricting the supply for these positions and their monopolization by the owners of educational certificates.

The concern with regulation and monopolization have been long-standing characteristics of social work education, as exemplified in the COS's establishment of a School of Sociology, and continues throughout its subsequent development. In this chapter I want to draw attention to what I consider are the two principal functions of social work education. The first of these, which I term the 'external' function, has to do with the manner in which social work education has been used to forge a professional and expert identity for social work and to demarcate and claim a slice of social welfare activity for itself. The Charity Organization Society's development of a formal social work course provides a particularly clear example of the way in which social work education has been used as a strategy to enhance the image of social work and as a tactic to close off an area of activity.

The formation of the School in 1903 marked an extension rather than a new departure in the COS's attempt to assert its influence over social reform policies. It was the explicit objective of the Society from its foundation in 1869 to co-ordinate and regulate all existing forms of

---

1. More detailed support and analysis will be found in my thesis (1977) and in an article on the foundations of social work education (1976). Hopefully the references will aid those who want to seek greater clarification. In this solitary note I would like to acknowledge the support of many friends in writing this chapter and especially Tony Novak.

philanthropy and not to become yet another relief agency among the many thousands already operating in London. Although the Society never achieved this goal and did get drawn into relief work, it never shifted from its overall aim of wanting to prohibit what it considered as harmful relief policies and to establish itself as the fountainhead of knowledge and expertise in all issues pertaining to the relief of working-class destitution.

The actual timing of the establishment of a formal social work course was not fortuitous and indeed reflects the external functions of social work education as a regulatory and image-creating institution. Throughout the 1890s the COS's position as one of the most influential and respected organizations concerned with preventing destitution was coming under increasing threat and attack – not from the working class itself, which had long before rejected the COS's methods of investigation and its assertion that the primary cause of destitution was the immoral character of the poor (Loch, 1906, xvi; B. Bosanquet, 1901, 297), but rather from other 'advanced' sections of the upper classes, who like the COS were concerned to formulate modern and 'scientific' social policies to deal with the miserable plight of substantial segments of the working class. This opposition to the COS came from a diverse collection of groups and individuals which included the Fabian Society (Townshend, 1911), John Hobson (1909), Charles Booth, and even one-time members of the COS such as Cannon Barnett and Violet Markham. Despite important differences separating them, their common attack was on the COS's intransigence over the role of the state in relief policies other than the poor law. It was the Society's contention that the state was incompetent for the task of 'improving' the condition of the working class and that any large-scale relief programmes initiated by the state, whether old age pensions, free school meals or work projects for the unemployed, were all short-term palliatives with long-term disastrous consequences. For example, both free school meals and pensions were deemed to undermine family responsibilities and encourage the poor to look to the state rather than to their own resources and efforts for maintenance.

The COS maintained that the bulk of working-class poverty and squalor was occasioned by the inadequate 'social habits' of the poor – 'a weakness of will and poverty of spirit', Charles Loch, the influential secretary of the Society, wrote in 1906. According to the theorists of the Society – Loch and Helen and Bernard Bosanquet – the working class could be differentiated into three broad categories: 'first-class' workers and their families who had internalized those hallowed virtues of labour discipline, thrift, self-reliance and independence and whose behaviour and character meant that they were rarely without work and never a burden on society; an intermediate (and the largest) group who demonstrated some good social habits but had not thoroughly taken them for themselves, with the consequence that they were often precariously poised between independence and destitution; and finally a totally demoralized residual section of paupers, beggars and criminals, who were seen as a continual and major drain on resources and a threat to property, who never made any attempt to sustain themselves through productive labour preferring instead to survive on charitable doles and hand-outs.

From its very beginnings the COS set out to prevent any relief from getting through to this residual category. It was their contention that the only way to rid society of this cancerous burden was to ensure that its existence was made as arduous and unpleasant as possible. Thus if relief had to be given it should only be through the workhouse, managed in the punitive manner laid down in the 1834 Poor Law Amendment Act. Accordingly, the only legitimate domain for philanthropists was deemed to be the large intermediate category, or what the COS called the 'deserving' and later, the 'helpable' poor. Moreover, if demoralization was to be avoided, the charitable assistance offered had to be of a certain type and administered carefully. Merely dishing out soup or handing out doles as had been done in the past would do nothing, the COS claimed, for strengthening the character and social habits of this group. In fact such an approach would result in the pauperization of the deserving poor given their already precarious grasp of the virtues of self-reliance. Consequently, it was one of the central messages of the COS that the only form of effective relief work which would enable the deserving poor 'to regain their full and effective citizenship, that is, to restore them to a proper self-dependence and independence' (Holman 1912, 26) was that which would strengthen their character and moral fibre:

> The only way of really helping a man is to strengthen him by education, timely assistance, opportunities, what you will, to meet his own difficulties and organize his own life ... only by their own efforts can they develop progressive interests, and only by purposes and progressive interests can they organize their lives successfully. [H. Bosanquet 1897, 277.]

It was from this well-formulated position of social casework that the COS criticized the activities of those philanthropists who handed out material goods to the poor without making any attempt to educate the recipients or ensure that they only dealt with the deserving poor, and opposed the proposals for state intervention.

From its very origins therefore, social work has not only been concerned to socialize its clients in what it regards as the appropriate social habits, but it has also been in conflict with sections of the dominant classes and at times governments, about what *strategies* are best suited for reaching the common goal of maintaining and reproducing a reliable working class. In developing an adequate understanding of the role and history of social work education, it is most important that we recognize this dimension of intra-class conflict as well as the more obvious character of social work as an activity imposed on the working-class poor.

From the inception of the Society a training programme was implemented, not only to ensure that its social workers were instructed in the appropriate methods such as how to decide whether a claimant was deserving or not, but also to regulate the activities of those it termed 'indiscriminate almsgivers', who were handing out material goods and cash in an *ad hoc* manner to beggars and the destitute. It is clear in the writings of the Society's leaders that they hoped that training programmes, even of the apprenticeship mode they initially adopted, would impress upon philanthropists that their intervention in the lives of the working-class poor should not be whimsical or guided by their emotional response to squalor but should instead be informed by a wider and longer-term perspective of the character of the working class and its place in society. In other words it was the Society's contention that philanthropy could no longer be seen as a passing duty of the aristocracy or its bourgeois mimics but was a delicate task requiring considerable skill, knowledge and above all training. Always adept at borrowing the jargon and concepts of the more established professions – a continuing characteristic of social work as Wootton (1959b) has noted – these early social work leaders maintained that social workers should be regarded as social practitioners to the ills of society in much the same way as doctors who tended to the ailments of the body. Just as 'doctors have to be educated methodically, registered and certificated, [so] charity is the work of the social physician. It is to the interests of the community that it should not be entrusted to novices, or to dilettanti, or to quacks (Loch, 1906, xix).'

Through an extensive system of publications which included not only books, articles and letters in the leading journals and papers of the period, but a monthly journal (*The Charity Organization Review*), and through its emphasis on training, the COS set about to 'modernize' and educate its own class in the need for a thoughtful and 'scientific' approach to social policy. For as Helen Bosanquet (1902, 138) wrote: 'Perhaps the greatest obstacle to getting a sound public opinion on matters of social policy lies in the general ignoring of the fact that scientific principles are as much involved in them as chemistry or architecture, or any other of the arts of life.' In this task the COS was joined by many other 'advanced' sections of the professional and middle classes who were similarly convinced that many of the problems Britain was facing at the turn of the nineteenth century were due to a deep streak of amateurism and patronage in many parts of the administrative apparatus of the state with the subsequent lack of expertise and ability (S. and B. Webb, 1911, 331).

However, in social policy what was once a conflict between the amateur philanthropists 'who lacked any understanding of labour questions or feeling for citizenship' (Hutchins, 1913, 51) and the 'experts' of the COS, became by the beginning of this century a struggle between experts, in particular between the COS and the Fabian Society.

Throughout the first decade of this century these two societies battled with each other for influence. The Royal Commission on the Poor Laws which sat between 1905 and 1909 was a major site of this struggle, with its membership divided between the COS and Fabian camps, and it resulted not surprisingly in two reports, the majority representing the COS line and the minority that of the Fabians. As I have already indicated, the conflict centred over the role of the state, with the COS maintaining that state relief policies would be as demoralizing in their effects on the working-class poor as had been indiscriminate almsgiving, whereas the Fabians, and especially the Webbs, were committed to state intervention and a dynamic managerial state as being capable of ensuring a disciplined and efficient (but still capitalist) society.

It was in the course of this conflict that both Societies established their own training and educational institutions. The COS had its School of Sociology and the Fabians had their School of Economics. Both Societies had understood the importance of infusing their own brands of experts into the administration of the state as a means of extending their respective influences. There is no doubt that the COS recognized the importance of establishing a formal educational institution of university status as a means of advancing its claims of expertise, as was demonstrated in the report of the sub-committee which was formed to explore this possibility: 'If the educational functions of the Society were more fully recognized by the public it would lead to a much wider appreciation of its work and influence' (1898, 137). The next sentence of the report also portrays the Society's hope that such a school would expand to become the principal route to philanthropic activity for those so interested: 'They would like to see in the Society the nucleus of a future university for the study of social science, in which all those who undertake philanthropic work should desire to graduate.'

It would be interesting to explore further the conflict between the Fabian Society and the COS, which eventually resulted in the School of Sociology being 'mopped up ... by that confounded School of Economics' (B. Bosanquet, cited Woodard, 1961) in 1913 to form the Department of Social Administration at the London School of Economics. But my concern here is to highlight the manner in which social work education has been used by the profession as a tactic for enhancing its prestige and power, often in the context of intra-class and factional disputes. The origins of formal social work courses merely provide a clear example of this external function of social work education.

Throughout the expansion of social work services since 1945 we can also trace the manner in which professional courses in social work and the attendant processes of certification have been used in a similar fashion to carve out an area of activity and establish the legitimacy of the social work strategy for dealing with a specific cluster of problems. In this contemporary context most of the struggles have taken place within the state between various agencies and 'professional' groups. Unlike the early days of social work, the majority of the disputes are now between the various categories of state-employed 'experts' working in similar and neighbouring fields, such as the police, health visitors, teachers, doctors, psychologists, housing welfare, social security officials and of course social workers. Most of these groups not only share many common features but often have their own preferred strategies and legitimating theories. At points of conflict, therefore, the weight behind their respective claims of expertise in pressing for a certain course of action rather than another is of some significance in determining the outcome. Doctors, for example, are renowned for the ways in which they parade their extensive training and education in pursuit of their objectives. Whereas the police force have become embittered in recent years over what they see as a vast interference in their work by 'experts' such as social workers. According to the deputy chief constable of West Yorkshire, they are a 'hindrance who made it a work of art getting some young offenders to court. We are fed up with the softly-softly, namby-pamby, pussyfooting approach to the vicious elements who have never had it so good' (cited in the *Daily Telegraph*, 19 April 1976).

It is little wonder then that social work has fought so hard over the past thirty years to achieve professional status and recognition and to exorcise its image as an activity which can be undertaken by anyone with a sympathetic manner. In that struggle social work education has had a central role. For example, during the early 1950s social work successfully fought to keep its courses in the university sector despite the opposition from many social studies departments, which maintained that their presence lowered their own claims for academic status and respectability (cf. Silcock, 1950). Younghusband (1951, 172) opposed any move from the universities on the grounds that it 'would lower the standards and status of the courses' and as Stein (1968, 55, 58) so acutely observed, a university base was of considerable importance to the occupations's professional claims:

The single most important influence now affecting its capacity to meet these criteria of a profession is the extent to which the preparatory education is rooted in a university base. ... It is fair to say that where it has become professionalized ... the principal index and influence ... has been the gradual incorporation of social work education into universities.

Likewise, the recent tendency to rename postgraduate qualifications in social work to masters degrees from diplomas has to be considered as yet another example of the image-creating manoeuvres of social work.

This 'politics' of expertise is not, however, simply restricted to the factional or doctrinal disputes within the state apparatus or ruling classes but is also directed at the working class. The most notable aspect of this inter-class dimension has been the manner in which authority and legitimation are articulated and exercised. More and more aspects of social life are now coming under the rule of 'experts', who claim that their authority to intervene and advise people how to live their lives, raise their children and so forth, is based on a body of knowledge, a science. With its images of neutrality, rationality, universality and truth, science and technology have become the *lingua franca* of domination. As Laski (1931) noted, the day of the 'plain man' has passed; he is considered too ignorant to be a judge on most matters, consequently whole areas of life are removed from public and political discourse and left to the appropriate expert:

> As social problems become the concern of professionals, the professionals become involved in a problem-solving domain where problems and their solutions are seen as technical rather than as structural and political. The positive implications of limiting the focus of the professional's concern and of accentuating the technological capacities at the professional's command also limit the ways in which the problems are interpreted, their solutions are formulated. Solutions to problems that are seen in their more delimited aspects and interpreted in technological terms will tend to be isolated from solutions pursued in the arena of structural social change and mass political movements in the society at large.
> [Galper 1975, 92.]

Although experts such as social workers become 'less easily understood and less susceptible to the control of public opinion' (Keith-Lucas, 1953, 107), this does not mean that the old cluster of moral injunctions and ideals – self-help, self-reliance, thrift, conforming behaviour and so forth – are less omnipresent; rather they are being presented in a new language of science. No less applicable to the case of social work are the remarks of Davis (1938, 65) on the way psychiatrists tend to handle their patients: 'Disguising [their] valuational system [by means of the psychologistic position] as rational advice based on science, it can conveniently praise and condemn under the aegis of the medico-authoritarian mantle.'

I now want to focus on the content of social work education in order to illuminate how one of the regulatory institutions confronting the working class has become secularized and made liberal use of the prestige of science to enhance, legitimate and neutralize its specific class objectives.

This focus on the content of courses brings me to what I consider as the other major function of social work education, namely an 'internal' concern with the qualities of social workers. Although I have distinguished two major functions of social work courses, there is a necessary inter-relation between the two, for it is to a large extent through the actions and manner of individual social workers that the expert image of the profession is articulated. Furthermore, whether we are considering intra-class or inter-class tensions, and the accompanying processes of regulation and secularization, we cannot ignore the individual social worker. The scientization of many of the basic precepts of social work for instance, do not merely confront the client but the social worker as well. Intervening in the clients' lives, requesting information, often of a most private and intimate kind, removing children from their parents, directing families' lives are activities which pose moral dilemmas for social workers. To be able to claim that these activities are informed by a 'scientific knowledge base', and that one's training helps in resolving these dilemmas, sustains the individual social worker in the belief that what he/she is doing is *right* and proper, just as it communicates to the client that what they are doing is *wrong* in a much more effective manner than a mere reliance on overtly moral categories and concepts.

The concern of social work leaders to instil a specific consciousness or 'faith' among prospective social workers was evident from the origins of formal courses. As well as signifying an extension of the COS's tactics to gain influence and prestige the formation of the School of Sociology was in part occasioned by the growing realization that the old apprenticeship approach to training was incapable of instilling in new social workers the principles and theory which underpinned and guided the social work strategies of the COS. *Education* as well as *training* in social work was seen to be needed if social workers were to achieve 'good' social work practice.

The need for social workers to have grasped and internalized a particular view of the world – a social theory – which was what the concern for education implied, has been restated often during the past seventy-five years. According to Professor Wilson (1949, 354), who was head of the social studies department at Hull University: 'The primary aim of a department of social studies is to give potential social workers an education, not a technique for handling other peoples' problems as life hurls itself at them in the shape of other peoples' troubles as well as their own perplexities.'

And it was the contention of T. H. Marshall (1946, 17), that without a social theory the social worker 'is at the mercy of a thousand discouragements'. Both of these short statements illuminate an important point about social work, namely that social work is recognized as a problematic and arduous activity which imposes certain hazards for the ill-prepared social worker. Implicitly, they reflect something of the class character of social work. Most fundamentally, and this is applicable to both the social work of the COS and the contemporary period, how do social workers manage to sustain a predominantly individualistic approach and perspective to the problems presented by their clients, especially when most of those problems are often the product of material and structural deprivations and inequalities of one kind or another? In both periods the prime target groups of social workers have been and are particularly hard-hit sections of the working class, whose concentration in specific areas of cities and towns and run-down council estates highlights the collective character of their problems. Moreover, social workers have in the main been drawn from the middle classes, often with a genuine desire to help the 'less fortunate' and with little or no direct experience of the squalor and hardships faced by their prospective clients. All these features point to the need for social workers to be 'immunized' or 'educated' so that they can penetrate these nether zones of our society without becoming demoralized. As one of the first social work tutors at the School of Sociology so succinctly wrote:

> We must train ourselves in a greater faith – the faith which never doubts that beneath the unequal, fettered, unlovely and unloving social conditions, as beneath the perplexed, half-sorrowful, half-hopeful religious questionings of today, there lies hidden a new heaven and a new earth which ... will one day be realized in their midst. Only through such a faith can our self-control become strong enough to stand by and see suffering and misery and evil go on untouched by us.
>
> [Bannatyne, 1902, 342–3.]

The faith or social theory which social workers had to come to believe in, and which the totality of course content constituted, has remained remarkably unchanged since the time of the COS. Cormack could write in 1964 (30) that 'by 1914 social work ... already possessed so many familiar features that many of us would find ourselves almost at home in its small world – much more so than in many other Edwardian circles.' Similarly Leubuscher (1946, 20–21) commented on the COS courses:

> 'In reading their prospectus and syllabuses one is struck by the degree to which they embodied principles and methods which, with few modifications, have been retained up to the present day.'

Although there are differences between the theoretical bases of social work in the two periods, which are significant and usually of a 'middle-range' character as we shall see, there is a crucial continuity in orientation and overall intent. While there is always a danger of simplification when attempting to draw out 'essences' or underlying themes, it is possible to argue that social work courses since the time of the School of Sociology have been concerned to inculcate a broadly similar social theory to social work students. Whether the subjects taught have been called ethics, citizenship, charitable methods and principles or human growth and behaviour, sociology, social work methods, it is possible to identify certain common and unifying themes which have been taught to students to legitimate and sustain the social work approach.

One of the dictums of this social theory has been the centrality accorded to the personality or character as the prime determinant of an individual's social condition. Thus whether an individual enjoys comfort and security or poverty and hardship is considered to be largely a question of his or her personality, which in turn is shaped decisively by the patterns of socialization early in life in the family. Long before the arrival of Freud, the theorists of the COS were proclaiming the family as one of the most important of society's institutions (Bosanquet, 1906). 'We take it', wrote Loch (1890, 10), 'that the family is the civic unit. A sweet and wholesome family life is the first condition of good citizenship.' Likewise, drawing attention to both the physical and moral aspects of family functioning, Helen Bosanquet (1906, 99) argued that 'a proletariat residuum is impossible where all young people who go out into the world are trained to habits of labour and obedience, as well as being strong and capable.'

Fundamentally this stance of the COS on social problems is the same as that held by the contemporary social work enterprise. In terms of juvenile delinquents and problem families, which constitute their primary target groups, it is still strongly maintained that 'the problems facing the caseworker are rooted in the life of the family and [are] not peculiar to the environment' (FWA Minutes, 1953).

Around this idealist view of clients and social problems, social work has constructed a coherent and congruent body of knowledge. Drawing from a wide range of social science theories in an explicitly eclectic and pragmatic fashion, a social work perspective has been developed which consistently undervalues structural and class determinants of social conditions and focuses attention on the individual and the family. It is a social theory which is presented to students throughout all the subjects taught on a course. Sociology for example, despite its many drawbacks, could be considered as a subject which might give social work students a greater awareness of the social dimensions to the issues with which they deal; Heraud (1967, 14), however, discovered from his survey of a number of social work courses and exam papers that, apparently, 'sociology, to those who set the papers, is mainly concerned with questions about the family and this is the main reason for having sociology in the course.'

Although sociology has never been one of the 'core professional' subjects taught to students – 'it is not necessary for the professional functioning of a social worker' (Heraud, 1967, 9) – the manner in which social work teachers have reacted to some of the critical and radical developments, especially in deviance theories, does graphically reflect the central intent of social work education to socialize students into a particularly conservative and unquestioning view of the world. Munday (1972) and Wilson (1974) have both criticized lecturers in the sociology of deviance for their teaching of social work students, on the grounds that their claims that deviance has to be considered as a political phenomenon understood in the framework of a capitalist society demoralizes prospective social workers and leads to confusion and despondency. According to Wilson (1974, 9) the 'dangers of undermining the professional commitments of novices in the field parallel those of putting a viper in the cradle of an infant' Munday (1972, 4) similarly wrote that:

> Current theories in the sociology of deviance pose the greatest threat of all to social work students, with their clear message that society creates deviants for its own ends and that social workers as part of the system of social control, are used to create and amplify deviance rather than improve the lot of the deviant. The ideas of writers like Matza, Becker and Cicourel are intellectually fascinating and persuasive but quite ominous for the social worker.

Ideas such as those presented in the sociology of deviance can be threatening because they turn upside down the entire approach and theories of social work. A set of theories which attributes the problems of a working-class residuum to their character and upbringing clearly sustains the individualized and educative approach of social casework. This is not the case when those problems are attributed to the social structure and relations of capitalism.

To be blunt, we must never forget when discussing any aspect of social work that we are investigating one of the regulatory apparatuses of the state which is *imposed* on sections of the working class. Consequently, social work education despite its liberal facade is not in any other business than trying to produce a group of people who will be strong, self-disciplined and trustworthy, to be 'guardians of the social trust'. Through rigorous selection and assessment procedures, followed by a sequence of carefully constructed courses, the hope is to produce 'super citizens', 'whose own good citizenship is at the same time rational and infectious' (Gardiner and Judd, 1959, 195) and capable of being a model for clients to copy. As one COS worker wrote, the best social workers 'must be the best human beings, those whose conduct of their lives is most nearly what we wish the conduct of all lives to be' (Gow, 1900, 110).

A study of social work education however, sensitizes us to a number of important features about the state and the manner in which its domination is sustained and exercised. State rule may be 'abstract' or ideological in many instances but equally it is undertaken by people, many of whom have no vast propertied stake in society, do not own any means of production and undertake their work simply as wage labourers. Social work, like a number of other vocational employments, is complicated further by the fact that many social workers are motivated by compassionate and humanitarian impulses. Although we can trace in the writings of the leaders of the COS an explicit concern to regulate and control the working classes, we would be hard-pressed to discover a similar consciousness among the vast majority of contemporary fieldworkers or even the charity workers of seventy years ago. There are no simple answers to the question of how people become state officials, but through social work education we do gain some insight into the processes involved in the production of one group.

In this production two features stand out. Firstly the selection of the 'raw material'. As one social work teacher noted: 'The course really begins ... not with the lectures and academic session, but with the selection of students of appropriate background and academic standards' (Heywood 1964, 9). Or as another argued:

> 'The most important thing is the appropriate selection of appropriate people, rather than what to do with, or do to students once they are on a course' (Bibby, 1976, 3).

Selection policy has always been important for social work. No amount of teaching can ensure that the prospective professional will embody the virtues and perspective required to bring wayward clients 'into closer conformity with society' (Rodgers and Stevenson, 1973, 184). Using its own theoretical schema, social work expects that these values if they are present will have 'been laid down and securely founded in early life, and have again been thought out and incorporated ... in adolescence' (Heywood, 1964, 9). Consequently, social work courses attempt only to confirm and strengthen a predisposition of support and conformity to the prevailing social system; they do not create it.

This leads on to the second feature: the filling out of this orientation with the middle-range theories and methods which both guide the social worker and sustain him/her in the belief that the activity is necessary, helpful and right for their clients. It is within this middle-range cluster of theories and methods rather than at the level of the overall idealist and consensual view of society that there have been the most significant changes in social work education during the past century.

The take up of psychoanalytic theory by social work in the 1950s and '60s provides one of the best examples of change and continuity in social work education and theory as well as illuminating the character of scientization and secularization. Despite the talk of 'psychiatric deluges' in social work as a result of the dominance of Freudian theory since 1945, it is most significant that its take-up did not involve any fundamental shift in social work's stance or orientation. As I have already indicated, the COS theorists at the end of the nineteenth century had insisted that patterns of familial socialization were the clue to most of the problems presented by their working class clients. Essentially, this was also the message of Freudian theory, as utilized by social work. Psychoanalytic theory was, however, far more sophisticated with its Oedipal complex, and concepts of id, ego and super-ego than any presented by the Bosanquets or Loch. Indeed, the 'scientificity' of Freudian theory was undoubtedly one of its great attractions for contemporary social work, providing the occupation at last with an esoteric vocabulary of accepted science to replace what were explicitly moral categories. Corner, in the lecture to the Association of Social Workers in 1959 (14), captured what many social workers perceived and welcomed in this shift to a scientific base:

> Slowly but surely, a change of emphasis has taken place. We speak no longer of the immoral but the immature; the lazy good-for-nothing of those days is the inadequate of today; the harlot and fallen woman have been transformed into call-girls; the pervert has become a deviant; the drunkard an alcoholic whom we try to help by psychiatric treatment. ... In casework in fact, we are not judgemental but analytical. ... We do not regard our client's problems as moral ones but as emotional ones. ... I suggest in fact that moral values are no longer at the core of things in the practice of casework.

Armed with such a scientific body of knowledge, social work had at last achieved the firm foundation from which to launch its claims of expertise and professional status. It undoubtedly enhanced the confidence of individual social workers to penetrate into the inner core of their clients' lives without the taint of moralistic interference, as well as sharpening the claims of a then fragmented profession for unification and a greater share of the social welfare action. The importance of language and conceptual imagery to social work was most succinctly expressed as early as 1904, and the remarks of Urwick (1904, 182), who was then the director of the School of Sociology, are no less pertinent for contemporary social work:

> The trained workers of today must be more than mere administrators; they must be the apostles of true doctrines and they must preach in the language of their generation. They may grasp and hold firmly enough the very essence of the principles outlined above, and yet they may seem too old-fashioned and too negative to make converts. The terms in which our truths are expressed often belong to a past age; have we not all been at times uneasily conscious that the mere appeal to fundamental principles of self-help, independence and thrift and the like has lost much of its force, and that these principles must be recast,

brought into new connections with current ideas and ways of thinking, clothed in new language. For it is unquestionably true that the new generation is receptive enough but, as always, demands a new preparation of its food.

For social work, this was one of the great achievements of Freudian theory; it provided the new language in which to clothe its fundamental principles and enhanced the apostolic character of social workers as preachers of true doctrines. Howard Jones (1975, 169) was surely accurate when he wrote: 'What we have of course been witnessing in the evolution of professional social work has been the gradual scientization and humanization of the basic ideology of capitalism.'

It would of course be crude merely to assert that social work embraced Freudian theory solely on account of its scientific gloss. To grasp fully the changes in the middle-range theories of social work and content of social work education we must look closely at the specific historical contexts in which such changes took place. Very briefly, social work moved towards psychoanalysis at a time when its client was changing. After the Second World War there was growing concern about the immense costs incurred by growing numbers of juvenile delinquents and the burden of problem families on the expanded range of welfare services following their reorganization between 1945 and 1951. The Freudian concepts of immaturity and the unconscious proved especially attractive for explaining the perpetuation of a cluster of problem families at a time when many thought that the combination of economic prosperity and welfare services had eradicated primary poverty. Furthermore, the desperately squalid conditions of many problem families resonated with the Freudian notion of irrationality – how else could one understand the self-defeating behaviour and squalor of such families and of many dilinquents? Above all, Freudian theory held out the hope of treatment and improvement, unlike the earlier theories of the COS which maintained that the undeserving residuum were incapable of being restored to self-actualizing citizenship. And treatment rather than simple regulation was seen as a pressing necessity if the cycle of deprivation was to be broken into and much needed reserves of labour (especially in the immediate post-war period) were to be opened up rather than allowed to degenerate among problem families.

Consequently, while Freudian theory did not disturb the cluster of domain assumptions about the nature and purpose of social work, social problems and society, it did enable a general sharpening up and increased precision within contemporary social work. Significantly, it gave shape to and permitted a shift to a 'softer' approach to problem families who had earlier been considered as part of the irredeemable and undeserving residuum. Freudian theory offered a precise identification of developmental sequences of the personality, stressed the importance of parents and early childhood, and suggested prescriptions for remedial action. The theory justified, however, and mapped out a notion as to how even the most recalcitrant deviant might be treated. Above all, it legitimated a greater degree of state interference in family life through the welfare agencies, on the grounds that if the children could be appropriately socialized from an early age then the immensely costly cycle of deprivation could be broken. The take-up of Freudian theory by social work typifies many of the changes that have taken place within the occupation and its training courses over the past century, and is now being repeated in the case of systems theory which is fast becoming the central 'middle-range' theory on many social work courses. Even if many of the changes are of a cosmetic nature, they nevertheless have consequences and implications. This is so despite the fact, in my view, that there has been no fundamental shift in social work's generally conservative orientation.

Concluding remarks

An analysis of social work education provides an empirically rich standpoint from which to further our understanding of the state. It highlights, for example, the way in which the state is a site of class conflict, and not simply between classes but within them as well. The struggle of social work to achieve professional status, in which social work education played such a central role in establishing and presenting an expert image, was primarily a struggle within the dominant classes, and latterly, professional groups employed by the state, over what constituted the appropriate strategy to deal with specific problem sections of the working class. Above all, social work education focuses our attention on the manner in which state officials are 'produced'. Just as a factory worker is not born a factory worker, but has to be brought within a particular set of social relations, the same applies to social workers. Moreover, given that social workers have as one of their central tasks to bring wayward clients back into the capitalist fold, it is particularly important that they are fully committed to that 'fold'. Social work education, as I have noted, attempts this task first of all by selecting what it regards as the appropriate raw material and then by presenting them with a body of knowledge which makes sense of the world, in a manner which permits and legitimates social work intervention and carries with it the adornments of neutrality and science.

The success of social work courses in realizing these goals is however mixed, and there are increasing signs of tensions and problems. For example, although many courses have attempted to restrict teaching posts to those qualified and experienced in social work, they have not been able to escape the influences of radical and critical developments in the other branches of social science. Many students entering social work training now know something of 'new criminology' or radical critiques of psychology or the research in social policy which has highlighted the perpetuation of structural inequalities. It was hardly surprising that Gould's (1977) document on radical and marxist penetration in higher education should pinpoint teacher and social work education as areas of prime concern, for these are two of the most important occupations concerned with transmitting the prevailing social values to those groups – children and clients – who have not yet fully internalized them. A problem of probably greater significance is the growing distance and tensions between the 'field' and the courses. Space does not permit a detailed examination but the principal issues concern questions of professional autonomy in an increasingly bureaucratized and proletarianized occupation following the Seebohm and local government reorganizations in the early 1970s, coupled with the growing recognition by social workers themselves that social work is being developed and funded by the state as a general servicing/dustbin agency for the welfare apparatus as a whole. This reality of social work practice is rarely reflected in the content of the professional courses, many of which remain committed to an autonomous image of the profession somehow balanced between the clients and the state. Consequently, increasing numbers of local authorities are complaining that the courses are failing to produce the product which they require. In a letter to *Social Work Today* (25 January 1977, 24) Mary Hope, the training officer of Hillingdon Social Services remarked that:

> Regarding the appropriateness of the training job, it is almost universally acknowledged that the CQSW prepares students for a task that it is not possible to do within the current local authority social services organization. There is also the problem that many courses omit basic knowledge and skills required by social workers.

The recent development of the Certificate in Social Service (CSS) is no more than a glorified form of in-service training where the student remains an employee of the local authority and attends the local college on a day release basis. The course of study is jointly designed by the college and the local authority and excludes teaching in the potentially contaminating behavioural sciences. It is more narrowly focused and more pragmatic than courses leading to the CQSW (CCETSW, 1975, 18). This document is itself one of the more self-evident responses to the current tensions and the signs are that this is just the opening shot in a campaign to completely restructure the profession and its educational system.

5

Care and control in local authority social work
Carole Satyamurti

Introduction

In recent years, the notion of a 'crisis in social work' has become a cliché. The idea refers to a loss of a sense of direction among social workers, and a growing uncertainty about what they are doing and what they have to offer. This loss of confidence particularly affects social workers in local authority settings (rather than, for instance, those working in hospitals or voluntary agencies), and it is largely as a result of protest by those placed in local authority departments about the irrelevance of conventional social work training that social work tutors have, belatedly, come to doubt the value of much of their course content.

A number of factors have contributed to the 'crisis'. Part of the explanation for it lies in the growth of radicalism in higher education since the late 1960s, which has affected many more people than would identify themselves as politically left wing, and has led to a scepticism towards individualistic explanations and solutions of social ills and to an 'end of ideology' with respect to casework. Another factor has been generally increased reluctance to take social inequality for granted and, consequently, a greater awareness, not always formulated, of the shortage of available resources.

But another important factor, to which little attention has been given, relates particularly to local authority social workers' position as state employees and to what may be seen as a gradually crystallizing contradiction between different elements of their occupational role. On the one hand, social workers are supposed to provide a caring service, responsive to the needs of the client. This is what most people have in mind when they become social workers, and social work in this sense is part of a long philanthropic tradition. But local authority social work also has its roots in the poor law and is directly involved in control functions towards the deviant and the dependent.

These two aspects of official welfare provision – care and control – while analytically inseparable were, until relatively recently, institutionally distinct. The thesis of this chapter is that the increasing convergence of these two strands, and their incorporation into the role of local authority social worker, confronts social workers with irreconcilable objectives and is a major factor contributing to the sense of crisis. Thus the situation today is a crisis in the true sense of the word, in that it represents a heightening of tendencies that have been developing for some time.

In pursuing this line of argument, I want, first, to look at social work in historical perspective, from the point of view of the developing relationship between care and control. And, secondly, to discuss some of the consequences of this relationship for the social organization of contemporary local authority social work.

Care and control in historical perspective

In considering the emergence of social work over the past one hundred years or so, it first has to be thought of as submerged in the general development of intervention in the welfare field by the state, and by large-scale, organized private bodies.

There is a complex and ongoing debate[1] concerning the origins and basis of public welfare provision in the nineteenth century, a debate which involves the identification of a multiplicity of contributory factors, and a disagreement about the relative weight to be attributed to these factors and the nature of their relation to each other. Older views, which saw the development of welfare in terms of the growth of humanitarian concern and the extension of citizenship, have been displaced more recently by accounts which emphasize other factors – concern that Britain would fall behind in international competition as a result of the inferior quality of her workforce; concern about the poor physical condition of men available for military service; pressure for reform coming from the labour movements and from an enlarged electorate; an interest in stimulating and maintaining consumption capacity in the population; fear of unrest and a sense that the propertied classes must pay 'ransom'[2] for their privileges in order to secure social stability; a fear that, if left entirely to the vagaries of the market economy, men who would otherwise be regular workers would during times of unemployment lose both the physical capacity and the moral incentive to work; and a concern with buttressing the nuclear family which can be seen as the main institution responsible for both the physical and the ideological reproduction of labour power.

1. See, for instance, Saville (1957); Titmuss (1958 and 1968); Bruce (1961); Marshall (1965); Mencher (1961); Hallam (1974); Stedman-Jones (1971); Wilson (1977); Gilbert (1966); Cormack (1968); Mishra (1977).
2. Joseph Chamberlain, in a speech in 1885: 'What ransom will property pay for the security which it enjoys?'; quoted by Saville (1957).

These factors, contributing to increasing state intervention in the field of welfare, are clearly not mutually exclusive. Indeed, as Gilbert (1966, 448–52) points out, the development of the welfare state should not be seen in monolithic terms; rather, it should be understood that different facets of welfare provision had their origins in differing political, intellectual and moral climates. I do not wish to give a detailed account here of the debate referred to above, but to draw attention to a thread (emphasized by several other contributors) which runs through the development of welfare provision up to the present day – an over-riding preoccupation with the able-bodied poor, and a perennial distinction made by the middle class between the respectable and the unrespectable working class; the 'deserving' and the 'undeserving'; the genuine worker (albeit temporarily unemployed) and the 'residuum'; the poor and the pauper. The importance of this distinction (which denoted a difference in kind, not simply one of degree) for the formulation of state policies and voluntary activity has been documented by Stedman-Jones (1971) for the late Victorian period, and it underlies subsequent and recent discussion of such issues as universalism versus selectivity in the social services and the 'cycle of deprivation'.

The crux of the problem, as policy-makers have perceived it, may be stated as how to ensure that members of the deserving poor do not join the ranks of the undeserving. The danger of this happening has been seen to reside both in insufficient *and* in excessive intervention. Left without help in times of hardship, some members of the respectable working class would sink into a state of physical ill-health or moral degradation such that they would become incapable of resuming work and independence. Or they might, in desperation, throw in their lot with the disreputable and become a socially disruptive force. But on the other hand, the help given to the respectable in times of hardship, and the help given to the unrespectable at any time, must on no account render them better off than the lowest paid employed worker, otherwise incentives to work and to be independent would be undermined. The problem has sometimes been expressed in terms of the need to maintain work incentives, sometimes in terms of the need to ensure social stability, and sometimes in terms of the necessity of supporting the independent, normally functioning family. But it remains the case that, as Mencher (1961, 45) has put it:

> The effect of assistance on dependency has probably been the most persistent problem of social policy since the period of the Reformation. Although the nature of assistance and the concept of dependency have changed markedly during the last four centuries, the expectation, or, more accurately, the fear, has persisted that any effort resulting in benefits beyond those obtainable through the normal economic institutions of society will discourage maximum assumption of responsibility.

This conceptualization of the 'problem of poverty' in conjunction with emotional attitudes of compassion on the one hand, and hostility on the other, has given rise to policies embodying both care and concern towards the poor, *and* punishment and control, as the attempt has been made by successive generations of policy-makers and practitioners to resolve their dilemma.[3] Historically, these two aspects of welfare, care and control, were institutionally distinct. On the one hand was individual-oriented attention to particular need; on the other, punitive, deterrent rule-governed activities. The first was the sphere of private philanthropy, from within which the occupation of social work developed. The second was the business of the poor law. However, as the role of the state in social welfare has expanded, and ways of operationalizing the distinction between the respectable and the unrespectable have changed, these two functions have increasingly converged, notably today in the role of the local authority social worker.

The new poor law of 1834 set the tone of Victorian public policy towards the poor and destitute. It sprang from a rejection of practices existing under the old poor law – practices which included the Speenhamland system of wage subsidy, and outdoor relief on a large scale. Mencher describes the new poor law as a move to break up a system based on the ability to claim subsistence from the rates as a status right and to shift the population into a state of total dependence on wages, based on the principle of contract. Under the new poor law, the distinction between poverty and pauperism was to be strictly implemented. The workhouse and (subsequently) labour tests were designed to ensure that assistance under the poor law would be 'less eligible' than the lot of the lowest paid labourer, and that only the pauper, and not the poor would come within the scope of the poor law.

A vast and complex structure of philanthropy existed side by side with the poor law, and however patronizingly administered, was supposed to address the plight of the deserving poor, and help prevent pauperism. The two systems of relief were closely related, however. They were related in practice, since close ties often existed between the two systems at local level, and the same individuals were often involved in the administration of both (see McCord, 1976). And they were related in principle, in that they were aspects of one, over-all public approach to poverty whereby paupers

3. The success of the drive to separate the interests of the deserving and the undeserving is perhaps reflected in the statement by Alfred Marshall in 1893, that 'the leaders of the working men would be as firm as anyone in insisting that scamps and lazy people should be put to a severe discipline', (quoted by Mencher, 1961, 56). If this was true, it would seem likely that factors operating within the working class itself were also responsible, and not only the ideological achievements of the middle class.

could be punished on the basis of an assumption of individual responsibility for destitution, while the deserving could be treated as the exceptions that proved the rule.

The formation of the Charity Organization Society (COS) in 1869 constitutes the first major step in the convergence of these two separate strands,[4] not because its work represented a totally new departure,[5] but because it formulated as coherent principles and methods practices which had hitherto existed on a random basis – principles which later formed the basis of the casework method on which professional social work is founded.

Gareth Stedman-Jones (1971) has given a detailed and convincing account of the way in which the COS arose in the context of class relationships in late nineteenth-century London. The geographical separation between rich and poor in London, and in particular the existence of a huge solidly working-class area in the East End, was a source of great concern to the middle classes of the day. They felt that the opportunities for control and influence that had existed through the face-to-face contacts between classes possible in small communities had been lost, with a resulting danger of mob violence and unrest by the 'dangerous classes'.[6] The middle classes were apprehensive, not about the behaviour of the poor as such, but about the 'demoralized' section of the population, the casual poor, who were seen as lazy, improvident and unscrupulous. An important factor contributing to this 'demoralization' was thought to be 'indiscriminate alms-giving', whereby, when poverty was most widespread and protest seemed a serious threat, charitable donations were pumped into the East End. It was thought that the disreputable could make an easy living by going from one charity to another, thus providing a corrupting influence on the respectable members of the community. The COS was set up with the aim of channelling and co-ordinating charitable endeavour, and of making sure that only the deserving received charity, the rest being left to the rigours of a stricter reformed poor law.

At first sight, this development looks as if it was designed to make more rigid the division between the deterrent, punitive controlling areas of activity, under state auspices, and the more compassionate approach embodied in charity. From another point of view, however, it represents an attempt by the COS to infuse into the latter some of the characteristics

4. For a detailed account of the history of the COS and its successor, the Family Welfare Association, see Rooff (1972).
5. Thomas Chalmers had been working along similar lines in Glasgow, cf. Young and Ashton (1956, 67–78).
6. These fears were not confined to the inhabitants of London. See the similar sentiments expressed by W. Rathbone of Liverpool, quoted by Fraser (1976, 10).

of the former – that is, to introduce criteria of eligibility and rationality into the giving of charity to individuals, to fuse the application of principles with detailed attention to individual circumstances.

Under the auspices of the COS, a style of work developed in which the seeds of modern casework can be traced. The giving of charity was only undertaken in the context of personal contact between a worker/visitor and the recipient, and then not on grounds of need alone, but on condition that the gift would help the recipient to improve his situation and recover his self-respect. Supervision was provided by the visitor to aid this process of improvement and the supervision was a condition of receiving material aid. An example of work on this model was the supervised housing schemes initiated by Octavia Hill, who was one of the early members of the COS. The major emphasis was on the personal contact between the worker and the poor person. The COS laid a great deal of stress on the scientific nature of their methods. Initial investigation and assessment was to be thorough and detailed records kept. Visits should only be made with a specific purpose and only on the request of, or with the consent of, the client. All cases were to be followed through until a satisfactory outcome was arrived at. When one looks at descriptions of this early social work, it is clear that the exercise of authority and control was an important aspect of what they were doing. But it was a control redeemed and disguised from the worker, if not from the client, by a relationship in which concern for the individual was central – a relationship on the maternal model.[7] It was thus rather different from the impersonal application of rules, backed by statutory authority, that operated under the poor law.

In the division of function between the poor law and the voluntary organizations as regards control on the one hand, and care on the other, the capacity for deterrence exercised by the poor law was, by the end of the nineteenth century, felt to be under severe strain. This was because the guardians' responsibility for the treatment of the destitute sick had produced a situation 'making the treatment of the sick pauper the envy of the poorest self-supporting patient' (Pinker, 1971, 80). The poor law inspectorate itself advocated the removal of medical services from poor law jurisdiction, so that 'it would once again be possible to follow a vigorously deterrent policy against the able-bodied' (Pinker, 1971, 81). This proposal was made to the Royal Commission on the Poor Laws (1905–9) and was in line with the recommendations of the Minority Report. But the failure of the Commissioners to agree on a common set of

---

7. 'Octavia Hill, for instance, had the warmest maternal feelings for her clients, and never went back to the country without bringing back innumerable bunches of flowers for her enormous family.' E. E. Irvine, quoted in Halmos (1965, 53).

recommendations was probably the main reason for the poor law remaining much as it was, and the new developments in the welfare field (notably pensions and insurance) in the years up to the Second World War largely taking place outside it.

The development of social work thus continued within the non-statutory sphere of activity. During the first half of this century, social work developed as an occupation with a recognized training, and with claims to professional status. A key aspect of this development was the adoption of psychoanalytic ideas as the basis of casework practice which, it was felt, made social work a more rational and objective undertaking.

With the major reorganization of social services of all kinds following the Second World War, the situation altered. Following the eventual demise of the poor law and a rethinking of the scope and nature of state intervention, the distribution of care and control functions – or, as Clarke (1979) puts it, 'the balance between consensual and repressive processes' – became changed. Social work on a casework model, based on cooperation and assumed agreement about goals on the part of the client, had been carried out largely in the voluntary sector; coercive, deterrent and repressive activities had been carried out under the poor law, backed by the judiciary. But now, for the first time (first time except for the probation service) trained social workers entered the statutory sphere, bringing a further development in the convergence of care and control functions by fusing them within a single occupational role, that of child care officer.[8] Casework soon became the dominant ideal or model of work in child care. But CCOs also took on control functions – the initiating of 'Fit Person' orders, the supervision of foster homes, and so on.

Since the 1940s, the functions of care and control have further merged. During this period, the range of powers and duties vested in local authority social workers has greatly increased.[9] Many of these powers and duties involve the exercise of authority, within the framework of a relationship that is ostensibly focused on the good of the client but where there is room for substantial difference of interpretation as to what the good of the client is. The whole area of work with young people arising out of the 1969 Children and Young Persons Act is a case in point. The reorganization of the personal social services in the 1970s has meant that the control functions involved in work with old people, homeless families and the mentally ill have been added to those involved in child care work, as part of

8. Trained social workers went mainly into the child care service. In welfare departments, there was no recruitment of trained social workers, as far as I know, until the introduction of Certificate in Social Work courses in the late 1950s, and even after that there were very few.

9. For a survey of these developments, see Forder (1971, chapters 6–9).

the role of the generic social worker, and this has made social workers more conscious of their role as rationing agents and authority figures (see Brill, 1972). Whether or not a social worker is actually exercising authority in her dealings with a given client, she might have to do so – perhaps even against her will, in response to other pressures – and the client knows this. The 'one door on which to knock' introduced by reorganization means that the client finds it difficult to invoke the help of one social worker in dealing with another.

In recent times, criteria whereby the poor (as clients mainly are) could be assigned to the status of respectable or unrespectable have themselves become blurred. Increasingly, official policy has embodied the view that the social services in general, and local authority social work services specifically, are for the benefit of the whole community and are to 'reach far beyond the discovery and rescue of social casualties'.[10] Yet the tension between collectivism and individualism, portrayed by Dicey (1905) for the nineteenth century, is still with us. A preoccupation with safeguarding the incentive to be independent still pervades policy at national and local government levels, and social workers are constantly reminded of it.

The merging of the strategies thought appropriate to the deserving and the undeserving respectively within one occupational role means that the task of distinguishing between the two categories becomes located within that role. In the nineteenth century, if people applied for help from a charity, the decision as to whether they deserved help or not was made at that point. Classification of people was an event, not a process. But if modern local authority social services are supposed to be for the use of everyone in the community, then the task of making the distinction which, it is felt, is still important to uphold, falls on the individual social worker, confronting the individual client in the context of a continuing relationship.

This introduces an endemic ambivalence and wariness into the social worker-client relationship – on both sides. It is very different from the model of social work contained in the textbooks, which sees social work help as centred on the client's needs, and as being something which the client is free to accept or reject. And it is different, too, from the ideal of 'helping people' with which most social workers enter the occupation.

Care and control in practice

In the interest of brevity, the foregoing account has oversimplified what was undoubtedly a complex set of developments. Now, as in the past, the

10. Report of the Committee on Local Authority and Allied Personal Social Services (Seebohm Committee) (1968, 11).

question of what may be counted as care and what as control is partly a matter for interpretation. The two ideas were, and are, relative to one another in the same way as are the ideas of deserving and undeserving. There is a considerable area of interaction between social worker and client in which the client may feel subject to control to some degree, while the social worker sees herself as acting only out of concern.

But it is clear that there are aspects of local authority social workers' role as state employees which involve them in the direct and unambiguous use of authority, and that they are, by virtue of this fact placed in a contradictory relationship to clients. The discussion that follows, based upon fieldwork[11] in a London social services department, indicates some of the implications of this situation for the social organization of local authority social work.

A distaste for the exercise of authority seems to be universal among social workers (see, for instance, Clarke, 1971). All those I interviewed said that they disliked it, although many said that they had come to accept it as a necessary part of the job. Some gave examples of cases in which they themselves felt reluctant to exercise authority, but were being pressed to do so by their seniors, or by other statutory bodies. Sometimes the responsibility could be shared with someone else, as in the case of compulsory admissions to mental hospital, where the decision could be shared with a doctor. Some social workers mentioned ways in which they tried to avoid being seen as an authority figure. For instance:

'Sometimes I can take responsibility myself for insisting on something against the client's will, but other times I fall back on the requirements of the law or the hierarchy. It's possible to use mystification in a situation where the client doesn't know where the decision-making power lies, to give them the impression that it's out of your hands. I tend not to use this very often, and then over small things, I don't like being authoritarian. I think social workers in general don't; they want the approval of their clients.'

Several social workers said that although in principle they disliked the aloofness implied in the idea of a professional relationship, in practice they felt they had to maintain some social distance between themselves and their clients, as otherwise it would be more difficult to exercise authority if the necessity arose. Sometimes what they had in mind was an eventuality involving direct coercion – a compulsory reception of a child into care, or admission to a mental hospital, for instance. But perhaps more often, in the case of families, the authority situation they most readily envisaged was one in which the client asked for money and the social worker would have

---

11. During 1970–72, I carried out a study of social workers in the children's department (and, subsequently, the social services department) of a London borough, 'Thamesham'. See Satyamurti (1978).

either to refuse or to impose conditions on the client.

Social workers were also aware that, although as generic workers they were supposed to be providing a service for the whole family, their capacity, and sometimes their obligation, to intervene in practical ways could involve them in alignments with some family members against others, having to choose to support the interests of one section of the family against another.

The ways in which social workers maintained distance between themselves and their clients included both symbolic aspects of interaction, and shared ways of conceptualizing clients, their needs and the role of the social worker in relation to these, so as to produce a distancing effect. Part of what was involved was a diminishing of the client's status as adult and as citizen, which is reminiscent of (though more subtle than) the ways in which, in the nineteenth century, those who received poor law relief often had to accept a way of life and a social identity that was stigmatizing and diminishing.

It seemed to me that the creation of distance was a strategy of survival which social workers needed to engage in, not only to enable them to handle more easily the transactions that involved them in the exercise of control, but also to minimize the pain that was inherent in the work. The pain derived from being closely associated with the suffering of clients, perhaps contributing to it, or at least being able to do relatively little about it. And the experience was made worse by the privatized way in which the work was organized, with each worker operating largely alone, with largely ineffectual supervision and leadership.[12]

There were various ways in which social distance between social workers and clients was symbolically created and maintained. Most of them had gone unexamined for years, as they formed part of the accepted idea of professional conduct, and although few of the social workers studied found any value in this model of professionalism, they did not feel safe in giving up the practices associated with it. These included not accepting gifts or hospitality from clients, apart from a cup of tea; not having the client use the social worker's Christian name, although the social worker might call the client by his or her Christian name; discouraging the client from showing any interest in the personal characteristics and off-duty activities of the social worker; and having strict rules about clients not being allowed anywhere in the department building except the waiting area, even when accompanied by a social worker.

The exercise of authority could be felt as more tolerable if it could be seen as in some way asked for by the clients themselves. If clients could be

---

12.   I have no way of knowing how typical this feature of the Thamesham department was.

seen as inviting control, either directly, or by virtue of their behaviour or personal characteristics, then this made the social worker's job easier. Thus, although social workers complained constantly about their clients, in fact they had an interest in sustaining the client stereotype with which they worked.

One aspect of this stereotype was to see clients (particularly child care clients) as irresponsible, disorganized, demanding and dependent. Many clients did indeed manifest dependency on their social worker, constantly ringing up to ask advice and so on, but it was clear, both from the files and from observing interaction between social worker and client that, in some cases at least, this was learned behaviour. Social workers' expectations of the client often had a self-fulfilling quality, and they were even actively discouraging of independent behaviour by their clients. One worker, for instance, complained about a client of hers, a young separated mother of two children, that she never did anything for herself. On one visit, the client said that she had been in touch with a charity to see if she could get a grant for clothing, but had not had a reply. Rather than suggesting that the client write to them again, the social worker said that she would write to them herself, implying that she would be able to get a better result than the client. Similarly, a social worker in another team was having a telephone conversation with a client of hers, telling the client in some detail what she should say to the supplementary benefits officer. At one point, when the client had apparently suggested something that the social worker did not approve of, she said: 'If you do that, all my work with you will have been wasted and my patience isn't unlimited.' At the end of the conversation she put down the receiver and remarked to a colleague: 'Isn't it dreadful to have to live someone else's life for them!'

Social workers varied considerably, and in a way that did not seem to be patterned with reference to training or experience, in how they reacted to and handled clients' dependency and demands. Some, consciously or otherwise, actively encouraged it. Others encouraged it in some clients, but not in others. Some encouraged dependency up to a certain point and then were rejecting of the client. Others could tolerate dependency of some kinds but not of others – for instance, demands of a practical kind might be tolerable, while emotional dependency was not, or vice versa. Dependency on the clients' part was, for some social workers, the same thing as a good relationship with the client, and they experienced it as a much needed confirmation that they were able to offer something of value.

Stereotyping the client involved emphasizing some qualities and ignoring others, so as to render reasonable a situation in which social workers were often behaving towards clients as parents towards children. Attention has been drawn (Wilkins, 1967, 85; Young, 1971) to the way in which a stigmatizing label acquired in one area of a persons' life has a tendency to contaminate other areas. Some clue to the process whereby this occurs can be seen in the way in which social workers used the label 'client'. People quite often, in discussions and meetings, referred to 'our clients'. Sometimes the term would be 'our inadequate clients' or 'our problem mums'. What was being suggested was a description of a total life style, and it betrayed a widespread, though not universal, assumption by social workers that being a client was somehow incompatible with being anything else that was at all responsible or effective. The use of these terms, in contexts in which they seemed on the surface to be merely descriptive, was in fact an affirmation and reinforcement of particular stereotypes. When social workers came across instances which violated the stereotype – when what was conceived of as a 'client' and a 'non-client' style of life were combined in one person – they would often experience this as uncomfortable and confusing, and might seek to reduce this discomfort by denying or invalidating one or the other aspect of the person's social identity.

In one instance, a mother had to be admitted to hospital suddenly and left her children with a neighbour. The neighbour was willing to look after the children until the mother came out of hospital, but the social worker insisted on their being received into care. He said that he could not allow the children to remain where they were because the neighbour 'could have been a client' and for this reason was not suitable as a foster mother.[13] In this case, someone perceived primarily as a client was not being allowed to assume a socially responsible role. In another instance a woman who was well known in her block as a source of information and general help approached the department because she was in financial difficulties and owing money for electricity. At the team allocation meeting, people felt that this was an interesting case and possibly a way of getting to know the community in which the woman lived, using her as a contact person. In practice, however, the social worker who took on the case found the ambiguity of the woman's situation very difficult to tolerate, and she in fact dealt with the difficulty by firmly rejecting and ridiculing the woman's claim to be other than a client: 'She's so manipulative I can't stand her. She thinks she's better than other clients but she's not.'

Sometimes the stereotyping process worked in the other direction. One social worker, J. K., an enthusiastic advocate of the 'heartland'[14] method

13. The social worker may or may not have been right about the neighbour's suitability for looking after children. What is of interest is the way in which he justified his action.
14. That is, the practice of each social worker having his or her own geographical patch, and taking on all cases arising in that patch.

of working, formed a contact with a man, who was the secretary of the tenants' association of a small housing estate in the social worker's patch. J. K. was someone who was very dependent on a range of symbolic and other barriers between himself and his clients. He tended to have short interviews with his clients, and to insist on their sticking to the point, as he saw it. He would often conduct an interview standing up, and he refused to accept cups of tea from any client on grounds of hygiene. He regarded the tenants' association secretary as a fellow worker in the estate, and frequently dropped in for a cup of tea with him and a lengthy chat. Yet this man was also a client. He had a mentally handicapped son and he had a married daughter who had been referred to the department for rent arrears. The married daughter lived in another part of the borough, but the son lived with the parents and J. K. would logically have been their social worker. In fact another social worker in the team had taken him on and J. K. did not refer to the son in his conversations with the man.

What was at stake in instances such as this was the question of whose definition of the situation would prevail, the client's or the social worker's. The social worker had an interest in seeing the client only as a client – as the kind of person to whom certain things tended to happen and towards whom certain behaviour was legitimate. The client, on the other hand, sought, where possible, *to* invoke other social indentities, whether in order to avoid stigmatization – which was expressly the case in some instances – or to improve his chances of getting resources which he felt would otherwise be denied him. Thus clients quite often invoked their status as ordinary citizens or constituents in writing to the press, or trying to obtain the support of their councillor or MP, in seeking to increase their chances of a favourable decision on the part of the SSD or to get an unfavourable decision reversed. Such behaviour was called 'manipulative' by social workers.

The use of the word 'manipulative' is but one example of a range of linguistic and classificatory devices whereby social workers distanced their clients. Sometimes this was to avoid pain, as when a complex and harrowing experience on the part of the client would be reduced, by the social worker describing it, to flat clinical terms. At other times, as with the words 'manipulative' or 'difficult', it was to invalidate clients' claims, which were seen as a threat. The threat was one of being engulfed by demands. Social workers had a kind of 'siege' perspective which led them to feel that clients had to be kept at bay and resisted. Not only were existing clients seen in this way, but the whole community was seen as consisting of potential clients, who had to be deterred from approaching the department, partly by the department not making too public what it had to offer and partly by not treating current clients in such a way as to encourage other people to apply for help. This applied most of all to financial help.

I would not want to suggest that social workers viewed their clients entirely as a threat, or that they derived no satisfaction from relationships with clients. But this tendency was sufficiently strong to drive social workers back on each other as the main source of satisfaction and support, and it was a major influence on the social organization of the social work team. In the struggle to survive in the job, in which many social workers were engaged, the support of colleagues was of very great importance – of much greater importance than anything that seniors were seen as offering. Colleagues were there to listen, to reassure, to endorse decisions one had made, to console when one had made a mistake, to give one information, to protect one from a client one could not face. Such dependence on colleagues, and commitment to behaving well as a colleague oneself, militated against innovation or fresh thinking about the work. Team meetings were almost invariably expressive outpourings of dissatisfaction or grievance against others, inside or outside the department. They were rarely problem-solving occasions.

The giving of money was the area of statutory activity that occasioned most worry to both social workers and management. Under Section I of the 1963 Children and Young Persons Act, local authorities are empowered to make financial grants to families to prevent the necessity for children being received into care. In Thamesham, expenditure under this provision was considerable, and management was concerned with the question of the efficacy of Section I payments. Did they help to restore a family to financial independence, or did they, on the contrary, encourage people to become dependent on receiving extra financial help from time to time? And what was the effect, for instance, on all those tenants who managed to pay their rent regularly, of the department paying the arrears of those who did not manage to do so?

The solution to these problems, as far as management was concerned, lay in the controls that social workers were to exercise in conjunction with the giving of money. These would ideally ensure that the financial problems would not recur, and would also deter potential applicants by making the receipt of help seem less attractive. The matter was not put quite as directly as this on the whole. Section I payments were not supposed to be made (though they sometimes were) except in the context of 'ongoing casework' with a client, and that was not seen as being a form of control. But many people were aware that for the client it often meant having to put up with a social worker visiting, asking personal questions, perhaps collecting the rent, possibly insisting on administering the family allowance money, and so on; in other words, that the client was going to have to accept a number of disagreeable consequences if help was to be forthcoming.

The view was widespread in the department that the degree to which a social worker could resist client pressure to give financial help was an index of professional maturity, since, it was felt, a good social worker should be able to offer some alternative to money. At one level, social workers shared this view, and would often feel depressed and guilty about giving money. At another level, they were conscious that often clients got into financial difficulties because their income was inadequate, and felt concern for the family's need. They were thus caught in a dilemma between care and control, between a wish simply to help, and a wish to behave responsibly by the department's standards. Decisions about amounts under £5 caused more heart-searching than much larger amounts, because the small amounts had to be given on the spot, and they often became the subject of what was seen as a battle of nerves between social worker and client – the 'siege' being here experienced by the social worker in its most acute form. There would be talk of 'not giving in', of 'calling (the client's) bluff'. Social workers disliked doing this, and sometimes could not bring themselves to do so, even though they might be apologetic to the senior and accept the implication that to fail to take a firm line was a sign of weakness.

Summary

In this chapter, care and control have been identified as complementary aspects of public policy towards the poor and deviant. These two elements, originally separately institutionalized, have converged in the role of local authority social worker. The implications of this for the social organization of contemporary local authority social work have been explored, and it has been suggested that the difficulty of reconciling care and control, humane objectives and statutory duties, within a single occupational role is partly responsible for the 'crisis in social work', and for the ways in which social workers attempt to survive.

6

The balance of medicine, law and social work in mental health legislation, 1889–1959

Clive Unsworth

Since the late nineteenth century, the orientation of legislation for the civilly committed insane has undergone radical change. Whereas the Lunacy Act (1890) reflected a preoccupation with the procedural protection of individual liberty, subsequent legislation culminating in the Mental Health Act (1959) has sought to restrict and modify formal legal safeguards on the ground that they impede early and effective professional treatment of psychiatric disorders. Traditional explanations of this reversal, which may be exemplified by the work of Kathleen Jones (1972), have emphasized the role of such developments as the rise of the medical and social work professions, advances in psychiatric treatment, and the growth of humanitarian concern for disadvantaged groups. More recently, however, theorists basically critical of the paternalistic tendencies in modern mental health legislation have analysed its emergence in terms of broad movements of political change. The following discussion represents a contribution to this redefinition of the historical roots of the legislation and emphasizes the need for a re-evaluation of the part played by the medical, legal and social work professions. By way of introduction there follows a summary of the main provisions of the relevant legislation and of the arguments originally advanced in favour of their adoption.

The Lunacy Acts Amendment Act (1889, incorporated in the consolidating Lunacy Act, 1890) introduced the requirement of certification by a justice prior to confinement in an asylum as a private patient where the order of a relative supported by two medical certificates had previously been deemed sufficient,[1] and imposed a ban upon the future grant of licences for the establishment of institutions for the reception of the insane on a commercial basis (s.56). This more stringent legislative approach was justified by its purveyors as a response to popular alarm at the apparent ease with which people could be incarcerated, and embodied the substance of the demand persistently voiced by élite

1. The Lunacy Acts Amendment Act (1889), s.2 (1). Judicial certification had been required since the early nineteenth century for long-term detention as a pauper lunatic.

members of the legal profession that procedural safeguards for the protection of the liberty of the subject be strengthened. The injection of further elements of legal procedure and lay control was seen as providing a check upon the autocratic authority of medical men, especially of professional 'alienists' who were suspected of over-enthusiasm in identifying the symptoms of insanity in their patients.

The act of 1890 could be seen as the culmination of a century of reform designed to afford the insane an adequate system of legal protection against wrongful detention, exploitation and abuse, following in the tradition of the Lunatics Act (1845). However, it actually represented a sound defeat for the medical and bureaucratic establishment of the lunacy system who had supported earlier legislation. The Lunacy Commissioners, led by their chairman Lord Shaftesbury, the veteran pioneer of lunacy reform, and the Medico-Psychological Association, the professional organization of doctors engaged in treating the insane, strenuously resisted change, arguing that legal intervention had already progressed far enough. In particular they claimed that the extension of judicial participation in the processes of admission would produce a decline in the rate of cure by deterring patients, or relatives acting on their behalf, from seeking psychiatric assistance when their malady was still at an early 'curable' stage. The prestige and experience of this opposition, and their ability to refer to the findings of the 1877 committee of the House of Commons which had counselled against the adoption of the main reforms embodied in the 1890 act, were to no avail. A determined campaign by the legal profession and the active support of a succession of lord chancellors ensured that the measure ultimately became law, even after broader popular interest had faded.

The Mental Treatment Act (1930) introduced voluntary admission to public mental hospitals (s.1) and authorized the compulsory hospitalization of 'non-volitional' patients for a maximum of one year on the basis of two medical recommendations without judicial certification (s.5). It also expanded the powers of local authorities to make provision for the insane into the pre- and post-institutional phases of care (s.6), and replaced such designations as 'lunatic' and 'asylum' by their medical equivalents 'patient of unsound mind' and 'mental hospital' (s.20).

These innovations represented a rejection of the earlier libertarian and legalistic proceduralism and reflected a new idealism in relation to the possibilities of medical science in the field of psychiatry. They were broadly in accordance with the recommendations of the Royal Commission on Lunacy and Mental Disorder (the Macmillan Commission) which, reporting in 1926 (15), proposed a new approach to legislation on the basis that 'there is no clear line of demarcation between mental and physical illness distinctions operating only at the superficial and misleading level of the form taken by the symptoms.' The Commission urged that the legal and administrative framework should be designed so as to facilitate the assimilation of the treatment of psychiatric disorder to that of physical illness. It was argued that the legal formalities of the Lunacy Act should be relaxed rather than strengthened as, in the Commission's view, the main danger to be guarded against was not so much the infringement of personal liberty as the deterrent and stigmatizing effect of 'criminalizing' procedures such as certification by a magistrate. Echoing the Shaftesburyite position of the 1880s, Macmillan (15–24) held that voluntary or medically controlled compulsory admission would eliminate damaging delays in treatment and finally allow psychiatry to realize its potential as a genuinely curative enterprise.

Although only an amending statute, the Mental Treatment Act considerably modified the legal structure bequeathed by the late Victorian lord chancellors. In practice, the new compulsory procedure was not much used as an alternative to traditional certification, but voluntary admission became widespread, varying regionally from 45 to 94 per cent by 1952 (*The Lancet*, 1952, 2, 972). It was the Mental Health Act (1959), however, which carried the approach endorsed in principle in 1930 to its logical conclusion. Magisterial certification was abolished, and replaced by procedures which essentially left compulsory commitment to medical decision.[2] The main safeguard against unjustified detention was the introduction of a system of mental health review tribunals (ss.3, 122–4), each tribunal to be composed of a legal chairman, a doctor and a layman possessing some relevant qualification, such as experience of social administration. Although the reference of cases to tribunals resembles an appeal procedure in that it can only take place subsequent to the issue of an order for compulsory admission, their jurisdiction is limited to deciding the applicant's fitness for discharge at the time of the review and the validity of the original decision to detain cannot be challenged. Furthermore, only certain categories of compulsory patient can apply to the tribunal.[3] It was envisaged, however, that the use of compulsory procedures would continue to decline dramatically, being used only as a last resort in clear cases, and that voluntary admission, which the act completely informalized, would be the norm. A preoccupation with legal safeguards may have been

2. The main forms of compulsory admission under the 1959 Act are for observation (s.25), treatment (s.26) and emergency observation (s.29). Ss.25 and 26 require the application of the nearest relative or social worker supported by two medical recommendations. Under s.29 the application may be by any relative and requires only one medical recommendation.

3. Patients detained under s.25 (maximum duration 28 days) and s.29 (maximum duration three days) have no access to a mental health review tribunal.

appropriate when psychiatry was fulfilling a predominantly custodial function, but was considered damagingly anachronistic once it was perceived as having become a dynamically therapeutic and curative activity. Rather than creating a need for more safeguards, it was felt that the evolution of new treatment techniques went far to disposing of any threats to liberty which might be inherent in the psychiatric enterprise, by reducing periods of hospitalization and transforming the deprivation of liberty sometimes involved from mere detention into a paternalistically warranted means to the alleviation of suffering and the promotion of cure.[4]

The Mental Health Act did not simply promote the assimilation of the practice of psychiatry to general medicine, however. It was also intended to herald a fresh chapter in the history of the mental health services, in which many of the mentally ill would be liberated from institutional confinement. By reinforcing the powers of local authorities to make provision for psychiatric patients beyond the walls of the asylum, the authors of the act marked their approval of the fashionable concept of 'community care'. The ideal of desegregating the mentally ill had an almost messianic appeal, promising a new enlightenment in which an oppressed minority was finally to be accorded social justice. Accordingly, the Mental Health Act was seen not only as a recognition of the medical character of insanity, but also as a product and a symbol of the humanitarianism and social concern of the welfare state.[5] Furthermore, it was perceived as a highly liberal measure: the rhetoric of liberalism which had formerly attached to the deployment of legal safeguards was now transferred to the process of facilitating the relief of suffering by their removal. This redefinition of humanitarianism and liberalism temporarily submerged the issues of civil liberty which were at the forefront of the debate about the treatment of the insane in the late nineteenth century and which have re-emerged in the decades since the passage of the Mental Health Act. It is to the respective roles of professional organizations and broader social and political change in generating this radical shift in thinking about legislation for the mentally ill that the remainder of this discussion will be addressed.

In Kathleen Jones' view (1972, 153) the pattern of historical development which has just been outlined can be understood in terms of the contributions of different professional approaches. Three such approaches are distinguished – medical, legal and social – which are identified respectively with the medical, legal and social work professions.

4. See, for example, the Report of the Royal Commission on the Law Relating to Mental Illness and Mental Deficiency, para. 317.
5. See the speech of R. A. Butler, as home secretary, to the annual conference of the National Association for Mental Health for 1958, in the report of its proceedings, especially p. 7.

These perspectives are associated with specific items of legislation: the Lunacy Act is identified as reflective of the legal approach, the Mental Treatment Act (1930) is characterized as medical in its assumptions, and it is implied that the Mental Health Act (1959) represents a combination of medical and social approaches. According to Jones, this legal–medical–social sequence corresponds to changes in the relative power and status of the professional organizations concerned.

This presentation of each profession as possessing a characteristic occupational world view which determines its stance on legislation for mentally ill obscures the fact that the professions concerned have at certain historical junctures adopted 'uncharacteristic' positions. The medical approach is described as blurring the distinction between mental and physical disorders and emphasizing physical treatment. Doctors are portrayed as the natural opponents of a legal or lay interventionism alien to their experience in physical medicine. However, the medical profession have not always comprised a harmonious and united pressure group. As Ewins (1974, 57) points out, the Medical Practitioners' Union voiced anxiety in the 1950s at the prospect of the power to detain being removed from magistrates and conferred upon members of the medical profession, fearing that this would harm the doctor–patient relationship. The leading professional organizations, particularly the British Medical Association and the Royal Medico-Psychological Association, broadly favoured such a transfer. Ewins's explanation for this divergence is that it reflected a conflict between the professional imperialism of the medical élite and the preoccupation of 'grass-roots' doctors with the facilitation of their routine transactions with patients.[6] However, the historical evidence shows that there had been divisions prior to this period and suggests that broader issues of principle and strategy were responsible for tension within the medical profession, both over the specific question of the procedure for compulsory commitment and the whole issue of legal interventionism. In

6. For the position of the Medical Practitioners Union see the letter from Bruce Cardew, its general secretary, to *The Times* (17th February 1959). This small association consistently opposed the medical establishment, but there is conflicting evidence as to the dimensions of dissent within the profession as a whole and as to whether it was basically confined to general practitioners. The British Medical Association and the Royal Medico-Psychological Association claimed that their memoranda of evidence to the Royal Commission of 1954–7 were compiled with maximum reference to the opinion of their membership, and they were ratified in council and at AGMs. But it was claimed by some MPs, for example by Dr A. D. D. Broughton, a psychiatrist, that there was widespread concern in the medical profession that the transfer of compulsory powers to doctors would harm the doctor–patient relationship and was a responsibility which they did not have the competence to assume. (Hansard, House of Commons Select Committee Report Session 1958–9, cols 279–82, 306).

the mid-1880s *The Lancet* had 'uncharacteristically' joined the legal profession in demanding further legal restraints upon the power of doctors to admit the insane to asylums, a position exemplified in this quotation from a contemporary editorial (7 February 1885): 'In truth, medical men ought to have no more to do with the legal and social disabilities of the mentally diseased than they have with the moral characters, the financial position or the educational attainments of their patients. ... No single power is needed by physicians engaged in the medical treatment of the insane which the common law does not give every citizen.'

In the 1920s, there was debate within the ranks of the Medico-Psychological Association itself as to whether magisterial control of compulsory commitment should be endorsed or rejected. In the preparation of the memorandum of evidence submitted by the Association to the Macmillan Commission (1926, II, appendix 24, 962), those 'radicals' who wanted to oust the magistrate were defeated and the document affirmed the principle that 'the authority for detention, discharge and continuation orders should entail the responsibility of some authorized person not acting in a medical capacity.' Furthermore, the Medico-Psychological Association's suggestion for a compulsory order short of certification retained the participation of a magistrate, and it was proposed that where full certification was invoked formal legal safeguards should actually be strengthened.

The position articulated in the editorials of *The Lancet* could be interpreted simply as an expression of a fear among doctors not primarily engaged in treating the insane that the involvement of medical men in the processes of detention would bring the profession as a whole into disrepute with its wealthier patrons, particularly as this was a time when well-publicized lawsuits were being brought against members of the medical profession by aggrieved upper-class patients complaining of wrongful detention in an asylum on medical recommendation. But the above quotation illustrates that *The Lancet*'s position was dependent upon a particular conception of the professional role, indicating that the issue was also one of principle. That conception corresponds closely to the ideals of classical liberalism. It requires that the professional expert inhabit the narrowly prescribed province of the technician. He is defined as essentially a consultant whose skill should be at the service of the consumer on request. Where his specialist competence might be abused in such a way as to threaten the liberty of those whom he purports to serve, as might be the case with the bureaucrat or the psychiatrist, it is imperative that his activities be subjected to restraints incorporating a lay element in order to protect individual freedoms.

This definition of the proper boundaries of professional discretion may be contrasted with a competing conception, in which the scientific character of the expert's knowledge, with its promise of maximizing the efficiency of the decision-making process, is valued more highly than the formal preservation of individual liberties. The logic of this position requires that procedures which notionally subject professional discretion to democratic and disinterested lay control be sacrificed as a measure of rationalization. In a psychiatric context, these professional conceptions correspond to different views of the appropriate relationship between the medical expert and the machinery of legal coercion. In the first, the psychiatrist's role can only be advisory, and the actual decision to detain should be a moral, legal and social issue for determination by judicial process rather than medical diagnostic procedure. In the second, however, the psychiatrist is the only figure who possesses the expertise necessary to decide whether compulsion is in all the circumstances likely to be conducive to recovery or to the protection of the general public. The use of coercion ceases to be divorcible from the need for treatment and becomes a therapeutic question.

There is a wealth of reference in the professional literature in the period with which this chapter is concerned to the uneasy position of doctors engaged in the treatment of the insane, in being expected to play the contradictory roles of gaoler and healer.[7] The desire of psychiatrists to impose a convincingly medical image on their work played a major part in shaping their attitude to the reform of mental health legislation. Two strategies were available for the resolution of the legal dimension of this problem of role contradiction. The medical profession could leave decisions affecting patients' liberty to legal or lay authorities and in that way distance themselves from the operation of the apparatus of coercion, or they could assume control of compulsory powers themselves, and by ousting the authoritarian figure of the magistrate and eliminating formalistic procedure, attempt to portray their use as an integral part of the therapeutic process.

These alternatives correspond to the two competing professional conceptions outlined above. As we shall see, the second conception accords particularly well with the collectivist political ideology which was in the ascendant during the first half of this century, so that it is perhaps not surprising that the medical profession chose to pursue the second alternative. It would be misleading, however, to suggest that changing professional conceptions alone have determined the attitude of medical men to the use of compulsion in psychiatry. It was assumed by the

7. See, for example, the oral evidence of Dr Herbert Wolseley Lewis FRCS to the Royal Commission on Lunacy and Mental Disorder, question 4649.

Medico-Psychological Association from 1911 until the late 1920s that the legislature would not grant them greater legal powers and this was a good argument for moderating their demand in that direction. The belief of some medical men that magisterial certification should be retained can also be explained as simple self-protection: in the 1880s and again in the 1920s, doctors were under severe threat of legal actions for wrongful detention, and if the responsibility in law for commitment could be placed squarely upon the magistrate, then this would confer a certain legal immunity. Nevertheless, the prevailing ideological climate from the early decades of the century onwards favoured the increasing unity of the medical profession behind demands for less legal and lay intervention in the procedures for the detention and treatment of mental patients.

Kathleen Jones describes the legal approach as stressing procedural safeguards against illegal detention, and portrays the legal profession as characteristically opposed to any extension of the discretionary power of the medical expert in the psychiatric context. It is true that concern for the formal protection of individual liberty is a fundamental element in legal ideology, and that while the decline of the classical liberalism of the nineteenth century has in general transferred the emphasis from individual rights to social need, the legal profession has remained primarily interested in the former. The legal profession's most notable intervention was in the 1880s, when they campaigned to extend the role of the magistrate in the commitment process by requiring a magistrate's order for admission to an asylum for private as well as pauper patients, and by defining his role as judicial rather than merely administrative in character. As we have seen, it was the persistence of three lord chancellors, actively supported by the judiciary, which finally changed the law. In the 1920s, when a movement for lunacy law reform developed similar to that of the 1870s and early 1880s, it received some momentum from legal sources. Lord Justice Scrutton, in *Harnett* v. *Bond* (1923, 2 KB 517) went out of his way to attack the laxity of current legislation and demanded more effective procedural safeguards against wrongful detention.

The legal profession had no substantive interest in this sphere, and their intervention was confined to the ideological plane. The high level of interest which they took in the late nineteenth century may best be explained as a by-product of the more more material conflict between judges and doctors over the sentencing of mentally disturbed offenders in the criminal courts. In challenging the aspiration of the medical profession to decide questions which affected individual liberty, lawyers were counterposing the traditional trial model for the ascription of guilt with which they were intimately familiar to the therapeutic model for the diagnosis of illness which in their view undemocratically placed decision-making power in the hands of experts guided by esoteric knowledge rather than laymen or lawyers whose thinking theoretically incorporated commonly accepted standards.

However, in 1926, the Macmillan Commission with its legal chairman and its majority of legal over medical members submitted a report which urged the dismantling of procedural safeguards as far as public opinion would allow on the ground that they were inconsistent with the medical view of insanity as an illness. Ewins (1974, 50–51) attributes this about-turn firstly to the influence of a changed social and political climate in which élite opinion was becoming more favourably disposed to the claims of science and medicine, the role of experts, and solutions to social problems which emphasized efficiency rather than liberty. Yet in 1924 the lord chancellor's committee on insanity and crime had firmly rejected the Medico-Psychological Association's proposals for the abolition of the McNaghten Rules, which allowed the defendant in a murder trial to be found not guilty by reason of insanity in circumstances considered by psychiatrists to be too limited in the light of contemporary medical knowledge. This indicates that there had been no general accommodation between law and psychiatry. Secondly, he emphasizes that lawyers had no substantive interest in this field and so would be likely to make concessions to the view that procedural safeguards be reduced when the general direction in which social legislation was moving favoured this. They would not appear to be adopting an eccentric position when they had no material interest to protect by doing so. This would account for the apparent difference in the legal profession's attitude to psychiatric intervention in the criminal trial and the regulation of psychiatrists' routine medical activities. However, the remarkable smoothness of the 'conversion' of the legal profession is perhaps better explained as a product of widespread disenchantment with the effectiveness of magisterial or other lay intervention as a safeguard, given the almost universal deference of the layman to 'expert' medical opinion in the light of the dangers to person and property of the ill-judged discharge of mental patients.

Kathleen Jones characterizes the social approach as emphasizing 'human relations', and associates it with the centres of moral treatment and non-restraint[8] in the early nineteenth century, and with the social services of the modern welfare state. While the social approach shares with the medical approach an antipathy to 'legalism', its distinctive feature is its emphasis on the social dimensions of deviant behaviour and a faith in the restorative power of skilful environmental management rather than the physical treatments traditionally favoured by medical men. As advocates of

8. A movement to abolish the use of mechanical restraint in asylums.

the social approach, social workers are presented as the ideological descendants of the 'moral managers' who were early potential challengers of the medical profession's emergent monopoly of the treatment of the insane.

The theory of moral treatment was originated by William Tuke at 'The Retreat', an asylum for Quakers near York. Tuke opposed the contemporary practices of confinement under inhumane conditions and crude physical restraint and held instead the positive and optimistic belief that orderly behaviour could be cultivated in the insane by the operation of a calculated system of rewards and deprivations. Briefly, he argued that appropriate environmental conditions could catalyze recovery. Advocates of this alternative therapeutic philosophy denied the effectiveness of the treatments being used by doctors, but for a variety of reasons it failed to generate an occupational group of lay therapists with the capacity to rival the medical profession.[9]

The social work profession has come to be associated with a similar 'social approach' which likewise threatens medical hegemony of the psychiatric sphere in that it stresses social factors in the genesis of mental disorder rather than individual pathology and encourages the employment of treatment techniques which do not demand specifically medical skills. But social workers have not always identified with this approach. In the early twentieth century, for reasons that will be examined in detail below, social and political conditions favoured the professionalization of the management of human relations. At the same time, the state intervened to provide a limited measure of economic security through public and insurance channels and this diverted the attention of those engaged in philanthropic work from the direct distribution of financial relief to the social and psychological adjustment of those whose way of life transgressed the dominant social norms. Psychiatric social workers (who became established as a distinct subdivision of the profession in the late 1920s, when a system of training was instituted and a professional association, the Association of Psychiatric Social Workers, formed) early adopted Freudian psycho-analysis as the theoretical basis for their approach to the problems of psychiatric 'maladjustment'. This emphasized their close association with psychiatry which gave them an élite status within the social work profession, but this association also had disadvantages. Psychiatric social

9. Scull (1975, 259–61) attributes this failure to three main factors: (1) the theory of moral treatment was not an appropriate basis for claims to expertise, as it emphasized common skills in human relations; (2) its leading adherents were magistrates and 'upper-class philanthropists whose social status made it unlikely that they would personally engage in the administration of treatment to lunatics and (3) it did not constitute a sufficiently distinct theory of insanity, remaining reliant on medical terminology.

workers were entering a field in which the medical profession had already established its dominance. Psychiatrists were in a strong position to impose a narrow and subordinate interpretation on their functions, excluding them from high-status work with the patient and burdening them with more routine auxiliary tasks.

It was the growth of the community care concept, the vogue policy of the 1950s and 1960s, that offered psychiatric social workers the opportunity to develop an independent role. As a policy prescription, it offered them the advantage of increasing access to the patient as the importance of the mental hospital, medicine's institutional base, became eroded. As a conceptual framework, resting on the sociogenic view of mental disorder, it offered them the advantage of a distinct theoretical basis for their practice. So, community care was enthusiastically taken up by psychiatric social workers, who began to emphasize the social approach. Although the theory of psychiatric social work is still indebted to medical concepts and terminology, community care's emphasis on the therapeutic value of living in the community as opposed to living in an institutional environment, supplied a vital element of distinction from the medical approach. To the extent that psychiatrists supported the ideal of community care, they were forced to justify their special competence to play a leading role in translating it into practice and it is noteworthy that in the 1960s there was a movement within the medical profession back towards the idea of promoting the integration of psychiatric treatment with general medicine.

Psychiatric social workers' self-protective insistence on maintaining the standards of their training helped to ensure that they were produced in very inadequate numbers which then had to be divided between hospitals, child guidance clinics and local authorities. As a result, many of the mental welfare workers in the local authority health departments set up in 1948 under the National Health Service Act were former poor law relieving officers and mental welfare officers who had worked for voluntary associations with the mentally deficient. The duties of the relieving officer were inherited by the 'duly authorized' officer. These were statutory duties under the Lunacy Act (1890) – to make application to a justice for certification of rate-aided patients, (here they had discretion not to follow medical advice to take proceedings) and, under s.20, to bear sole responsibility for detention for up to three days in an emergency (although in practice this was in some areas the usual prelude to certification). The designation 'mental welfare officer' was adopted by the duly authorized officers, whose association amalgamated with that of the original mental welfare officers to form the Society of Mental Welfare Officers in 1954. They aspired to transform their traditionally narrow legal and administrative function into a social work role which would be respected as an integral contribution to the effort of the clinical–social team. Supported by the recommendations of the Mackintosh Committee on the 'supply, training and qualification of social workers in the mental health service' (1951), the mental welfare officers pressed for training into this new role. They too adopted the social approach, both to underline their claim to social work status, and to continue to differentiate themselves from the approach of the doctors, with whom they were in conflict over the distribution of power between duly authorized officer and medical adviser in the compulsory detention process.

The position of social workers in relation to the reform of mental health legislation has not been characterized by the shifts and divisions noted in the cases of the medical and legal professions. Nevertheless, the evidence of the Society of Mental Welfare Officers before the Royal Commission on the Law relating to Mental Illness and Mental Deficiency, which sat from 1954 to 1957 and on whose recommendations the Mental Health Act (1959) was based, indicates an ambiguity in the theoretical basis of their approach which reflects their transitional position between a legal-administrative and a social work role.

In their evidence, they explicitly challenged the idea that compulsory hospitalization was essentially a medical decision. They cast doubt on the reliability of medical opinion and its expert status, and defended their discretion to disregard medical advice in the execution of their statutory duties. Such a militant position hardly seems an appropriate basis from which to bid for admission to the 'mental health team'. Indeed, the evidence of the Royal Medico-Psychological Association, as it had by now become, clearly states the disquiet of psychiatrists at the insistence of Mental Welfare Officers upon maintaining an independent and at times unco-operative role. They see the solution in training under medical auspices to re-educate them into a medically acceptable conception of their responsibilities: 'only by training them do we hope that they will realize the need for co-operation with the psychiatric specialist. At the moment ... there is a real danger sometimes of a duly authorized officer ... making his own decision over the head of the person concerned' (1957, 317).

There seem to be two strands to the argument of the Society of Mental Welfare Officers. The first is representative of the social approach and the desire of duly authorized officers to establish themselves as qualified social workers. 'The duly authorized officer is concerned with the patients in their social environment and on this question of an order takes into account the factor of the safety of the patient or of others, in considering whether the patient should be removed from his environment. That is the question at issue ... not the question of the person's medical state, when it is a question of removing him' (1957, 208).

The second strand is more 'legal' in origin, in that in claiming that the decision on compulsory hospitalization is not solely medical in nature it stresses the fact that liberty is involved, and the corresponding need for lay intervention of some kind. 'It has been suggested in some quarters that admission to hospital is a medical matter and no one else should be concerned in a decision to admit. We strongly hold that such a decision would be undemocratic ... and do not think that there is any precedent in holding that one profession alone should have virtually undisputed authority concerning the liberty of a very considerable number of people' (1957, 195).

Accordingly, there is sympathetic comment on the role of the magistrate in certification and at points the mental welfare officers almost seem to envisage for themselves a quasi-judicial layman's function to compensate for the reduction in the justice's role which they expect to follow new legislation.

It is Kathleen Jones' contention (1972, 153) that after 1845 the movement for further reform became an affair of pressure groups, and that it was the ascendancy of the medical and social work professions which accounted for the later decline of the legal approach to legislation for the mentally ill. However, we have seen that the professional organizations concerned did not consistently champion the distinctive viewpoints which she ascribes to them. This point is of particular importance in relation to the passage of the Mental Treatment Act (1930), the radical character of which consisted in its incorporation of the principle common to both 'medical' and 'social' approaches, that the facilitation of psychiatric treatment by maximizing informality of procedure should take precedence over the provision of safeguards for the protection of individual liberty. Not only did the legal profession endorse rather than resist this legislative orientation, but it would be incorrect to attribute responsibility for its initiation either to the medical or to the social work professions. The latter profession was at an early formative stage in its development, while the proposals canvassed by the former to the Macmillan Commission were notable for their moderation and caution. It was in fact the law-making personnel of the state themselves who took the initiative in promoting a substantial reform of the existing legislation. The Medico-Psychological Association's witnesses before the Royal Commission expressed surprise when the commissioners themselves suggested in the course of the submission of oral evidence that any new compulsory order short of full magisterial certification should be six months in duration (question 16, 927–30). They had themselves proposed a one-month order.

Furthermore, the legislation enacted by the Labour Government of 1929–31 was more enterprising in this key respect than the recommendations of the Commission, dispensing with the requirement of the magistrate's participation in the proceedings for the alternative compulsory order despite Macmillan's advice that this would be too far in advance of public opinion.

If it is accepted that the Mental Treatment Act was not a response to direct pressure from the medical profession, an alternative explanation might be that it reflected official recognition of successes achieved by the medical profession in the treatment of psychiatric illness. Ewins (1974, 35) argues that the development of new 'curative' physical treatments played an important role in generating the new approach to legislation, in that these 'cures' enhanced the persuasiveness of the medical model as a framework for interpreting and making social provision for insanity. However, the essential shift in the legislative perspective took place in the 1920s, pre-dating major 'advances' in medical technology such as electro-convulsive therapy and psychosurgery. Although a successful treatment had been found for general paresis, and confidence in the capacities of medical science had been increased by progress in general medicine, there were ample grounds for therapeutic pessimism. New treatments such as glandular therapy were still at an experimental stage. Medical evidence submitted to the Macmillan Commission indicates that there was little emphasis in the asylums on psychotherapy or on physical treatments developed specifically for use in psychiatry, and instead there prevailed a reliance upon general medical care, routine custodial management and the imposition of disciplinary regimes which included a substantial element of deterrent punishment. The cure rate, measured as the proportion of recoveries to direct admissions had actually declined from an average of 39·97 per cent in 1880–89 to only 34·3 per cent in 1924.[10] Baruch and Treacher (1978, 10–11) recognized the chronological obstacles to attributing a decisive or significant role to treatment advances in bringing about a change of attitude on the part of the legislature. Nevertheless, they do claim that such new methods of treatment as there were did play some part in that although not demonstrably successful as cures, they were construed as being successful, and so legislators were encouraged to accept the medical view of insanity as illness and modify the legal framework for its treatment. However, the Macmillan Commission and parliament were aware that there had as yet been no dramatic

10. Annual Report of the Lunacy Commissioners for 1890 and the Board of Control for 1924.

therapeutic breakthroughs.[11] That this did not constitute a barrier to reform of the law in the direction of freeing the medical profession from 'legalistic' restraints in treating the insane is a measure of the optimism with which the future potential of psychiatry was viewed. Psychiatric stagnation was actually blamed upon the rigid legal framework within which doctors were forced to work, the medical argument being accepted that they were largely condemned to providing mere asylum for hopeless cases because the stigmatizing procedure of magisterial certification deterred curable cases from seeking treatment in time.[12]

The explanation for this growth of faith in the psychiatric enterprise is to be found in the broad social and political context within which the shape of legislation for the insane was being considered. The early years of the twentieth century were a critical period of ideological transition, especially in relation to domestic social reform. Ideas were generated which created within the governmental and political élite a climate of opinion sympathetic to the psychiatric enterprise and to a 'scientific' approach to the management of social problems. In this atmosphere, concern for the legal protection of individual liberties became secondary, and a 'medical' model of legislation for the insane was accepted without it being necessary for psychiatry to prove itself by the demonstration of effective cures, the state being receptive to an optimistic evaluation of its ultimate curative potential.

During the Victorian period, classical liberalism had prevailed at the ideological level while state intervention was increasingly practised. From the last quarter of the nineteenth century, however, a number of pressures converged to precipitate an ideological crisis, which Searle (1971) has described as 'an exercise in self-criticism conducted from within the ruling class'. The growing power of the working class both as an organized movement and electorally, following the Reform Acts of 1867 and 1884 and later with the formation of the Labour Party, posed a serious threat to the established social, political and economic order. The rapid ascent of Britain's major trading competitors and imperial rivals, notably Germany, which had benefited from more recent industrialization and an autocratic political and social system, raised the spectre of her decline as an international power. Meanwhile, social surveys of the urban working class, such as those by Booth and Rowntree and the Report of the

11. See the Report of the Royal Commission on Lunacy and Mental Disorder, para. 226. Some MPs perhaps exaggerated the extent of psychiatric progress. Dr Hastings, MP, in the debate on the second reading of the Mental Health Bill announced, 'I have seen cases of severe insanity treated and cured by ordinary medical treatment or by a relatively simple operation on the nose.'
12. See for example, the Report of the Royal Commission on Lunacy and Mental Disorder, para. 46.

Interdepartmental Committee on Physical Deterioration (which inquired into the rejection of substantial numbers of recruits during the Boer War as physically or mentally unfit), revealed extensive poverty and disease. The ensuing awakening of the ruling class to the dimensions of social malaise reinforced both its fear of revolution and its sense of the nation's inadequacy to compete effectively with her international rivals.

The result was a reaction in some sections of the political establishment against the tenets of nineteenth-century liberalism and the ascription of a positive value to the interventionism which had become an increasingly obvious fact of life during the later Victorian period. Political historians have traced the emergence in the first few years of the twentieth century of a new ideology which has been characterized by Searle (1971), following Gilbert (1966) as 'the ideology of national efficiency' and by Semmel (1960) as 'social-imperialism'. This ideology counterposed to the atomistic individualism which underpinned classical liberalism as an organic conception of the state in which the anti-social became identified with the immoral. Taking as their model the envied autocratic systems of Germany and Japan, its adherents were prepared to subordinate individual liberties and democratic procedures to the pursuit of social efficiency. The instrument for this was to be a remodelled and expanded state apparatus, employing scientific method and guided by experts unfettered by democratic controls. 'Sectional' class-based demands could not be permitted to endanger the welfare of the nation as a whole, although in order to build an 'imperial' race and to create an ethic of service to the state, a far-reaching programme of domestic reconstruction and social reform was seen as essential. This emergent ideological fashion cut across orthodox party political boundaries. The policies of some Conservative politicans, notably Joseph Chamberlain, contained elements of it, as did those of the Imperialist wing of the Liberal Party. It also found manifestation in the proposals of the Fabians and the supporters of Eugenics. However, its authoritarian tendencies repelled both Conservative traditionalists and Liberal Party radicals.

The relationship of this ideology to medicine and social work is a complex one, but some connections can be indicated here. Its philosophical basis lying in the neo-Hegelian conception of the state as an organism naturally lent itself to articulation in terms of medical analogy. Thus social conditions which were identified as harmful to the development of a strong, cohesive and internationally competitive nation were deemed 'pathological' and in need of what the leading Fabians Sidney and Beatrice Webb called 'preventive and curative treatment'. This affinity with medical concepts possessed a definite political utility in that it allowed social policies draconian by the standards of the old liberalism to be couched in a scientific and humanitarian language which made them sound more plausible and attractive. This is nicely illustrated by the phrasing of a proposal contained in the majority report of the Royal Commission on the Poor Laws and Relief of Distress (1905–9, 317), a document which to some extent reflected this new kind of thinking:

> The Detention or Continuous Treatment of Certain Classes of Persons Receiving or Applying for Public Assistance.

> The term 'detention' is perhaps infelicitous. It is generally associated with the idea of punishment by imprisonment. Our primary object in proposing detention is neither punishment nor imprisonment. We aim at obtaining opportunities for applying ameliorative treatment to particular individuals over a continuous period. We desire to substitute for the present period of incontinuous and inefficacious relief, a continuity of care and treatment. ... To secure this ... some powers of control are necessary, but these powers of control are intended in the vast majority of cases to be curative and stimulative rather than punitive, nor need they necessarily be always exercised in an institution.

The classes affected were to be 1) extreme age or extreme youth; 2) illness or disease of mind or body; 3) persistent indulgence in vice or pernicious habits: a) unmarried mothers; b) adults repeatedly becoming chargeable through wilful neglect or misconduct.

Other connections between psychiatric aspirations and the ascendant collectivism can be detected in its cult of the expert and of scientific method. Furthermore, the preference of its adherents for 'prevention and cure' of social problems over the 'inefficient' distribution of mere relief of their symptoms coincided with the psychiatric profession's desire for early access to the patient to escape institutional isolation with 'incurable' chronic cases.

At a very general level the new ideology can also be seen to share similar assumptions to those of social work. The interventionist and directive social policy of relief conditional upon the abjuration of anti-social behaviour favoured by adherents of national efficiency such as the Webbs corresponds with social work as the regulation by professional experts of the social and personal relations of the deviant and the deprived. It is noteworthy that the term 'social work' itself originated in this period, indicating a redefinition of the charitable enterprise away from its individualistic Victorian conception and towards the notion of work on behalf of the state.

Of particular relevance to the reform of mental health legislation is the reflection of this ideology in both the conservative majority and the more far-reaching Fabian minority report of the Royal Commission on the Poor

Law.[13] They proposed the abolition of the deterrent poor law system on the ground that as it provided mere relief and made this conditional upon actual destitution, it prevented public agencies from gaining access to the whole range of social ills which were the root causes of poverty. An alternative interventionist 'preventative and curative' approach was recommended which would entail the provision of financial, medical, social and educational assistance in accordance with the broader criterion of need. This was intended to facilitate earlier and more extensive expert penetration of the lives of the deprived and thereby promote social efficiency.

This recommended pattern of reform is paralleled by the provision of the Mental Treatment Act (1930). In this context the stigmatizing and deterrent status of 'pauper' was joined by that of 'certified lunatic', which made treatment conditional upon the manifestation of clear and therefore advanced symptoms. The introduction of the alternative temporary order and of voluntary admission were mechanisms for circumventing this with a view to expanding the psychiatrist's sphere of operations. The liberal overtones of medical terminology facilitated a policy of enhancing psychiatric efficiency in combating 'irrational' deviant behaviour. It is noteworthy that the political divisions on the Mental Treatment Bill were similar to those which took place in relation to the ideology of national efficiency: the opponents of important elements in the bill were traditionalist Conservatives such as Viscount Brentford and radicals such as Josiah Wedgewood, a Labour fugitive from the Liberal Party who had battled against the Eugenicist-inspired Mental Deficiency Bills of 1912 and 1913. He naturally found support from the ranks of the Independent Labour Party which had inherited the mantle of radicalism from the Liberal Party. One of the bill's leading parliamentary advocates was Earl Russell, whose statements in a debate on the Mental Treatment Bill (1923) indicate his sympathy with Eugenics.

This characterization of the Mental Treatment Act and of the reorientation of the legislative perspective which it represented may be clarified by comparison with that proposed by Ewins (1974) and adopted subject to certain modifications by Baruch and Treacher (1978). Ewins is primarily concerned to explain the transfer of the control of compulsory admissions from judicial to medical authorities partially effected by the Mental Treatment Act (1930) and completed by the Mental Health Act (1959). He interprets this legislation as the expression of an alliance

13. Much of the strategy advocated by the minority was shared by the majority, but the latter nevertheless wished to retain a modified special destitution category and to accord a large role in the future to voluntary organizations.

between the medical profession and the political authority. In his view it embodies an almost contractual transaction in which the medical profession was granted greater legal powers to treat and detain psychiatric patients, in return for the essentially political and economic rewards which the political authority expected to flow from more pervasive psychiatric intervention in the community.

In the nineteenth century the medical view of insanity had gained acceptance on the ideological plane as a result of its capacity to explain irrational and bizarre behaviour in such a way as to neutralize its disturbing and threatening qualities. Ewins claims, however, that it was the development of psychiatric 'cures' which facilitated its translation into the basis for concrete legal and administrative reform. This allowed the medical profession to be perceived as a powerful agency of social control which, if given sufficient legal power, could employ its technology to eliminate politically threatening[14] irrational deviance and eradicate it as an economically damaging source of unproductiveness. This was the perspective in which these developments were seen by the governing political parties from the early decades of the twentieth century as there had evolved a consensus in favour of Fabian ideology, which emphasized the interventionist and sometimes authoritarian solution of social problems within the existing social and political framework.

We have already seen that the development of cures cannot have played such a prominent role. In addition, while Ewins's accentuation of the social and political dimensions of mental health legislation represents a great advance upon the work of Kathleen Jones, whose thinking is conditioned by the ideology of that legislation and treats its paternalism as unproblematic, his exclusive concentration upon the compulsory provisions leads him to misconceive the nature of the social control strategy which the legislation contains. For the expansion of medical control over compulsory admissions was accompanied by a simultaneous movement towards voluntarism and informality of admission. These features seem to contradict his thesis in that they ostensibly limit the formal dominatory power of doctors over their patients. This does not, however, mean that the legislation is not better understood as part of a strategy for greater social control rather than as a response to advances in psychiatric technology or a discrete instance of liberal and humanitarian initiative. Rather, the reliance upon informality and voluntarism indicates that the essential mechanism

14. Baruch and Treacher (1978, 12) describe Ewins as working with 'a romantic and yet essentially rationalistic conception that the mere existence within a society of people who transgress normally accepted ways of thinking is a source of potential threat to the dominant groups within a society.'

for expanding the domain of the psychiatric expert was not to arm the medical profession with more extensive coercive powers but to promote the *accessibility* of insanity as a social problem. This was to be achieved by restricting and ultimately removing the barrier of certification, which was perceived as a deterrent and stigmatizing process analogous to pauperization and similarly counter-productive. Ewins's central analysis forces him to dismiss the frequent explicit references by legislators to the need to diminish stigma as a mere humanitarian gloss. For him, it was not the 'real' reason for the reform of compulsory admission, which was the transfer of power to the medical profession. But as we have seen, the Poor Law Commissioners had themselves emphasized the need for the removal of impediments to contact between the necessitous and expert assistance. The stigma of certification was regarded as a real deterrent to early treatment and it was therefore natural to seek to eliminate it in the interests of psychiatric efficiency.

It would be a mistake, however, to interpret the Mental Treatment Act as the direct and systematic implementation of policies derived from collectivist ideology in the forms in which it was manifested in Edwardian Britain. The extreme interventionism of its more radical exponents is rather an 'ideal type' of collectivist strategy to which items of welfare state legislation have more or less closely approximated. Ewins describes modern mental health legislation as the manifestation of a Fabian ideology which has dominated Labour Party thinking and penetrated the conceptual apparatus of the Conservative and Liberal parties in the process of electoral competition. But, prior to 1945, reform in the direction of greater state responsibility in the field of social welfare was piecemeal and pragmatic. The Liberal Government to which the Royal Commission on the Poor Laws had reported in 1909, chose national insurance as the main method for alleviating social distress in preference to the proposals of either its majority or its minority reports. Insurance was a conservative mode of reform, perpetuating reliance upon 'negative' financial relief at the expense of a 'preventative and curative' strategy. Nevertheless as Jordan (1976, 119) has noted, the Liberal measures did effect an unprecedentedly high level of bureaucratic regulation of the working-class. In the inter-war period, the threat to the social order posed by prolonged massive unemployment ensured that, albeit unsystematically, reform in the direction of greater state responsibility for welfare did take place. Whatever party was in power, the survival of the political system required measures of social reform which would integrate a potentially revolutionary working class into the established political order, even if that implied the considerable modification of that order. Such measures would at once involve more state intervention in their lives and satisfaction of their more moderate demands. As social intervention became increasingly accepted as a necessary feature of political life, so the technique and the efficiency of intervention took priority in debate over concern for individual liberty. The themes of the ideology of national efficiency became incorporated in the philosophy of an emergent welfare state – the elevation of the expert, the veneration of science and its application to social phenomena, the displacement of legal formality and lay control. The Mental Treatment Act, with its emphasis on the principles of prevention and cure, was comparatively advanced in these respects and no doubt provoked little opposition because of the powerful logic of the medical view of insanity and because the treatment meted out to the insane had always been on the margins of political discourse.

The Mental Health Act (1959) should be understood as a more radical application of similar ideas. Its radicalism reflected a more advanced stage of development of the welfare state following upon the reorganization of its services in 1944–8 which finally abolished the administrative remnants of the poor law and opened the way for a vigorous emphasis upon the 'prevention and cure' of social problems. In the psychiatric sphere, this entailed an expansion of the discretion of medical and other experts at the expense of traditional legal procedures and lay involvement. The emphasis upon a strategy of prevention and cure, however, accrued to the benefit of social work rather than to the medical profession in that its predominant expression was the policy of community care with which social workers claimed special identity. Thus the potential was created for a medical-social work territorial conflict to replace the temporarily dormant medico-legal controversy.

The present balance of medicine, law and social work in mental health legislation is therefore ultimately the product of major change in the social, economic and political order. The processes of this structural reform were accompanied by complex changes in the attitudes of the professions concerned with the treatment of the insane to the question of how legislative provision for psychiatric treatment should be designed, and it is in the pattern of professional alignments in the early part of this century that a key can be found to the underlying origins of the theoretical revolution in legislation for the insane generated during that period.

7

Critical sociology and radical social work: problems of theory and practice
John Clarke

In recent years, social work has increasingly been seen as going through a period of crisis. This has been variously identified – a failure of nerve, a loss of confidence, declining professional standards, incorrect techniques, inappropriate political sympathies, or social work's place in the national economic crisis and cuts in welfare. I do not want to provide another analysis of what that crisis is in this chapter, but to move on from there and look at one of the attempted solutions to that crisis.[1] One clear element in the recent debates and arguments about social work has been the disenchantment of practising social workers with the traditional professional theories and techniques of social work – a disillusionment with the therapeutic casework ideal. And one of the attempted solutions to that dilemma has been the search for a radical social work.

Part of that search for a radical alternative has involved social work practitioners in an often uneasy and uncomfortable alliance with the sociological critics of social work, and it is the dilemma of that alliance that I want to look at here. But in order to reach those dilemmas, it is necessary to explore briefly some of the conditions which made that alliance possible in the first place.

The attack on traditional and consensual sociological theories in the late 1960s involved the development of new, radical and eventually, Marxist-influenced variants of sociology – variants which involved themselves in the task of criticizing existing social institutions and arrangements. Many of these criticisms, especially in the area of the sociology of deviance, came to focus on the exercise of social control through a variety of agencies, including social work. Social work came under attack as a form of social control exercised under the humanitarian disguise of caring, and this attack

1. This essay has grown out of talking with a large number of people, all of whom have contributed to its final shape, even though they may not agree with it. But in an unequal society, some debts are inevitably bigger than others, and I am especially grateful to the NAPO Members Action Group, Paul Corrigan, Hilary Walker, Boa Sousantos, and Roisin McDonough for their help, and to Bob Kornreich and Phil Lea for their comments on a first draft.

was developed into a more theoretically sophisticated analysis of the controlling and ideological functions of welfare in the capitalist state. These analyses attempted to undermine the legitimacy of professional definitions of social work in a number of forms. They aimed to demystify the professional claims of social work by pointing to the moral and political issues that were concealed by professional theories and techniques. They attacked social work knowledge and practice for tending to individualize what were essentially social problems rather than individual failings. Finally, they argued that this form of practice operated as a system of social control within capitalist societies, both directly through its effects on the client/victims of social work; and indirectly through ideologically disguising the nature of social problems in capitalist societies.

This trend of criticism from the 'new' sociology has often been treated as sufficient to explain the disillusionment of social workers with traditional methods by those who have attempted to defend or reconstruct that professional ethos. The decline in organizational or professional commitment among social workers has been explained (or, more accurately, explained away) by pointing to the evil and corrupting influence of machiavellian sociology lecturers who have laid their poltical hands on the naive enthusiasm and humanitarianism of social work students in order to lead them away from the path of true professional knowledge (for example, Gould et al., 1977; Lewis, 1977). It will be obvious that I have little sympathy for this theory of corruption through bad company as an explanation for disaffection and disillusionment among social workers, but its importance should not be underestimated. It has provided a significant rationale for exempting the social, political and organizational structure of social work from any scrutiny that might have revealed sources of strain and contradiction there which produce the destruction of professional and organizational loyalty. And it also connects with the far wider debate about the danger posed by the 'Marxist infiltration' of education, as identified by Julius Gould, the Sunday Express and the National Front, among others.

But whatever its ideological significance, it seems nevertheless extremely inadequate as an explanation for the amount of disillusionment, doubt and cynicism to be found among social workers about their work. More powerful explanations seem to me to lie within the changing position and practice of social work itself, particularly within the expansion of social work and its consequences. That expansion at the end of the 1960s and beginning of the 1970s was accomplished in a particular form – that of bureaucratization, in which considerable emphasis has been placed on the construction of a hierarchical system of managerial control, coordination and supervision. In a sense, this managerial structure has come to provide an organizational embodiment of the traditional 'professional conscience' of the social worker. The increase in bureaucratic coordination, together with the increases in statutory requirements, have acted to prescribe the work roles and practices of the social worker. These changes are also an index of the changed social position of social work itself – a consequence of its move from being a relatively marginal and fragmented collection of roles and practices to a central and systematically organized element of the state's welfare apparatus. This, in turn, has had its consequences for the characteristic experiences and self-definitions of social workers themselves – crudely, a shift from a relatively independent semi-professional into a paid employee.[2]

It is within these structural changes that we can also find the sharpening or intensification of several professional problems and contradictions – the apparently perennial concerns about whether social work is an agency of care or control; whether its primary loyalties are to the client or to society; and over the problem of client self-determination. These disputes take on a new and different significance when they take place within the social, economic and political conditions of a state bureaucracy. We may point to the decline of confidence in the model of psychotherapeutic casework as being in part caused by the failures of this style within the new bureaucratic structure – failures involving the hostility of the organization to providing the time and resources to do 'proper casework', and the failure of the central themes of traditional social work knowledge to cope with the experience of the social, economic and political constraints and conflicts which social workers find surrounding themselves and their clients.

These comments provide nothing more than a rough outline of the conditions under which both critical sociologists and disenchanted social workers have converged, and out of which the attempt to find or create a radical social work has come. In the rest of this chapter I want to look at some of the consequences and problems of this convergence, especially where they have come to focus around an argument about the connections, or lack of them, between theory and practice.

The theory-practice problem

The relation between the sociological critics of social work and social work students and practitioners has, in the past few years, been anything but the wholesale seduction of the innocents by the professional corruptors envisaged by the defenders of professionalism. Instead, it has been an extremely unstable and tense liaison, full of doubts, mistrust and

2. For a discussion of some of the tensions created by the expansion of social work, see Seed (1973, part 3).

arguments. These tensions have most often surfaced around the failure of the 'theory' of the sociological critics to generate any prescriptions for professional practice. The 'it's all right for you to talk' syndrome, so accurately identified by Stan Cohen (1976), has characterized much of this relationship between sociologists and social workers – a syndrome in which sociologists have stuck to their task of demystifying social work and attacking its social control functions, while social workers, though agreeing with many of these attacks, have failed to find any guidance or solutions to those dilemmas.

I want to suggest that this syndrome has had particular consequences for the way in which the discussion of radical social work has gone, and unfortunate consequences at that. The division between theorists and practitioners, has, I think, tended to produce a division in the positions taken up about radical social work, a division marked not only by the content of these positions, but by different assumptions which govern them. My belief is that there has been a tendency to polarize discussions about radical social work into two models – one for the theorists, and one for the practitioners. Here I want to present a crude characterization of those two positions, crude in the sense that it certainly reduces the complexity and sophistication of both, but still, I hope, presents them as accurately as possible.

The more theoretical side of this division comes first. Here the demystification of social work, although it has become more complex and sophisticated, has signally failed to develop beyond this basic stance of criticism. It has, however, provided us with important analyses of social work and its relation to class and sexual struggles. Perhaps most importantly, it has insisted that the analysis of social work must involve seeing social work as part of the welfare apparatus of a capitalist state. Overall this theoretical attack has been important in shifting attention from internal and professional considerations of social work functioning on to the political and structural determinations of social work practice.

But in spite of these accomplishments, the theoretical analysis of social work has been diminished by some important inabilities and weaknesses. Most significant among these has been the inability to transform theoretical criticism into political outcomes and strategies. It has been a form of politically abstract criticism which has remained the *intellectual* guardian of revolutionary purity: it has sought and found its politics primarily in intellectual forms, namely the article, book and lecture. In response to attempts within social work to find new strategies, it has only been able to offer relatively abstract criteria of criticism, as each new initiative is found to be still fixed within the orbit of the capitalist state, and therefore subject to the criticism of being yet another variety of social control.

To be more specific, this mode of analysis has failed to move from sociological criticism to political critique, to connect its analysis to action. However much it has drawn on the concepts of Marxism for its analysis of social work and the state, it has so far failed to produce an analysis which is capable of identifying the forms and directions of possible struggles *against* the dominant structure and practice of social work. Instead it has focused on the larger and more abstract determinants of welfare – the structures of the state, rather than the contradictions and struggles within and against them. In part, it is this failure to translate the broader concepts of the structure of capitalism and the capitalist state into more specific and localized analyses of particular apparatuses and branches of the state which underlies its inability to intervene in the 'present moment'.

So I am suggesting that this theoretical side of the discussion of radical social work must be considered not just as theoretical, but as *theoreticist*, preoccupied with the production of theoretical sophistication rather than the production of 'really useful knowledge' – knowledge that applies, or, more importantly, can be applied to particular situations. This is not, it must be stressed, an argument against theory itself rather an argument for theory that informs groups acting in particular circumstances, for a theory that guides on the basis of critical analysis, rather than merely providing criticism.

A second problem of this approach lies in the form of some of the theoretical criticism which it produces. There is a tendency towards a functionalist view of welfare in capitalist societies, which reduces the complexities of the class struggles in the state to simpler concepts such as social control (with its implication of one side imposing itself on an unresisting victim), or of welfare serving in a simple way the economic or political needs of capital. This tendency stems from an approach which places most emphasis on the conclusions or outcomes of particular struggles over welfare, rather than looking at the struggles themselves. And further, since these outcomes have (to date) always been accomplished within the organizing principles of capitalist development and the capitalist state, they become equated with serving the needs of capital. Thus, for example, from this standpoint the National Health Service is equated with the need of capital for a healthily maintained work force, an equation which misses the effectiveness of working-class demand and pressure in its creation, and the political work of struggle and compromise which is involved in containing such a demand within the logic of the capitalist state. To put it crudely, this perspective suggests that as there has been no revolutionary overthrow of capitalism, all of what continues is one-dimensionally capitalist, and this leads to a failure to consider the contradictory nature of welfare provision in capitalist societies, and from there to a political immobilization (if everything is created and controlled by capital, what is there that is worth fighting over?). I shall come back to some of these theoretical and political consequences later in the chapter.[3]

These comments are, of course, not new. They have been directed at the sociological critics of social work from a variety of sources, and often focusing on the failure to develop beyond the work of analysis to the world of action. Further, they are usually directed at sociologists in the name of 'relevance', or in the name of 'practice', in a plea for something that will concretely help social workers to do their work in a different way. This leads us to an alternative to the critical intellectual stance: a concern with radical social work which focuses explicitly on the creation of radical practice. But I want to argue here that the narrow focus on practice leads to an inversion of some of the errors of the critical intellectual position – with equally unfortunate consequences.

The concern with practice, especially when it is conceived of as finding new ways to do the job, often leads to an omission of precisely those things which the critics are good at: the analysis of the structural conditions under which practice takes place. There is a tendency not to look at the class dimensions involved in welfare as they are expressed in the bureaucratic, managerial and professional determinations of the social work task. That is, 'practice' tends to get separated from the ways in which it is structured, and this produces a *voluntarism* about practice. By voluntarism here, I mean a belief that new or radical methods could be evolved which could be introduced independently of any changes in the structure or relations within which social work is organized as a state activity. It is an underestimation of the constraints which are built into the organization of social work to direct it towards certain forms of practice. One example might illustrate this. An attempt to overcome the 'individualism' in the practice of social workers and probation officers in relation to crime and delinquency must involve more than the attempt to 'take into account' social factors or to do group work. For social and probation work is organized through the pattern of the criminal justice system, a system which is organized to produce crime in the form of 'individual cases', and which consequently exercises considerable control over the ways in which social work practice in relation to crime can be organized. This principle of 'individualization', although dear to the heart of traditional social work, is not peculiar to social work: in this instance it is lodged firmly in the

3. For a more detailed criticism of this Marxist functionalism, see Corrigan (1976). As I am not attempting to scapegoat particular individuals here, the errors of this position are quite clearly demonstrated in Clarke (1976).

operations of other state agencies, and is not subject to immediate overthrow in social work practice.

Secondly, because of the concern with practice in the job, the reference point used to assess whether or not some aspect of practice is radical tends to become the existing structure and practice of the agency itself. This seems to me to manifest itself in two forms. In some contexts, the adoption of an anti-agency or anti-management stance is seen to be the guarantor of radicalism: the proof of radical credentials, the avoidance of agency regulation, the refusal of instructions, the practice of one-up-manship against the hierarchy and so on, may, in the context of the daily round, take on considerable symbolic importance for the social worker (Pearson, 1976). But while these forms of 'primitive rebellion' may be significant in creating solidarity among basic grade workers, and contribute to making the experience of the job more bearable, they cannot be said to constitute a political analysis or solution. They are more a form of negativism, based on an inversion of expected behaviour within the agency, and tend not to have a point of political reference outside the agency.

The second form which is taken by this use of the agency as a point of reference is in the tendency to equate radicalism with the adoption of, or demand for, roles or forms of practice which do not currently form part of the agency's repertoire, for example, welfare rights work or group work. Here again the use of existing agency practices as a guideline to radicalism does not form a very reliable criterion for the political assessment of forms of practice. These new forms of practice may in some way be radical, but novelty itself is no guarantee of that. More importantly, such a perspective, lacking external political orientations and guides, is a potential victim to the process of co-option by the agency since it provides no means of assessing which approaches can be comfortably assimilated within the prevailing definition of social work practice. Thus, for example, the apparent radicalism of welfare rights can be diluted by being treated as part of the social work function to be accomplished through the normal professional casework skills (Rose and Jakubowicz, 1978). This process of assimilation may also embroil social workers in the expenditure of considerable time and energy to produce something which becomes nothing more than an adjunct to the normal mode of working.

The third problem, which is connected with this narrow focus on practice, is that by minimizing the question of the structural determinations and constraints of social work, the attempt to find a radical practice can fall victim to becoming an extension of the liberal values of social work, rather than standing as an alternative to them. This again, seems to fall into two main parts. First, such a radicalism tends towards a pro-client stance, seeing them as oppressed or hindered by the existing practice of social work. The radical alternative then becomes a matter of finding better, more humane, less coercive and controlling forms of practice. This tends to narrow the question of radical alternatives to the types of worker-client interaction that are possible, and again to remove attention from the broader questions of the structure, functions and operation of social work as part of the state.

The second element of this slide back into the core values of social work involves the attempt to extricate the 'caring' elements of social work practice and ideology from the dehumanizing and controlling elements of bureaucratic control. These efforts to find a new practice are guided by a wish to dissolve the tension between care and control and thus free the elements of care and help. In this sense it involves a radical accentuation of the liberal values of social work – a belief that in some sense 'pure' social work can be redeemed or rescued from its deformation and distortion by the organizational context in which it is practised. This rehumanization of social work seems to me to ignore the extent to which care and control have been inextricably bound up in the development of social work. The history of that development warns us that there was never a 'pure' social work which became subverted by the introduction of elements of control, but rather, that the attraction of social work was precisely the belief that control could best be exercised through the medium of a caring personal relationship (Stedman-Jones, 1973; Jones, 1976). The tension in social work is not one induced artificially by the imposition of bureaucratic demands for control; rather it is inherent in the activity itself, being a tension which aims to control the client, on the one hand by offering care, and on the other, by transforming the caring attitudes of the social worker into a mode of control which is itself a form of exploitation. So I am suggesting that we should be wary of attempts to rescue 'care' which fail to question what purposes and interests are served by the provision of that care.

I have been arguing that these two approaches to the question of radical social work possess particular deficiencies which hinder the work of political analysis and action within and about social work. More specifically, I have tried to characterize them as inversions of each other, as reflecting the two sides of the dilemma of theory and practice. To summarize, the approach of critical theory tends towards an abstract structuralism and functionalism which denies the possibility of action, and which fails to focus closely enough on the processes, contradictions and struggles involved in social work practice. On the other side of the equation we are confronted by a crucial concern with practice, narrowly interpreted as the means by which the job is to be accomplished, which neglects the broader structures and determinations within which practice takes place, and tends towards an extension of the liberalism and voluntarism already present in social work theory and practice. Finally, I have suggested that these approaches are shaped by and certainly experienced by their protagonists in the form of a gap between theory and practice.

Theory and practice revisited

If this characterization of the approaches is correct, it is possible to envisage a number of responses to the dilemmas which they pose for us. The first is a simple and perhaps quite widespread one – to throw up one's arms in horror, cry a plague on both your houses, and retreat from the problems into a cynical and instrumental approach to doing the job and finding satisfactions and involvements elsewhere. The second is to attribute the gap between theory and practice to the bad faith of those involved in the discussions – to accuse sociologists of being unwilling to 'dirty their hands' with practical questions, of only being interested in radical social work as a viable area in which to make money out of publishing and teaching, of treating social workers as a captive audience on which to try out pet theories without taking any responsibility for the consequences. On the other hand social workers may be castigated for merely trying to find ways of making the job bearable, of being unwilling to face up to difficult political issues. While such a vision may be psychologically comfortable to its users, the attribution of these recurrent difficulties to bad faith, self-interest or 'failures of communication' is not likely to be very useful in resolving these problems. It is, indeed, more likely to produce a context of hostility, guilt and mutual mistrust, as if the situation were not already bad enough. The solutions offered by this approach can only rest on a series of moral injunctions (since the causes are identified as moral failings): 'let us talk to one another without bullshit, let us not exploit one another, let us not be guilty of bad faith.' These exhortations fail to deal with the circumstances in which problems of theory and practice are posed. Such a response treats us as if we were free individuals taking part in an equal debate, but one which fails to question the structures through which we engage in it. So, can there be a third alternative which may explain why and how this divide between theory and practice is persistently reproduced, and why we carry on living out that 'great divide' in the search for a radical social work?

I want to suggest that there is something *systematic* about this theory/practice division which cannot be explained by the motivations or failures of particular individuals engaged in these discussions. It is not accidental that taking sides on the theory/practice division usually involves academics or intellectuals on the theory side, and practitioners on the practice side, for this division indicates something about the way in which social work and education are organized as part of the division of labour within the capitalist state. Thus, while it is obviously not true that academics have no practice (they teach, write, organize courses and so on) and that social workers have no theory (they have theories about their clients and organizations), each group is shaped by a particular division of theory and practice within the state itself. This division one-sidedly accentuates the nature of the occupation and fixes particular occupational and social identities for us – identities either as theoreticians or as practitioners.

This division between theoretical and practical labour is a particular deformity which is systematically organized within the state. The encounters between theory and practice take place within carefully regulated and defined settings (courses, conferences and lectures), which prescribe how these contacts should be made. According to this prescription they should and do normally take place in academic settings separated from the world of 'practice'. The organization of this division both produces and is sustained by a variety of mystiques – about the elusiveness of theory, about its special, almost mystical qualities, and about the agonies, trials and sacrifices which have to be gone through in order to become a theoretical priest. Conversely, there are equally compelling mystiques about the irreducible qualities of practice, about the values of 'experience' over book learning, and about the irrelevance of theory to the complexities of the real world.

But these are not just mystiques and incorrect fantasies, for they involve real elements of how this division of labour is accomplished within the state. They are embodied in the historical separation of sociology from social work in university and polytechnic departments; in the conditions of work which tend to isolate the sociologist from other forms of practice; and in the intellectual and disciplinary boundaries which ensure, or attempt to ensure, the production of knowledge within certain prescribed limits. On the other side of the divide, they are built into the conditions of work which mean that social workers encounter 'theory' only in occasional and carefully regulated 'days out' from the real business of practice. The separation is also made stronger by forms of work organization that ensure (through high caseloads, long hours and so on) that the social worker is sufficiently preoccupied by and exhausted by immediate tasks that there is little opportunity to step back and consider the broader picture. These tendencies are further reinforced by expectations that social workers will work as isolated individuals with their own 'private' caseloads, separated from their colleagues. Also, in the post-Seebohm period there have been pressures to de-skill the social worker into a functionary, manipulating bureaucratic routines.

These, then, are the material conditions which produce and maintain this division between theory and practice within the capitalist state, a division which we perpetually recapitulate in the discussion of radical social work, since we ourselves are enmeshed in these conditions. They are conditions which at their strongest produce a double fetishism – on the one hand a fetishism of theory, and on the other a fetishism of practice. A fetishism of theory which divorces theory from the world (and thus from both its conditions and consequences) and turns it inwards on itself so that it becomes the practice of theoreticism (the endless cycle of theories criticizing theories in abstraction) in which the intellectual appears to himself – and others – as somehow standing outside the conditions and constraints to which everyone else is subject, and capable of making free (and correct) judgements from these Olympian heights. On the other hand, it produces a fetishism of practice, in which all is measured against the immediate demands and constraints of the job, and matters beyond that are irrelevant.

These conditions, however, are not eternal and fixed: they were historically created as part of a state concerned to manage the problems of a capitalist society, and they are subject to contradictions, changes and tensions which weaken their hold on those whom they are supposed to contain and constrain. The current attack from the radical educational right on Marxist and radical subversion in education (an attack which has the connection between sociology and social work as one of its focal points) is a response to the temporary and partial dissolution of both these fetishisms. It registers on the one hand a concern with the political and practical consequences of theory among intellectuals, and on the other, a concern with the consequences of practice, and attempts to both understand and change them among social work practitioners. Whatever its causes, there is no doubt that this convergence is a source of considerable concern both to the educational policemen of the right and to the employing agencies of social work (Gould *et al.*, 1977; Lewis, 1977). Out of this concern has arisen an attempt to limit the scope and styles of sociology where, however loosely, the latter is connected with political processes in contemporary Britain. Equally, methods were sought to select and recruit social workers who have 'agency loyalty' and not too much 'idealism' or 'immaturity'. There is a contemporary drive coming from senior social work managers to organize the encounters between sociologists and social workers – for example in social work education – in a direction which emphasizes the practical and skill-based nature of social work at the expense of the broader and more troubling 'philosophical' issues (Kornreich, 1978).

The political right have overestimated the convergence between mental and manual labour. Their assessment misses what I have been arguing is characteristic of the attempt to produce a radical social work – that in spite of the weakening of the ties of fetishism, we still have the problem of the division between theory and practice as it is produced for us by the state. The core of our problem is to find ways of overcoming that division. We must first recognize it as part of the social conditions under which we work rather than as a matter of individual failure. There is another aspect of the problem which seems to me to be equally damaging in its effects, and this is the *content* of the theory/practice division which we inherit.

How can we overcome the tension between theory and practice? I suggest the possibility of an alternative way of posing the theory/practice relationship: that of political theory and political practice. These questions of theory and practice lie outside the immediate contexts of either academic discipline or the social work profession, and require different conceptions of theory and practice, from among which specific means of doing the job in a radical way may emerge. This alternative demands the development of a theory whose main purpose is to allow us to analyse situations in order to identify the means and directions in which to act, and in the development of practice which is both informed by and helps to develop analyses.

There are, once again, good historical and structural reasons why the discussion of radical social work has not taken this form, but has remained vitiated by the weaknesses of academic criticism and professional concerns with practice. One of the central factors here is the absence of any developed politics of welfare within the working class and its political organizations in this country. I am not suggesting that the English working class has had no concern about welfare, for it has fought long and massively over the content and the nature of welfare provision, from the fight to reduce the length of the working day, to struggles to defend the 'social wage'. But these have essentially been struggles over the economic content of welfare, over welfare seen as a series of material benefits (see Corrigan, 1976, for a fuller discussion). This focus has tended to exclude or omit questions about the administration of welfare and its political and ideological consequences – precisely those areas in which the concerns of radical social work have developed most strongly. This absence has been, and still is, exacerbated by the class differences between those engaged in the provision of welfare and the bulk of the labour movement. The professional identification of social work has militated against the construction of links between the working class and state employees involved in welfare (and those analysing welfare as professional sociologists), and has proved a potent form of insulation of social work from trade union organization and connections. I do not want to suggest that academics, social workers, Ford workers and the unemployed all occupy the same class position (the view that we are all the proletariat now); but in spite of the economic and ideological divisions between the working class and professionalized state employees there are points where there are convergences of interest which need to be explored and solidified (for example, action against cuts, and the preservation of jobs).

This absence of a developed politics of welfare has had a hidden but important effect on the discussions of radical social work. It has meant that the debate has been conducted largely without any class dimensions and directions. On the one side, this absence has affected the academic discussions of welfare, inducing a functionalism about how the state serves the interests of capital, and the impossibility or futility of attempts to work within or against the state. A similar tendency can be seen in the general separation between the labour movement and Marxism in Britain – Marxism being enclosed and developed largely within academic forms and contexts removed from its possible political applications. On the other hand, it has led to a narrow focus on radical practice which has taken a pro-victim/pro-client stance, which has all too easily been confused with a socialist stand. The consequence of these developments has been to produce on every side an inability to offer a strategic analysis of social work – an analysis which is capable of evaluating existing practices and proposals for reform connecting them to their external political consequences.

Radicalism and the problem of progressive strategies

The central problem to emerge from this study of our current dilemmas is the failure to create a political analysis from which the consequences of different forms of action and practice can be assessed. Neither the theoretical nor the practical versions of the discussion have been able to generate the sort of criteria which would offer a systematic guide to action in particular situations, or in relation to a particular form of practice. At present, we are unable to point to specific elements of social work and say that some particular ones are worth defending and building on, while certain others should be fought against and removed. The reason for this is that we have no systematic criteria with which to assess the political character of social work practices. Consequently, the two polar positions tend always towards their own in-built conclusions. The critical theory assesses everything by the fact of its taking place within the capitalist state; hence no current social work practices can be regarded as being progressive. This is a political analysis from which no politics flow – a pessimism of control. Conversely, practical radicalism assesses everything by virtue of its novelty or absence from existing practice, and its politics are those of institutional inversion, and an optimism of care. Both contribute through their failures to a final form of political misjudgement – that of opportunism, in which our assessments are made uninformed by political criteria, but move according to which way the economic, parliamentary or agency winds are currently blowing. So, for example, we can be left in the strange position of defending a welfare state (including social work) against economic and political pressures, when, only a few years earlier, we had attacked that same welfare state as the most complex, sophisticated and accomplished form of capitalist manipulation and social control. In neither moment have there been sustained attempts to look beyond this apparent monolith of the welfare state to ask questions about which elements of it may be counted as progressive, and therefore in need of defence and enlargement, and which are oppressive and need to be fought against. But, I am arguing that it is only in the context of these questions that the discussion of radical social work can make either any sense, or any progress.

This is in a way, necessarily a chapter without a conclusion. I do not have specific criteria, or a political theory and practice ready to be handed down – and, indeed, this chapter is hardly likely to be the medium through which these issues can be resolved. I have tried tentatively to indicate what some of the directions involved are: there is a need to move from abstract theory to a more concrete assessment of the politics of welfare, such an assessment should have at its centre a concern for the distinction between progressive or oppressive elements and should also be concerned to identify any contradictions, sources of tension and weakness in the system upon which action should be taken. It would also be an analysis and a mode of action which could identify realistically the limits of particular struggles and areas of action rather than making the assumption that the creation of a radical social work is necessarily the only or final solution to the problem.

However, perhaps more important than these tentative suggestions is the fact that there are already processes at work which are making this movement away from academic criticism and professional practice more possible. Some intellectuals are attempting to move beyond the sterility of abstract criticism to engage more directly with the consequences for practice of political theory (for example, Corrigan and Leonard, 1978). At the same time, attempts by the state to cut welfare, to increase welfare workers' 'productivity', and to increase the repressive elements of their work, have produced collective responses and resistances which could potentially move beyond narrow conceptions of practice.[4] These

4. For example, refusing to take on new duties, resisting police involvement in case committees and so on.

developments, however unsteady and uncertain, stand to remind us once again that the conditions and constraints under which we operate are not as permanent or solid as they might first appear.

8

Social work and the family
Michael Rustin

This chapter is concerned with the relation between the development of social work as a profession and an activity since the war, and the institution of the family. It argues that social work was explicitly developed in support of a prescriptive model of familial care and control. It emphasizes the historical distinctiveness of this development, in comparison with the earlier history of industrial capitalism, and argues that the support of familial care by the state represents the strengthening of an altruistic principle within the dominant capitalist order. There is a continuing contradiction between this altruistic 'welfare' element in capitalism and the dominant market ethos. The chapter suggests that this contradiction is often overlooked by radical and Marxist critics of social work who over-assimilate social work to a dominant system of social control. A clear grasp of the post-war development of social work, in relation to the past history of welfare, and of the continuing contradictions between altruistic and market principles under contemporary capitalism, is necessary if the struggle for a more caring society is to be maintained and if social workers are to understand their part in this.

The rise of social work as a profession, and the rise of the family as an object of positive social policy in the post-war period are very closely linked. The connections can be seen in the official reports which advocated and legitimized the enhanced role of social work. The Ingleby Report on Children and Young Persons (1960, paras 11–12) for example stated:

> It seems probable, however, that those families which have themselves failed to achieve a stable and satisfactory family life will be the most vulnerable, and that the children brought up in them will be those most likely to succumb to whatever outside circumstances there may be in the outside world. If this be accepted, it becomes the duty of the state to discover such families and to help them in every possible way. ... The state's principal duty is to assist the family in carrying out its proper function.

The Younghusband Report on local authority social workers (1959, paras 675–6) also placed great stress on family support as a function particularly suited to social work. 'We agree that this particular grouping of services (social work with homeless, "problem" or other families, including unmarried and unsupported mothers) ... favours a general social worker because of the variety of problems and the many different ways in which these arise.' Similar arguments for preventive services directed towards families were presented in the White Papers, *The Child, the Family and the Young Offender* (1965) and *Children in Trouble* (1968). Taylor, Walton and Young (1975, 6–14), Clarke (1975, 1979) and Wilson (1977) have documented these connections.

The importance of the family can be seen too in the climate of ideas within which post-war social services were formed. Among the most influential contributions was that of John Bowlby (1952), whose work on maternal deprivation gave a scientific basis to the emerging aim of support for the family, and was also influential in later arguments by social workers for the importance of relationships rather than sanctions in the care and control of the juvenile delinquent. For the Younghusband Report (1959, para. 630) Bowlby's work was a paradigm example of relevant scientific advance.

> The growth of knowledge, even in the last decade or so, in sociology, psychology and psychiatry, has made possible a deeper understanding of the different groups of people within our terms of reference, and has therefore also made possible more consciously directed and effective work with them than heretofore. Some of this knowledge is now widespread among the general public, for example the effects of maternal deprivation or of continuing stress in the causation of physical ill-health.

Bowlby and his colleagues' work seems to have been prominent in their minds as the paradigm of a positively useful finding. Sociological work of the early post-war period (see for example Mays, 1954 and 1959) also provided some evidence to support the idea that deviations from the 'normal family', through emotional disturbance, break-up, and (for the time) abnormal size, could produce disadvantage. The discussion of changes in working-class community, and especially the reported decline of the extended family (Young and Willmott, 1957) emphasized the role of familial relationships in care for dependants, and exposed a vacuum which growing professional social services might beneficially fill. The emergence of the concept of a cycle of deprivation (Jordan, 1974) in the 1960s reinforced an emphasis on 'problem families' which had been present throughout the post-war period.

Thirdly, the predominance for a time of casework methods in social work thinking, and the influence of psychodynamic ideas, taught through 'human growth and development' courses during social work training, reflect this emphasis on the family as the main locus of social work effort. Psychodynamic theory seeks to explain the emotional dynamics of families, and their consequences for individuals, and its practice is designed as a therapy to improve this. Much of the literature produced for social work training purposes in the post-war period is dominated by this approach, (see for example Younghusband, 1965, 1966, 1967).

This stress in the 'official' literature of social work on the importance of the family is echoed in the writings of radical critics of social work. Their critique has rendered this familial emphasis of social work practice both highly visible and problematic. They have criticized the casework approach as individualistic, making into matters for personal guilt and responsibility what should, they argue, be seen as structural problems. They have criticized the psychological emphasis of social work training, (Cannan, 1972) advocating a political approach to the material determinants of individual problems instead (a complex discussion of these issues is provided by Busfield, 1974, and Pearson, 1974). They have attacked the ideology of the 'normal family', for legitimizing sexual or parental oppression, and for neglecting the diversity of family forms which actually exist. Feminist writing has recently given a specific force to this critique of the family, and of social work in so far as it enforces family ideology: Elizabeth Wilson's (1977) book is an important example.

This chapter will argue that there is a deeper convergence between liberal and neo-Marxist views of the family and social work in the post-war period than their common assertion of a strong interconnection. Each position, we shall argue, lacks an adequate sense of history and of conflict. In the post-war development of an ideology for social work in the various official reports and textbooks, we find a latent functionalism characteristic of much of the social science of the period. There is an uncritical assumption that the family's functions are a universal imperative for society, that the integration of individuals in 'healthy' families is 'natural', and that the good both of the individual and society are unproblematically achieved by securing this. The reliance on psychology as the social science of most practical use to social workers reinforces historical and universalistic assumptions about the social setting.

Certain somewhat class-specific assumptions seem to underlie the emphasis on psychotherapeutic methods at this time. The norm of verbal articulacy about relationships and feelings on which this method depends is clearly closer to the way of life (or aspiration) of the professional middle classes than to average working-class experience. The demonstrated lack of fit (Mayer and Timms, 1970) between working-class clients' expectations of social work, and the social workers' therapeutic definition of the task, has influentially pointed up this aspect of social work ideology, and undermined social workers' confidence in its universal relevance. As radical critics have pointed out, there is an assumption in 'official' writing about the role of social work that structural and material problems have been overcome, leaving the adjustment and resocialization of individuals and families into the social order an unproblematic aim.

It is as if a norm and ideal of family functioning predicated on the small nuclear family unit became naturalized in social work practice, as a domain assumption, for which social workers then became practical missionaries. Young's and Willmott's book *The Symmetrical Family* (1973) represents this norm in the form of a predictive theory about the development of the family in contemporary Britain.

The origins of the modern British welfare system are of course rooted in social and ideological conflict. Within the discipline of social administration, and in the arguments of advocates of the welfare system in the Labour Party and elsewhere, these conflicts of ideals between individualistic and laisser-faire market-oriented doctrines, such as those urged by the Institute of Economic Affairs, and altruistic and socialist ideas, were highly visible and central for many years. More recently, the terrain of debate has shifted somewhat from issues of principle concerning the construction and rationale of the welfare system, especially its degree of collectivism or market-orientation, which dominated the post-war period, to managerialist concerns. The latter debates have been influenced by systems theories employed in the hope of improving the integration and control of services, and this approach has dominated reorganizations of local government, the national health service, and social services, all in the space of a few years (Cockburn, 1977; Bains, 1972), Social work has grown out of the earlier phase of social democratic collectivism, and social work teaching has always given prominence to social administration and the work of the leading advocates of altruistic ideas of welfare, such as Titmuss and Townsend. But the task-orientation of social work teaching always made it difficult to incorporate these social objectives – objectives for society, rather than individuals – into social work practice. Instead, social work *assumed* the achievement of material security in conditions of dependency, and concentrated on personal support and help. A split between theory and practice referred to by Clarke (chapter 7, above) in regard to radical social work, can also be found even within the modestly pragmatic setting of reformism. The reforms, in effect, were assumed or left to others nearer the centres of power. The developing professionalism of social work accentuated this split between social and political objectives, which underlay the whole establishment of modern social welfare, but which were precluded as practical concerns for 'professional' workers and the casework methods which were deemed to be feasible. In the later period, when managerialist concerns for optimum effectiveness and organizational rationality come to dominate (see Rowbottom *et al.*, 1974), the split becomes wider, since even the social policy framework of welfare becomes depoliticized and 'neutral'.

It is in reaction to this situation that the radical critique of social work and social policy comes to have such resonance. While this has valuably exposed the limited and taken-for-granted assumptions of social work thinking, it must be said that the radical analysis has also achieved its own oversimplifications and reductions of the role of the welfare system under capitalism. We do not find, in this body of writing, much recognition of the active conflicts of principle and class interest which brought the modern welfare state into being. Indeed one of the influential models underlying this critique is an inverted functionalism translated from the psychologistic framework of individual integration into a sociological analysis which sees the system of welfare as itself integrative. The orthodox account of social work presupposes integration as a goal. The radical critique, following the prescriptions of critical phenomenology, one of its formative streams, renders visible this presupposition, and then, lifting the argument to a sociological plane, argues that the real integration is being accomplished in and by ideology, by the system of social work thought and practice.

The phenomenological component of this critique, which emphasizes reflexiveness and the relativity of standpoints as a critical lever on practice, does not contribute to historical awareness. The rather abstracted model of familial oppression (in the work of Laing, 1971, Cooper, 1971, and their colleagues) and of the interactions of social workers and clients as containing important aspects of control, assume rather than develop an account of the role of the welfare system in modern capitalism. And when this somewhat moralistic and existentially based critique becomes filled out as a sociological account of welfare and the family in contemporary capitalism, it often does so in functionalist terms. Debates on the reproduction of labour power in the contemporary family, on the role of state expenditure in post-war capitalism which treat welfare spending as the socialization of reproduction, and characterizations of new 'soft' modes of ideological control through the education and welfare systems, contribute to a new radical theory of the stabilization of post-war capitalism.

Social democrats had generally argued a positive view of the family (Townsend, 1975, 16,216), of welfare expenditure, and of the advance of therapeutic and medical definitions of social problems over juridical definitions, and had treated changes in these fields as gains of the post-war welfare system, achieved through political action. The neo-Marxist critique, which was directly aimed in some cases at reformist assumptions, argued on the contrary that these were functional imperatives of late capitalism, emanations of the ruling order rather than diminutions of its power.

An explicit theoretical functionalism enters this debate through

Althusser's influential writing (Geras, 1972; McLennan *et al.*, 1977). This work has the merit of recognizing different systems levels and components in the overall structure of domination. It thus opens the way to a coherent explanation of the role of education, welfare and the mass media in late capitalist society, and is a crucial advance on the base-superstructure model of Marxism which it attacks. But its *a priori* stress on the ultimate integration of a 'structure in dominance', and the invitation it offers to interpret all phenomena as in the end instruments of the ruling interest, are in effect a form of functionalism with the signs reversed from positive to negative.

This functionalism assumes that a social equilibrium is maintained by homeo-static mechanisms of which socialization into common norms is the most important. The problematics of 'reproduction' and 'system maintenance' are in fact somewhat similar, even down to a common emphasis on ideology in the one case, and shared values in the other as the matrix of social order. The spirit of Durkheim lies behind both Parsonian and, less directly, structuralist system theories (Badcock, 1975). It is not surprising, given the common endeavour to explain the conditions of stability of capitalism as the prime explanatory task, that Marxist functionalism has been more fertile in discovery of complex supports of the system, than of contradictions within it. The search has proceeded inwards into the self, as well as into literature, broadcasting, the law, and academic disciplines. Phenomenological modes of questioning provide support for structuralist analysis in considering all forms of consciousness as possible aspects of ideological control. The inherent determinism of this style of analysis, the stones of cognitive repression being only briefly lifted by the effort of reflection, and the difficulty of finding any ground uncontaminated by the dominant form of consciousness, render this work both pessimistic and élitist in character, though still illuminating.

Valuable attempts have been made, nevertheless, to characterize welfare policies in relation to the specific historical moment of the post-war reconstruction. The discussion of Fabian criminology by Taylor, Walton, and Young (1975) is one such contribution, though it is seriously flawed by its simplistic imputation of conservative intentions to what were seen by their authors as radical reforms. The baleful influence of the later *New Left Review*'s dismissal of the British working-class movement's actual politics can be seen in these authors denunciations of 'working-class myopia', which echo the rhetoric of Anderson (1968) and Nairn (1964). Work by authors connected with the Centre for Contemporary Cultural Studies is less dismissive, but all these writings have in common the absence of any apparent memory of the period prior to 1944. The goals and achievements of the post-war generation of the policy-makers, and the political workers and members who made legislative changes possible, cannot be recognized unless their historical setting, and their fundamental points of reference, are understood. When a return to more punitive modes of social control (in the guise of 'law and order'), to the displacement of collective forms of welfare by the market principle (for example in possible reforms to the education or health system), to the intensification of stigma for recipients of social security are all now active political possibilities, it is unduly sanguine to diminish the difference between these and social democratic forms of provision and control on the grounds that they are all operated within capitalism, (ignoring the balance of forces characterizing capitalism at these different moments). There are some uncritical convergencies going on, when criticism of 'therapeutic' attitudes towards criminals and advocacy of the comparative merits of punitive justice come both from neo-Marxists and from Sir Keith Joseph. The neo-Marxist critique is put into some disarray by its need to combine its exaggerated and one-sided picture of the integration of post-war British capitalism with its strong and possibly overdrawn sense of its developing crisis. What has been ruled out of account, *a priori*, are the oppositional and radical forces embedded in the post-war settlement, responsible for it, and committed to defending its gains. Among these should be included the public service occupations such as social work. By dismissing the role of such major factions, and of official working-class leaderships, the system is made to appear both more fully integrated than it ever was or is, and also more helpless in the face of crisis and conservative ideological offensives.

In fact the ideological space now available for such an offensive is significant. The right has adopted the same organizational tactics of pressure group, demonstration and sect as the left, and conducts increasingly explicit doctrinal and ideological argument in opposition to the dominant consensus of the centre. This tells us what has happened to the centre, and how far that now constitutes a terrain in which powers are substantially, though far from equally, divided between classes.

A further point can be made about the role of sociological concepts in this analysis. Whereas Parsonian analysis overworks the idea of normative consensus, making it, following a particular reading of Durkheim, a precondition for any society, the radical critique of social control overworks the concept of control. The existence of dimensions of control, in the work of allegedly provisive or benign agents such as teachers, doctors or social workers, is held to 'unmask' their real functions, on behalf of the ruling orders. This has been, it must be said, a valuable corrective to self-serving and meliorist conceptions of these professions, but it remains important to recognize, as Satyamurti (chapter 5, above) makes clear, the balance of provisive and control functions, and the distinctions between different modes of control and their implications for relative power. It is a naive theory of domination which collapses into each other the gun, the vote, and the intellectual treatise without regard to the different limitations of each of these forms of power. They have quite different implications for the relative powers of superordinate and subordinate classes, as Simmel (1950, 181–9) understood.

The consequences of both sociological and neo-Marxist functionalisms have been to emphasize the apparent stabilizing effects of policy reforms, and to diminish the conflicts of principle and intentions which led to them. The post-1968 split between the generation of post-war reformers and official Labour leaderships, and radical and neo-Marxist critics no longer identifying with the achievement of a limited social democracy, is the political context of this argument.

The family, in capitalism as in other forms of society, is an institution concerned with dependency. It is within its boundaries an altruistic institution, based on mutual care within and between generations. This assertion is not refuted by the demonstration that the care takes place on unequal terms, between sexes and between generations, or that other functions such as control are also important.

The main purpose of this chapter is to draw attention to the major shift in the state's relation to the family that has taken place especially in the post-war period, compared with the past. We seek to understand social work as an instrument of that new and more positive relation. To put the argument at its most succinct, the policy of the contemporary state is to intervene to support the family in its functions. The interventions of the nineteenth-century state, by contrast, especially in the period following 1834, were in effect to break it up. The foundation of that earlier social policy was of course, the hated poor law (Checkland, 1974; Fraser, 1976) and this was the central point of reference for social reformers in the construction of the contemporary welfare system. The dismantling of the poor law, through the National Assistance Act of 1948 and also the Children's Act of 1948, and the obligations put on local authorities to care for kinds of dependant defined by age and handicap rather than by destitution (Holgate and Keidan, 1975) marks a vital stage in the development of modern social work (on children see Middleton, 1971). It gave rise to its main organizational structures and specialisms including children's and welfare departments prior to the Seebohm reorganization. Titmuss's (1963) influential discussion of welfare problems in terms of dependency is an explicit assertion of universalistic social responsibilities, against the previous stigmatizing definitions. In fact, struggles over the continuation of 'poor law principles' by other names, in the contemporary welfare system continue to be central, and may well grow more fierce if further retrenchment in the welfare system is attempted in the next few years. It is odd in these circumstances that the centrality of the poor law in the minds of post-war reformers has been forgotten.

The prescriptions for family life embodied in religious and secular ritual, in commonsense belief, and in the legislative framework, impose obligations between family members that are as near to unlimited liability as any social relationships in society. Unlimited liability, that is to say, between spouses, by parents for dependent children, and formerly but now to a declining degree, by children for aged and dependent parents. In different and more extended family structures, obligations towards kin extend more widely. Functionalist analysis of the role of the family under capitalism, notably by Talcott Parsons (1943 and see also Middleton, 1974), has been clarifying in this regard, perceiving that the altruistic and caring functions necessary for any society under capitalism are concentrated and specialized in family relationships, while the economic and political spheres become, with the development of capitalist wage and market relations, increasingly impersonal, instrumental and contractual in character. It is of course a central criticism of capitalism as a way of life that it confines and limits altruistic relationships in this way to the familial setting, while defining all others as non-members and potential competitors.

This altruistic character of the family was insisted upon even in the harshest period of industrial capitalism (see Parry and Johnson, 1974, 2–9, on familial ideology). But it was insisted upon and enforced, in the period after the 1834 poor law reform, as a binding obligation upon adult individuals, while being in no way shared or supported by the state, for fear that this would undermine individual motivation. It was recognized that men would only undergo the sacrifices of industrial work for the sake of the collective self they recognized in their kin. To the degree that it neglects the sufferings undergone by male workers for the sake of their families, the account of the family under industrial capitalism as an agency of male oppression is somewhat one-sided. The doctrine of self-help required men to maintain themselves and their families (Finer, 1974, II, 110–26) and punished the family as a whole to enforce this norm. The state, and the churches and moralists who supported the dominant ideology, harshly insisted that altruism (that is care of family) was good and necessary for individuals, but would be disastrous and undermining for the community. Dependants, especially women, children and the aged, could retain a measure of dignity while they remained within families, and families had to depend exclusively on the self-help of breadwinners (or property) for their sustenance. Once individual self-reliance, and other altruistic obligations to kin had failed, or more often been defeated by material hardship, the state insisted that familial status and the status of citizen be taken away and be replaced by the single overwhelming status of pauper. The workhouse split up families. That was its most fundamental meaning. It cast men, women and children out of family relationships into uniform institutional degradation. This was the particular relation of the state and the family in nineteenth-century capitalism: the state prescribed and enforced familial obligations, but did nothing to positively aid or assist them.

The contemporary state exhibits a somewhat different relation. As a result mainly of Liberal and Labour welfare policies, the state now underwrites the family's caring functions. It does so through the provision of services such as health, housing, education, domiciliary and institutional care. It does so by financial provision, most notably by redistributing resources towards families and conditions of dependency, modifying the allocations arising from the labour and property markets to produce more 'altruistic' outcomes than would otherwise occur. (This is the effect for example of the recent child benefit allowances, compulsorily directing resources from wage-earning taxpayers, to child-caring mothers).

Preoccupation with the structure of the family as an institution (for example whether it be 'nuclear' or 'extended'), and with its function (socialization, or the reproduction of labour power, as functionalists and Marxists might respectively put it) can each obscure this important difference in the social relations of the family, and the different roles of the state towards it in different periods. The degree to which the family's caring functions are enforced by destroying all other caring resources in society, or are supported and supplemented by state action, (or are wholly or partially replaced by other agencies, such as the commune, kibbutz, or even the public school) are important variants and possibilities within our own recent history. We argue that it is the growth in the state's positive intervention in support of the family which explains the growth and nature of contemporary social work.

In the light of the history of state policy towards the family in the nineteenth century, it is not surprising therefore that the idea of a welfare state that would support the family's functions was regarded by socialists at its inception as a benign development, rather than as a mode of incorporation. The right to be cared for in dependency by kin, at a reasonable level of subsistence, had after all been systematically denied for much of the population for more than a century in a culture whose individualism had ideologically and morally entrenched the idea of a family as the natural locus of human care. English capitalism simultaneously urged and compelled the ideal of family life, while materially and legally denying its possibility in times of hardship. This culture had in a similar way propagated an ideology of individual self- development (a high point of its advocacy being reached in the writings of J. S. Mill, for example) while depriving most of its people of the means of it. The romantic protest against industrialism, so influentially described by Raymond Williams (1958), is the result of that second contradiction. The ideology of familial altruism is the outcome of the first. Because of this history and experience, the achievement of this long-contradicted possibility of familial care became a dominant metaphor for a better society. The equation of welfare with socialism, while a partial and limiting definition, was an understandable elision, asserting the claims of what even the dominant culture recognized as a fundamental human need. The claims of human need and fulfilment made against the dominant order are recognizably shaped by values formed within the dominant culture. Something similar can be seen in the respect in which the rule of law and parliamentary democracy are held by working-class radicals in Britain in the eighteenth and nineteenth centuries and since (Thompson 1968, 887 passim; 1975, 258–69). This cultural dialectic in which oppositional struggles take their form goes some way to explaining the national peculiarities of radical and socialist movements.

Against both functionalist and structuralist Marxist forms of analysis, which assert the 'fit' of family and its supporting social agencies with capitalism, we need, therefore, an account more sensitive to structural contradiction and historical change (see Goldthorpe, 1964 on functionalist and conflict approaches to social policy). In particular, the opposition between familial and market values, and the tensions within a capitalist order between these conflicting imperatives, need to be given their due weight. We shall argue that the changing relation of the state to the institution of the family should be understood as the result of a particular compromise in a continuing social conflict. It is a heavily over-determined compromise. The ideology of family life, in the post-war period, becomes central to a 'consensus' which can be seen as the outcome of what Rex, (1961, 127; Rex and Moore, 1967, 6–7) calls a situation of truce in a continuing class conflict.

On the one hand, we must note the importance of the assertion of the rights of citizenship (Marshall, 1963, 1975) in the wartime and post-war period, and their extension from political and legal rights to the rights to employment and to support in circumstances of need. The assumption of social responsibility for dependency, in the Beveridge Report and in the establishment of the National Health Service in particular, is a recovery of an idea of relationship destroyed as an operative concept for government during the industrial revolution. We have to recognize the attacks on human relationship, dependency and altruism brought about by industrial capitalism before we can comprehend the revolution implied by its recovery. The most important aspect of Bowlby's early post-war work on maternal deprivation is not its restrictive implications regarding the role of women, now so widely attacked by feminists and the left, but its demonstration and assertion of the importance of caring relationships for the development of infants. We have to remember how uninterested the psychology derived from the utilitarian account of human nature is in human relationships in order to understand the lasting importance of Bowlby's attempt to give a scientific demonstration of the importance of caring. The antagonism of much academic psychology to Bowlby's work is parallel to the hostility of liberal market economists to welfare policies motivated by social concern rather than individual choice. Elaborations and qualifications to Bowlby's thesis (indicating that others can provide continuous care besides mothers, that disturbed care may be even worse than separation, and so on does not refute his fundamental achievement, which was to demonstrate the critical importance of early relationships, and in so doing to establish the ground for adequately complex accounts, from psychoanalysis or elsewhere, of human development and relationship. Rutter concludes in his review of the literature (1972, 121) that later studies

> have amply demonstrated that early life experiences may have serious and lasting effects on development. This conclusion of Bowlby's, which was regarded as very controversial twenty years ago, is now generally accepted as true. We may now take for granted that many children admitted to hospital or to a residential nursery show an immediate reaction of acute distress; that many infants show developmental retardation following admission to a poor-quality institution and may exhibit intellectual impairment if they remain there for a long time; that there is a connection between delinquency and broken homes; that affectionless psychopathy sometimes follows multiple separation experiences and institutional care in early childhood; and that dwarfism is particularly seen in children from rejecting and affectionless homes.

The attention to early relationships, and the view of the family as the formative model for such relationships, is one important development underpinning social work's development in the post-war period. A second important contribution is the development of a social ethic of concern for need and dependency. This is partially socialist in inspiration, urging working-class experience of mutual help and solidarity as a model for the whole society. It also draws on Christian and especially nonconformist ideals of moral responsibility and social compassion. The inflection of socialism into an overriding concern for the weak, into the conception of a caring society, is an advance over the ideology of discipline, self-reliance and egoism. But it nevertheless represents a partial deflection of socialist pressure away from the sphere of production and work, into the subordinate institutions of welfare. The Labour movement, in its political institutions, becomes largely the spokesman for the 'caring' part of society, and as a result becomes permanently on the defensive. Spending on welfare, though enormously enlarged during this period, can always be presented, given this division of interests and powers, as a residual item, the margin left over after production and wages have been looked after. Intellectually the left retained an ascendancy in these 'welfare' areas throughout the post-war period (until the recent retrenchment), maintaining pressure on the education system in part through the findings of sociologists, and on welfare notably through the work of the London School of Economics group around Titmuss. These latter writers developed an interpretation of 'social administration' which was compassionate, uncompromising and sociological in its advocacy of socialist welfare measures.

The work of these writers is based on a predominant ethical altruism, most finely expressed in Titmuss's exemplary study. *The Gift Relationship* (1971). Their empirical studies re-establish the prevalence and scale of need, and connect this to conditions of dependency which for large numbers of working-class people mean unavoidable poverty under market conditions. They root their conceptions of mutual help in the study of working-class communities: this is perhaps the significance of the studies of Bethnal Green by Townsend, Young and Willmott for this group's social theory. Most strikingly they, and especially Titmuss, (1958 and 1963) attacked the ideologists and institutions of private welfare provision – private insurance and health. While choosing a Fabian and pressure group strategy, of influence through the Labour establishment, and working within the confines of the issues of income distribution and welfare policy, they nevertheless develop fully the implications of making needs the criterion of welfare policy. For all the limitations of a politics whose socialism is confined largely to welfare issues, they demonstrate what can follow from the post-war recognition that dependency is a community and not merely an individual responsibility. They articulate, in fact, the contradictions between the norms of the social welfare system in post-war Britain, and the dominant market economy.

While both psychodynamic approaches and Fabian social policy theory seek to restore recognition to caring relationships as a political ideal, we must nevertheless recognize that the adoption of the family as the model of this relational ideal is a limiting one in the post-war period. The problem of mixed economy capitalism after the war was how to reconcile the pressures for a more altruistic and egalitarian social order with the continued dominance of capitalist forms of production. Just as the deflection of the labour movement into 'welfare politics' was one resolution of this problem, so concentration on the family as an ideal of policy was another. The family embodies a principle of altruism and care for dependants, but confines it. Family income, in the post-war period, continues to derive largely from earnings in the labour market, and income differentials reflect the market's measure of worth. The exclusive reliance on the labour market for family subsistence, and the harsh punishment of families for whom the principle of self-help broke down, was no longer acceptable after the war. But it was possible to supplement and support the family in the exercise of its main responsibilities, without conflict with the continuing discipline of the labour market for able-bodied workers. Thus the dominant principle of self-help and reward in accordance with desert could be and was conjoined with a subordinate principle of state support for dependency.

In determining welfare policy, there is a central conflict between the principles of the market, distributing resources in accordance with the market value of labour, and welfare principles which would distribute resources in relation to need. This conflict can be resolved by contrasting operative principles. One such was provided by the poor law, whose principle of less eligibility, punitive status of pauper, and institution of the workhouse, gave the minimum recognition to the claims of need. The Beveridge Report proposed a somewhat more generous principle, laying down the ideal of a minimum subsistence income compatible with maintaining normal family life. Beveridge throughout his life was exercised with the problem of how to combine generous support to dependants, including children, with the maintenance of the incentive to work. In practice the stigmas of means-tested benefits and inadequate subsistence have continued to this day. A third principle which can govern relief in dependency is that of state-supported proportionality, that is wage-related benefits which, on the model of superannuation, support non-working dependants at a living standard proportional to income at work. This principle established the labour market as setting *relative* standards of subsistence, but uses taxation and compulsory insurance to ensure that incomes in dependency are maintained. The most radical principle provides for dependency exclusively in relation to need, without regard to the income level of recipients. Because of the superordinate principle of determining incomes in accordance with presumed desert, this radical principle is implemented only in the provision of benefits in kind, such as the National Health Service and education. Public goods can be provided on an egalitarian basis, everyone being entitled to the same high standard rather than to the same low standard of the subsistence minimum. It is their non-commensurable character which makes this possible, removing these services to some degree from the stratifying effects of the market. In practice, the co-existence of private markets in education and health, and various mechanisms biasing allocation towards the better off, make these systems less egalitarian than they might be.

These conflicting principles coexist in post-war social policy, though the shift to the more generous of them marks the progress already described in the social recognition of dependency. But even though the family is now helped in its caring functions, rather than driven to perform them, the dominance of rewards from work as the main source and legitimation of income ensures that it became as central an object of positive policy as it was earlier of coercive policy. Indeed, the priority given to enforcing the work ethic explains much of the continuing meanness and repressiveness of the system of income-support, with the dire consequences this had had for the roles of social workers (on this see Jordan, 1974 and for a different view Stevenson, 1973).

The family becomes economically and ideologically central during the post-war period. The main growth of the post-war economy was through industries which supplied domestic consumption. Expenditure on housing, on cars, and on consumer durables, were the main economic motor of the 1950s and 1960s. The supply of domestic capital goods, more convenient houses, and declining family size in its turn facilitated the increased participation of women in the labour market, supplying the consumer goods industries. Mass communications in this period, substantially funded by consumer advertising, propagated an image of the family as the centre of consumption. It was influentially described as a 'home-centred' society (see Zweig, 1961, 206–11; Lockwood and Goldthorpe, 1963, 141–2; also Clarke, 1979).

Familialism had the advantage of being potentially a basis for consensus, in a society deeply divided by class. Working-class families become to some degree assimilated to a culture of privatized consumption, in part through the break-up – via housing policies – of established working-class communities and extended families, and also with the decline in family size. A factor in the decline of these communities has been the move of industries away from class-conscious and highly unionized inner-city areas such as the East End of London. The family is a natural sacred focus of an individualist society which has few other institutions which can invoke total commitments. Post-war full employment, rising living standards and welfare policies made this an ideal which could be seemingly actualized for large numbers. For a declining power, turned inwards by the loss of empire, and deprived of its former basis of national pride, 'happy families' was a useful image of domestic consolation. The effective representation of the monarchy as a 'royal family' during the current reign, projecting an apparently domestic and dutiful life-style, is an index of this ideological thrust, which is also evident in the salience of the family as an electoral image.

Given this general ideological commitment to the family, the emphasis of social work in this period becomes explicable. Social work develops into a principal agency for supporting families in their caring functions. The assumption that normal families can and should 'manage' in the labour market constrains social workers not only to support dependency, but also to support the work ethic and financial responsibility as it is conventionally understood. Some of the dilemmas of 'care or control' described by Satyamurti (chapter 5, above) derive from the fact that resources from the community are intended to supplement, not replace, resources which are earned. Families therefore have to be helped to 'behave responsibly' and conform to the ethics of paying one's way, as well as helped in their caring tasks. The problem is not so much that social workers have to make help conditional on respectable self-helping by their clients, though this frequently happens; it is more that the resources available to social workers, under this norm of 'supplementary benefit', make it difficult for families to escape from economic difficulties unless they learn to 'manage' more like conventional families. The issues of care and control in working with poor clients are inseparably bound up; unless clients are 'controlled' to some degree, and their coping capacity improved, it will not be possible to help them in the long run.

In contemporary British society the values of self-help in order to care for one's own are widely shared. In this sense social workers are often supporting common values, even among their worst-off clients, when they urge better efforts to keep family and home together. Indeed, social workers as a professional group are usually more sympathetic to the difficulties of their poor clients than are the surrounding neighbourhoods of non-aided families. The attempt to 'radicalize' such clients by offering a political model of relationships to the welfare system (Leonard 1975, Corrigan and Leonard, 1978) analogous to the worker's contractual relationship to his employer, runs up against deep moral resistances as well as the obvious practical problems of mobilizing desperately unhappy and harassed people. Social work clients often have a commitment to those they care for – even husbands that may ill-treat them – and the option of refusing to carry on unless more is provided is usually a repugnant one. The inference that because families are reproducing capitalism's labour force, therefore families can bargain with the social services for a better return for their reproductive work, is false. Care for kin is a commitment which people make their own, and cannot be set aside as the value of material products in an alienated work-process can be. The relations of people to reproductive activities within families, and to productive work in the labour market, are asymmetrical.

The mixture of care and control functions, the ethics of the market and of family care, has generated great difficulties for social work theory and practice. The methods of casework are designated for the handling of emotional problems. Psychoanalysis as a theory of infantile development within family relationships is well adapted to these. It both accepts the family as a prerequisite of personal development, yet actively grasps its deformations, distortions, and negativities. It wants the family to work, yet it is not afraid to recognize that it does not. Its practitioners, and this includes skilled case-workers, are trained to be able to face and explore the frightening emotional states that arise when it has failed. Its techniques enable them to sometimes modify feeling and action in clients.

The rationalizing of family functions by technical experts is pervasive in advanced capitalist societies, replacing religious interpretations of human experience, among others. For an ever larger range of family functions, reliance is placed on impersonal, 'scientific' knowledge. This is disseminated through a hierarchy of cultural levels, from original scientific work, through its applications by professional workers such as paediatricians, counsellors, psychiatrists and social workers, to diffusion through the mass media in advice columns, 'phone-ins', and popular books. Some writers achieve great fame and influence as arbiters of family life – F. Truby King, Dr Spock, Dr Bowlby and Anna Raeburn for example. Deviant versions of family interaction have emerged: R. D. Laing's work can be understood in part as taking the side of the adolescent and reaching over the medical-scientific community to a popular audience in a counter-culture to do so. These various rationalizations of family, pre-family and anti-family life commonly start from the everyday experience and problems of their readers, which means experience in families. They tell people how to do what they feel they must do anyway, somehow or other. Social work in the post-war period carried one such influential theory and legitimation of family functioning.

The adoption of psychodynamic casework as a dominant methodology for social work presupposed that social workers would be able to specialize in the skilled support of familial caring. It was most successful, in psychiatric and medical social work, where these conditions came closest to being met – that is, where clients' problems were experienced by clients as having an important 'inner' component, and where conditions of work and training enabled social workers to practise casework capably. But it was generally supposed in the development of the profession that Beveridge had taken care of problems of subsistence, and that in any event other agencies would take responsibility for income maintenance. It was not recognized how ungenerous social support would remain for most of those who turned to the state for help, nor how implicated social work would become in instilling conformity to accepted economic values.

Psychoanalytic work can help individuals to learn about their feelings and free themselves from unconsciously based difficulties. But in the short run it often adds to rather than reduces burdens of anxiety and pain, as a part of learning. It is hardly, therefore, the best method of coping with dire material distress. The particular adaptation of psychoanalytic ideas which have been made in the development of 'casework' indicate the effect of this contradiction. It can be argued that the stress on 'supportive' relationships in social work practice, though a natural response to the state of need of their clients, is a distortion of the core psychoanalytic method, whose principle aim is insight, not comfort. We must add to the pervasive and overwhelming needs of clients the poor training and supervision which most social workers have received in casework practice, unavoidably given the huge growth of social services over a short period and the great difficulties of this work. Psychoanalytic ideas have become devalued under these pressures, into a superficial mode of channelling anxieties which cannot be resolved either materially or emotionally. The pervasiveness of the casework idiom in social workers' dealings with each other (even where it has been overtly rejected as a method) is an indication of what is amiss. It has often become a means of rationalizing social workers' own situations, and a defence against pain. These factors account for the widespread rejection and undermining of casework as a method.

While field social workers became a means of supporting families in their caring functions, residential work took on the functions of replacing the family when it could no longer maintain them. The children's home and the old people's home replace the workhouse as the residual caring institution. Officially, in those institutions under the control of social services departments, a model of family-like care is adopted as the norm, in place of the large-scale regimented custody of the workhouse. They have become, over recent years, smaller in scale and gentler in intention, though the extremely low priority accorded to institutional care of all kinds makes this substitute family concept far from realization. It is even more remote in some institutions which have the function of looking after those for whom family does not function – geriatric and psychiatric hospitals, prisons, and doss-houses for the single homeless, for example. The last remains closest, in virtue of the 'lost' statuses of its clientele, to the workhouse in its character.

This institutional provision demonstrates another side of the inadequacy of the caring services offered by the welfare state to those unable to maintain themselves. The specific concentration of altruism within the family unit may explain the difficulties of providing support to an adequate degree outside it. The unconditional, continuous, and lifelong relationship offered by kinship in favourable circumstances is difficult to replicate. The problems of doing so are scarcely yet adequately faced, even though the numbers of people who will be extruded from families by death or separation will inexorably increase. This is the obverse of extended survival into old age, of smaller families, and of increased choice and mobility to make and break relationships. Creating and filling vocations for 'caring workers', and also finding and releasing sources of altruism in the rest of the community, seem to be the key to this. The current concerns about the state of residential social work, and the emphasis on community-based social work, are the beginnings of a recognition of these problems.

We have identified the formative condition for the development of social work in the post-war period as the state's new positive commitment towards support for the family. This has been a major change in the relation of the family and the state, giving greater support to caring functions within the still-dominant market system. But we must note that these relations continue to change. Changes are in the direction both of a greater tolerance and pluralism and also of a greater measure of social intervention. The state's coercive relationship to family responsibility in the nineteenth century carried with it the enforcement of husband's dominance, parental rights, and obligations to dependants. In recent years, as the Finer Report (1974, I, 66 passim) excellently documents, under the pressure of more egalitarian concepts of matrimony, this repressive relation has been modified, so far as the jurisdiction of the divorce court is concerned. The easing of conditions for divorce, and their equalization between men and women, and for abortion, have altered the balance of rights, and a criterion of meeting the needs of family members has replaced concepts of desert in determining what should happen when marriages break up. The rights of children have been similarly given much greater weight in the court's decisions about families, and accompanying this is an increased willingness of the state to intervene to protect both women and children from harassment. Social workers have been active agents in these processes, acting on behalf of both women and children.

There is also evidence of greater tolerance towards 'deviant' forms of family life, for example in the recognition of the problem of, and special provision for, single-parent families, which the Finer Report signalled. While many of its provisions have yet to be enforced, there is no doubt that the climate of opinion on this issue has been substantially changed. While some radicals and feminists have argued that the repressiveness of a familial culture can only be ended by its overthrow (Mitchell, 1974) and by the overthrow of its roots in capitalism, there seem material reasons (for example of increased leverage of women in the labour market) to explain why more liberal and pluralistic family forms can and do develop in contemporary capitalism (Collins, 1972). The strength of familialism within this culture, and also in its relation to this economic system, suggests that greater tolerance of diversity will only strengthen the position of the family as a central institution. In the same way, the tying of economic rights in conditions of dependency to economic rights when in work serves to strengthen the legitimacy of the labour market as the source of economic rewards.

The relation of the competing principles of allocation according to need or merit remains more open and problematic, especially since this issue is now more heavily contested politically than at any time since the war. The labour market is failing an increasing proportion of people, through structural unemployment, and there has been some pressure on the state to dissociate the right to live under decent conditions from the right to work, which has had some limited effect so far as the short-term unemployed are concerned though less for those out of work for longer periods. There has been a similar recognition of the failure of the housing market, and an increased obligation by the state to provide reasonable housing for all. But it is unlikely to be possible to combine egalitarian and generous welfare policies with the continuation of substantial unemployment.

Both the costs and wastefulness of unemployment relief, and the difficulties of combining reasonable living standards in unemployment with incentives for the working, make it certain that the continuation of unemployment will drag down the living standards of the worst-off. Pressures for reduced taxation and assertion of the claims of the 'productive' against the welfare sector have also been growing, these being effectively claims on behalf of those possessing capital or scarce labour power against those with neither. Beveridge's conviction in the 1940s (Harris, 1977, 429–41), that generous welfare provision for dependants in a market economy depends on full employment, remains valid, especially since subsequent developments in social security policy have placed such stress on the principle of benefits being related to wages. Concern with the relative incomes of the best and worst off (which Donnison (1978) describes as a third stage in the post-war debate over poverty) is unlikely to be effective if the distance to be bridged is not merely between full-time workers, but between the highly paid and the long-term unemployed. The battles of the post-war reconstruction, for goverment intervention to ensure full employment, and to guarantee decent standards in dependency, now have to be fought all over again, against the same enemies of market economics and repressive social policy (Hall *et al.*, 1978). This fundamental conflict of interests and principles, between egalitarian and altrustic ideals of welfare and the ethic of economic desert, continues to define the framework of social work practice.

A recognition by social workers of their roots in these caring traditions, of human relations theories and ethical and political altruism, and some greater organizational capacity in pressing these goals would have some weight in this conflict. The idea of social rights has been extended and generalized in contemporary society, as T. H. Marshall (1963) has pointed out. Marshall drew attention to the shift from political and legal definitions of rights, to economic and social rights. Ralph Turner (1969) has subsequently noted that an idea of rights of personal fulfilment has become a third 'existential' stage of this development, also described in Hoggart's important, though devalued, phrase as concern for the quality of life. Their concern for relationships, and for example, the recent assertion and implementation of the idea of rights to welfare, have placed social workers in the centre of this process.

The current pattern of social services has represented a considerable step for this society towards humanity and fraternity, albeit limited and contradicted by the still dominant capitalist ethic. The history, and the specific contradictions facing welfare under capitalism, needs to be grasped. Only by a detailed attention to conflicting norms of policy, and to the institution of care, can any further advance be articulated and secured. Stan Cohen (1975) in his paper, *It's All Right for You to Talk*, argues rightly for a recognition of humane individual practice against academic radical critiques. But it is more than a matter of good individual intentions working against bad institutions. The radical traditions and potentialities within the welfare sector need to be 'rescued', and the next stages sought communally in the attempt to generalize to a whole society the ideal of human care.

9

Social work today: some problems and proposals

Noel Parry, Michael Rustin and Carole Satyamurti

The essays in this volume seek to examine the development of social work and social welfare from a sociological and historical perspective. They are mainly attempts to describe and explain, informed by differing views and emphases, and are not directly concerned to offer programmes for social workers or policy-makers. In this respect, the aim of the volume differs from much writing about social work which has been heavily prescriptive, advocating different approaches without always having much regard for providing a factual or analytical foundation for them.

Some social work practitioners may feel, reading these essays, that this commitment to historical and sociological analysis is all very well, but has little to do with the problems of social work today, and the difficulties facing both social workers and those concerned for the future of the social services. In our view, accounts of the origins and contemporary functioning of social work necessarily have implications for policy and action. And practical stances, including radical ones, which disregard deeply entrenched cultural and structural formations are not likely to amount to very much. Programmes deriving from fashionable theoretical systems (the way the Seebohm changes were implemented is a case in point), formulated with scant interest in the facts of social work practice, are unlikely to realize their objectives.

In this chapter, we turn to more 'applied' questions and, with the other contributions as a background, consider some of the problems faced by social workers and by social work as an occupation, and some of the factors which have a bearing upon the shape that social work might take in the future. The discussion is sociological in that it seeks to understand these problems in terms of the structural factors affecting their recurrence and replication, and to think about the future in ways which take proper account of the force of these factors and the difficulties of changing them.

There exists a fundamental contradiction in the way that the social welfare services are structured. If one were to look simply at the policy statements of successive post-war governments and, even more, at the way legislation has been framed, one would form the impression that basic needs – income, housing and health care – have been adequately met, and that social work and related services can concentrate on providing a service for those with social and personal difficulties. The Seebohm Report, particularly, envisaged the personal social services providing a universalistic service for the whole community, and not just for the stigmatized poor or the 'social casualties'. The emphasis is on service, and a service relatively unfettered by considerations of eligibility and constraint.

Yet not only do the local authority personal social services have a range of duties which involve social workers in exercising control over clients (with all that that implies for the service ideal) but, in addition, basic needs have been very imperfectly met in practice. There is still widespread poverty, often related to particular stages in the life-cycle (old age, families with dependent children – especially one parent families, for example), but also arising from the way the income maintenance services are administered; there is still large-scale homelessness and overcrowding; there are still major shortcomings in the provision of health care. And social workers' clients tend to be drawn from sections of the population which are subject to these kinds of deprivation.

These sections of the population tend also to be those who are affected by such factors as the decline of inner city areas, shortcomings in educational provision and communal facilities for children and young people, unemployment, especially for school leavers, and low-paid oppressive types of work for those who are employed, and so on. These circumstances impose marked distortions on the practice of local authority social work. Without wanting to suggest that all personal and familial difficulties spring from poverty and deprivation, it can be no accident that very many social work clients come from such a situation, and for social workers to be attempting to help, in a situation where they can do nothing about the background deprivation, presents them with an overwhelmingly difficult task.

Thus social work operates in conditions of material distress which often render its therapeutic orientations irrelevant. No one seems to think well of social work. It is attacked from the right both for being 'soft' and partisan towards scroungers and criminals, and for being unnecessary. (Thus, for example, an article in the *Daily Telegraph* of 3 October 1978 suggested that the social workers' strike, current at the time of going to press, demonstrated that social workers are redundant, since the withdrawal of their labour had no negative consequences.) It is attacked from the radical left for lending itself to the repressive forces of capitalism. It is criticized from all sides for ineffectiveness at times when tragedies occur (such as the Maria Colwell case). And social workers themselves often feel that, despite the commitment to a service ideal that brought them into social work in the first place, they are unable to be effective.

It is difficult in this situation for problems to be correctly identified by those faced with them. The scale of the problems, organizational constraints and inadequate training tend to throw social workers into a state of confusion, helplessness and piecemeal, crisis-oriented activity similar to the state that often characterizes clients, and for related reasons. We can identify a number of different diagnoses which are currently influential in the field, and with some of which we fully agree. The problem-definition of greatest recent influence has been the managerialist view implemented through the reorganization of social services following the Seebohm Report. This was based on the assumption that a more rational management and information system and the integration of the social services would enhance their ability to deal with social problems. Fragmentation was held to be the main obstacle to providing adequate social services, not structural inequalities or the absence of social service resources. Reorganization offered advantages to experienced social workers, in the form of substantial promotion opportunities and the establishment of more powerful bureaucracies, and its damaging effects in a de-skilling of social work and in a concomitant rise of defensive unionism have only become evident later on.

Recommendations for the development of social work practice and education since the war have given a consistently high priority to the development of a distinct and recognized social work profession, equating this objective as a matter of definition with improvements in the service provided. Such assumed identities between providers and provided-for cannot be taken for granted, least of all in the case of recent social service reorganization. Social work trade unionists, acting in response to their new more bureaucratized conditions of work, have taken a leaf out of the book of their 'professional-minded' superiors in making a similar equation of self- and social-interest, in militant terms. Those, on the other hand, most committed to social work professionalism seem to hold fast to an extremely individualized model of social work (influenced by the examples of medicine and psychotherapy), and while this places an important stress on skill and responsibility, it turns away from the more social and structural issues underlying the problems of most social work clients.

A number of contributions in this volume refer to the effects of large-scale societal forces on the conditions of social work – for example, the pervasiveness of the 'less eligibility' principle, and the way in which the distinction between the deserving and the undeserving, inherited from the poor law, still permeates thinking about welfare, especially where the provision of income is concerned. To an important extent it is this, and not merely parsimony at state level, that stands in the way of the rhetorical ideals of welfare legislation becoming realized in practice. In the day-to-day administration and allocation of basic services, need is not treated as a sufficient criterion for services being provided. Considerations that have to do with work incentives, motivation to be independent, and criteria of desert are an important aspect of policy formulation and implementation, and it is in this respect that the role of the state in facilitating an adequate supply of labour for capital – not just historically, but in the present – is most clearly discernible. In our view, genuinely adequate basic services are an essential prerequisite of social work effectiveness.

The question of how social work could operate differently if the basic services of income, housing and so on were being effectively provided clearly turns on the extent to which a preoccupation with incentives and desert is an *essential* part of state activity in a capitalist society. If one takes the view that the provision of welfare represents simply an aspect of the oppression of the working class by capital, mediated by the state, then one would tend to expect such preoccupations to persist. Such a view, however, seems to us to reflect too monolithic a view of the nature of the state. It appears to spring from a neo-functionalist perspective that sees the *status quo* as necessary and inevitable and makes it difficult to explain the shifts and developments in social policy that have in fact occurred.

An alternative perspective, which seems to us more plausible, is to see the activities of the state as the outcome of compromise between conflicting interests and welfare provision as being the expression of working-class gains, as well as taking some of its shape from the interests of capital (see Saville, 1957) and from influence brought to bear by intellectuals. The bourgeoisie is itself divided, with the more 'progressive' sections having always seen punitive and deterrent measures as less crucial to the survival of the existing social order than had traditionally been assumed.

A related feature of the development of the bourgeoisie has been the growth of a service class of (largely) state employees, those who administer the investment of state capital in the reproductive process. There is much to be said for Olin Wright's (1976) view that this category of employee has a dual class character, which derives on the one hand from the source of its remuneration – the state – and on the other, from its close involvement with members of the working class in the course of its work activity. It can be argued that out of this dual class identity emerges a set of interests that is all its own, distinct from the interests of either working class or bourgeoisie – interests centring upon the goal of occupational advancement. The pursuit of this goal, however, tends to some extent to operate in favour of the working class, or at least the client population, since it implies commitment to an expanding scale of welfare provision.

We argue therefore that the importance of the welfare sector in the provision of employment, including professional employment, generates an occupational interest by state employees in the defence of welfare provision. This interest should be considered over and above the interests of potential and actual consumers of state services. Here is a question not only about the interests of different segments of the labour force, but also most importantly about the division of the societal resources of capital. The involvement by the state in the reproduction of labour power, through education, health and welfare, requires substantial investment and creates influential bureaucracies. These also come to have a vested interest in their own growth, and to us it seems theoretically helpful to recognize a growing sub-division of capital invested in the welfare sector today. The relations and balance of power between private and state capital, and between capital invested in the industrial and social sectors, are matters for separate consideration. One influential mode of contemporary thinking argues against welfare expenditure on the grounds that it has to be 'paid for' out of industrial profits, though one could equally argue that without the benefits of such expenditure, which one can identify as health, education, and some basis for social consensus, there would be no industrial activity. One man's useful production is another man's consumer waste; one man's welfare extravagance is for another the basic means of life. Our own view is that while private capital remains dominant in this structure, its power has been increasingly contested.

While the welfare sector may be in the last resort subordinate (for example to the international capital market which can generate pressure to cut 'public spending' or internally through resistance by taxpayers to high levels of taxation), it is not simply a tool of private capital. The concept of relative autonomy is important here. Governments, however, cannot dispense with welfare expenditure which now forms an important part of the strategy of economic and social management. They have to rely on welfare expenditure not least because of the welfare system's labour intensiveness in times of growing unemployment. While welfare expenditure services the capitalist economy, it also asserts contradictory claims and can be no more easily pushed aside in this society than can trade unions.

There is, therefore, some basis for hope in the continuing struggle to provide decent and more equal living standards for all. While we share with other 'structural' analyses of the conditions of social work a view of the critical importance of material standards, we do not support the pessimistic and often defeatist analysis that accompanies this. Social work is best practised where the needs it responds to are not those of poverty, but of the kinds of dependency, disability and distress which can arise irrespective of class. The idea of a universal social service, provided as a condition of citizenship rather than as a kind of poor relief, depends upon success in the struggle to overcome gross material deprivation. The contemporary definition of poverty has become increasingly a matter of relative rather than absolute levels of income (Donnison, 1978). Exclusion from commonly shared standards of life, and the stigma and restricted opportunities which arise from this. are now rightly interpreted as the contemporary meaning of poverty. Priority to the conditions of the worst off, including specific categories such as the single homeless and the one-parent family, and some general redistribution of income towards the lower paid are the means by which many problems could be resolved at their root rather than left to the palliatives of social work as a service of last resort.

We believe it is important that social workers should continue to pay attention to these structural and economic determinants of their conditions of work. Social work is not only about the alleviation of poverty or struggles against inequality, but these issues remain fundamental to it. A sociological approach should lead social workers not to an exclusively political analysis, but to distinguish in the complexity of their work those factors which are primarily economic in origin from those which are not. The connections between personal and structural approaches are too often broken in social work, with a consequent misidentification of problems in practice leading to a deep confusion of occupational identity. Good social work depends on there being a viable provision of basic income and services, just as good health depends on nutrition as much as on medicine. But social work is not only the material services: the two are connected, but not the same. Social work needs a better form of occupational organization in order to be generally a more effective pressure group for the redistribution of resources towards its clients, and specifically towards social work services themselves. This is not an alternative to 'non-material' forms of social work, but a precondition of them.

We now turn our attention to some recent developments within the welfare field which provide other indications for possible change in the factors shaping social work practice.

One important trend has been the emphasis on welfare rights. This can be understood to derive from the principle of citizenship, the generalization and extension of which has been one of the moving principles of political democratization and of the development of the welfare state. An aspect of this tendency has been the development of grass roots organizations such as claimants' unions and tenants' associations. The redefinition of welfare provision as a right or entitlement, as opposed to the somewhat paternalist and discretionary principle of charity, provides, at least, a procedural and formal move towards equality, however inadequate this may be in terms of substance and content. This is also true of the caring activities which take place inside families and which in limited instances are now recognized as *work*, such as the payment of foster parents and the provision of attendance allowances. The social worker as a quasi-legal adviser to clients, in negotiations with the labyrinthine welfare bureaucracy, is in a less controlling and stigmatizing relation to the client than is the case when the social worker is placed in the position of relieving officer. A client's claim is likely to be taken more seriously given this form of support, in the same way as legal representation enhances respect for defendants and trade union representation respect for employees.

These developments, if made more extensive and widespread, could be seen as a kind of 'calling the bluff' of the welfare state, ensuring that services are fully delivered, at least up to the limits to which there is provision in principle. Welfare rights activity may also put pressure on statutory welfare agencies to make explicit the basis for their exercise of discretion and to publicize their criteria of eligibility. Some people, however, have criticized the liberal assumptions of welfare advocacy, pointing out that it is an illusion to suppose that by providing formal legal recognition and engaging in negotiations on behalf of individuals one is necessarily conferring any substantive economic equality. These critics argue that such 'rights' are a mystification, conferring legitimacy on a system which denies rights in substance. It has also been argued that if 'citizenship is an achieved rather than an ascribed status' (Pinker, 1971, 200), and is enhanced by the exercise of it, then welfare rights advocacy *on behalf* of clients diminishes the client's status as citizen.

It is interesting to note that the welfare rights movement, like many other innovative developments in welfare, has been influenced by the American example, where the individualizing limitations of this form of advocacy are most marked (see Handler, 1973, 9–10). But it may be that the translation of a liberal model of welfare rights to a class society such as ours, and the taking up of welfare rights in the context of collectivistic organization, has more radical implications. Welfare rights advocacy which is undertaken by collective organizations, and which is closely linked to pressures on policy formation (for example, by pressure groups such as the Child Poverty Action Group) can be seen as part of a wider social movement towards greater equality of economic as well as legal citizenship. (See Turner, 1969 for a discussion of the way in which social movements may seek to redefine phenomena that have been seen as misfortunes, and get them viewed as matters of injustice.)

A second important development has been the increased emphasis on community, as an essential dimension of social work effectiveness. One aspect of this has been the attempt to involve members of the community in the caring process. Another has been support for community organization and community action directed at achieving change in the local environment or in the level of community provision. This is important in that it recognizes that collective self-help, and a mobilization of altruistic capacities, is essential if real help is to be offered to those most in need. Caring functions cannot be provided wholly by professionals, even of this were desirable. Greater community involvement in caring could increase community control over the available services. Handing over to public employees responsibility for dealing with major areas of dependency (for instance, old age, mental and physical illness and handicap) is alienating in at least two senses. First, the character of these kinds of dependency is not given, but is, at least in part, socially constructed. The non-dependent community is involved in defining the nature and implications of such states of dependency, but shelves responsibility for the consequences of such definitions by calling in professionals and relegating people to institutions to the extent that it does. Second, by relinquishing responsibility, the community also harms the possibility of control over services which, after all, anyone might need at some point in their lives. In this sense the non-dependant are also showing disregard for their own futures.

Community involvement in caring does not mean the same as leaving the families (that is usually female relatives) of the dependant to cope as best they can – which tends to be the reality of 'community care' at present (see Titmuss, 1968). It partly means ordinary human concern manifested by one neighbour to another; and partly the continuation and expansion of the voluntary principle through organized activity of various kinds – church activities, Age Concern, activities integrating the disabled and the fit and so on. There is room for far greater community participation than is currently the case in the day-to-day life of residential establishments of all kinds. Such involvement might bring to wider public attention the depressing and positively scandalous conditions that often obtain in such establishments (see, for instance Oswin, 1971; Morris, 1969; Townsend, 1962; Page and Clark, 1977, among others), and go some way towards changing such conditions. There is also scope for involving members of the community on a paid basis in work such as the fostering of old people and the mentally ill, and escort work with the handicapped. And there is room for expansion in the area of self-help groups – people with similar problems forming associations for mutual help – and for drawing attention to the problems they experience. All this would not reduce the need for public expenditure in the welfare field, but would increase the extent to which resources could be concentrated on those areas of work really requiring expertise. Richard Crossman (1976) was correct in his view that the spirit of voluntary altruism was necessary to, and compatible with, the provision of professional social services by the state.

A second important aspect of community work is in its political function, in helping to secure and extend the rights and powers of citizenship in a collective way for the members of neighbourhoods experiencing common problems or grievances. Possibly these may be problems of general deprivation, but equally they may be more specific, related to facilities for the young or housing management for example. This is a collective analogue of welfare rights and can equally be seen as a form of social redistribution, strengthening individual and social capacities which the secure and professionalized take for granted.

Both these dimensions are important. A lack of community involvement in social care is a structural fact about highly individualized market societies. The experience of geographical mobility, smaller family networks less able to provide support, and higher aspirations for the quality of life have led to a vast expansion of professionalized state services. However, it is clear that these cannot themselves provide all that is required, now or in the future, nor is the model of a professional service the only one that is appropriate in the provision of care and relationship. And on the political side, involvement by citizens in the provision of social goods (analogously to the trade unions' defence of the citizen in regard to the provision of 'private goods') is essential if the standards of public services are even to keep up with the growth of national resources, or improve relatively, or effect any measure of redistribution.

Just as with the 'welfare rights movement', there has been a substantial influence from the United States in the recent growth of a 'community' orientation in social work. The concept of welfare rights arises from a forceful interpretation of the liberal idea of individuals equal under the law. The idea of mobilizing community resources for the common good draws on a related liberal tradition of voluntary association. We have argued that the extension of access to legal services has a different effect in a society with powerful class organizations, compared with a society where these are relatively weak. Consider for example the great importance of trade unions in enabling their members to obtain rights under recent labour legislation. In the same way we would suggest that a more active and participatory mode of organization based on community groups will have a different meaning in a society where politics is already organized on class lines. The domination of local government in working-class areas by often oligarchic labour groups has sometimes stifled local initiative, and a greater range and vigour of community action in such neighbourhoods is desirable, even if sometimes unwelcome to political leaderships. It seems at present to be urban areas of transition or mixed population which demonstrate the greatest proliferation of community activity.

The question of social workers' involvement with the community reveals a major blind spot in the current debates about the social services. None of the available organizational models for social work offers a participatory role to the social service consumer. Managerialism and bureaucracy, professionalism and unionism alike assume that social workers are either state functionaries or are an autonomous corporate profession. There seems to be no conception that the social services could or should be more directly accountable to their clientele or neighbourhood, in the way that even a private professional has to be to some degree to his clients through the market, or in the way that a trade union official is accountable to his members. In the development of social services there seems to have been a total victory for the state, including the local state, with marginal concessions to consumers' or citizens' involvement through community health councils and other weak participatory machinery. While there may have been some convergence of interests between 'welfare professionals' and the working class in the enlargement of welfare services, there has been little or none in their actual mode of organization. The 'professionalism' of teachers and social workers, for example, constitutes a barrier against the influence of the clients and consumers of the services they provide. In this field there are, however, signs of stirring, with arguments being heard for a stronger voice for consumers of public services (for example, the Taylor Report recently advocated elected parent governors of schools). There has also been criticism of the system of patronage by which are appointed the many semi-autonomous government bodies (QUANGOs) which are one characteristic means of controlling public provision.

However, such notions of participatory democracy are at present mainly honoured only in rhetoric or at best in timid marginal experimentation. The general structuring of relations in the work context is one root source of this weakness. Because the organization of employees against capital and against the state is largely oppositional, unionism is adopted as the best strategy of defence in the context of our market system; hence other possible models for collective initiative, control and responsibility for production are relegated to a marginal or merely theoretical role. Even where proposals for workers' control or industrial democracy are canvassed, they are opposed by the organizations of capital and of the state bureaucracies and for the most part are given only ambivalent and lukewarm support by trade unions. A clearly defined defensive function is found preferable by unions to the blurred boundaries and possibly emasculating and compromising effects of participation. The control and disposition of capital as a possible political objective is generally thought at present to be well beyond the reach of workers, except through the indirect and remote machinery of the state apparatus or to some extent through the negative exercise of union sanctions. This defensive model of class relations, described in theoretical terms as 'corporatist' by Anderson (1968) and Nairn (1964) and in its everyday assumptions by Hoggart (1957), extends from the workplace to the full range of 'their' institutions, including the institutions of welfare. Working-class defensiveness and passivity in the workplace extends to these contexts too, so that council tenants, school parents, patients and clients tend, with occasional exceptions, to treat these as services provided *for* them, but not as potentially controlled *by* them. It is phenomena such as this induced passivity which render the concept of hegemony a useful one.

It is easier to envisage the practical arrangements that such an extension of consumer participation might involve than it is to imagine the conditions for a change of will regarding the extent of consumer participation, both on the part of the professionals and on the part of the working-class community. There could for instance be fifty per cent user representation on the committees running old people's homes and children's homes ('users' in both these cases would include the families of residents). Social services departments area teams could have management committees on which clients would be represented, as could the various committees in the department as a whole. Patients could have active representation, to an extent sufficient to give them an effective voice, in the running of hospitals. Such arrangements would give concrete recognition to the fact that without the consumer, without the patient, the client and the resident, social service organizations would not exist. Only by putting social workers at the service, and in the employ, of their clients, in more than a symbolic and pietistic sense, can the fundamental alienation of professional as well as managerial workers from their clients be resolved. This distance arises from differences of status, of power, of skill and frequently of income, and only where some power is transferred to the recipient of services can ideals of common membership in a community be realized.

One kind of obstacle to client involvement in effective participation in the services they receive is the stigmatizing model of client status that is associated with the cluster of ideas inherited from the poor law. Another is a conception of professionalism that sees decisions about the services to be provided as a matter for experts. A third obstacle is the bureaucratization and managerialism associated with expansion and reorganization of social services. Professionalism may be preferable to managerialism in its present form. But both professional and managerial approaches to social work purchase status and power at a high cost, both to the social worker and to the client. Part of the cost is the splitting off of caring capacities from the community to the specialist workers, whose burden is thereby made impossible. There is also a cost which comes from the adulteration of benign and helpful motives with elements of domination and resentment, as a result of the controlling and rationing components which remain part of the social work task. Again, more adequate provision of basic services on universalistic lines would lessen the necessity for bureaucratic regulation, and make the introduction of consumer and/or community involvement in the provision of social services more feasible.

Another difficulty in the way of social workers viewing themselves as accountable to the communities in which they work is that at present they often erect practical and conceptual barriers between themselves and their clients, not for reasons of professional aggrandizement, but by way of self-defence in a situation in which their working lives are often intolerable. Apart from the changes in basic provision which would ease matters, there are signs that where there is a shift in the mode of working from a privatized, individualized workload to more shared organization of work, (see Carter and Barter, 1972) it becomes possible to view clients differently and to be less defensive and more responsive to community demand. Nevertheless, one should not underestimate the possibility of conflicts of interest within the community, nor minimize the implications for the social worker's relations with clients and potential clients of the fact that inevitably there will still be 'soft policing' functions to be performed – notably compulsory admissions to residential care of various kinds.

Such changes as we have discussed would necessitate some thought about the kinds of skills and training regarded as appropriate for social workers. The tasks of the personal social services can be seen as falling into four categories:

(a) the provision of routine caring and supportive services of a non-expert kind, for example, supportive visiting, a range of domiciliary services, caring and supportive services for those in residential establishments;

(b) specialist skills, for example, different types of social work expertise (such as family counselling), occupational therapy, an expert service for the blind and deaf;

(c) the mobilization of community activity, including participation in decision making, in the running of welfare services, and involvement in voluntary and paid capacities, in the provision of caring services;

(d) engaging in pressure for policy change at local and national levels, backed by research, analysis and experiment undertaken by members of social services departments.

These functions are extremely dissimilar, and a major problem for the social services is the way in which the range of functions and duties have been increased by legislation while clients' demands on social services have grown. Some social workers do require professional skills, though of rather various kinds not necessarily found in the same person, but much social work requires little specialist skill – if any. The pursuit of professional recognition, and the burden of 'professional responsibility' placed on social workers by legislation and public opinion, seems to demand that all the work be defined as 'professional', even though the meaning of that term remains muddled. The range of tasks required of social workers, together with the vigorous controversies between different theoretical orientations in social work, have led training courses to take refuge in 'unitary' and 'integrated' approaches in an attempt to hold all this diversity together in some single framework. But this is often an exercise in merely 'naming of parts', and placing them on a single map, and does not in fact unify either the range of tasks within the field or the educational inputs that might best relate to them.

In particular, we think there is a lack of clarity about what those who emerge from a basic social work training with a CQSW are supposed to be able to offer. Can they offer a casework service to clients, or a capacity to work with groups, have they adequate knowledge of rights and entitlements, or what? It seems to us that, in reality, CQSW courses offer very little by way of a training in any kind of expertise or concrete skill, though the general education they provide is no doubt valuable, particularly to mature students who have hitherto been deprived of the opportunity of further education. Perhaps this lack of specialist skill is appropriate, given the large amount of work that local authority social workers have to do which calls for little more than commonsense, goodwill, and a reasonable degree of efficiency – work which tends to be undervalued by social workers themselves as 'not real social work' but which is nevertheless very valuable to those at the receiving end, if properly carried out. Social workers feel that they ought to be able to do more than 'routine tasks', yet they have neither the skill nor often the time to do so.

The influential 'generic' model of social work at present can be compared with general medical practice with the critical difference that the social worker unlike the general practitioner has almost no back-up services or specialists to whom he can refer clients. Within the department referral of difficult cases is usually to those defined as superior in authority and not necessarily more expert in knowledge. Consequently, questions of authority and responsibility are more salient in social work than they are in some related professions where expert opinion rather than hierarchical position provides the grounds for decision-making. The style of case supervision yields another example where often, it seems, a model of direction by the superior is used, rather than a model of expert advice which would require the social worker to take responsibility for his or her own cases. In our view, without the development of specialist areas of knowledge and skill, the profession of social work will remain confused and often overwhelmed by its excessive range of tasks and problems. Not only can a better service to clients be provided if there is a system of referral from the generic worker, but generic work itself requires specialist areas of practice and knowledge in which intellectual resources can be developed. The field cannot be expected to advance in knowledge or techniques, if everyone is working in an identically diffuse and all-encompassing way. It is worth noting to what extent work in the contemporary 'generic' era has in fact had to continue living on professional capital accumulated in the period when psychiatric social work, medical social work, child care and other specialisms were separate occupations.

One possible solution would be to define clearly the CQSW course as only a basic qualification providing a general preparation for social work practice. This would include an introduction to the range of client groups, and to factors affecting inter-personal, intra- and inter-organizational relationships. There would be a grounding in social structural factors bearing upon aspects of the world with which social workers have to deal, a familiarity with the most commonly used welfare legislation, and with the functions of the other agencies with which social workers most frequently liaise. Encouragement should be given to students to think about and analyse aspects of social work practice. Course tutors should maintain a much closer link with the field than is usual now, and this could be done through the appointment of part-time tutors the rest of whose time would be spent as practising social workers. Arrangements should be made whereby full-time tutors would spend a regular period of observation and/ or practice in a social work agency. It is a particular weakness of social work training at the present time that its college-based tutors are without real professional responsibility for their students' work in the field, and are in effect suspended half way between an academic and a professional role. There is some similarity with the role of college tutors in teacher-training, which has been criticized for similar reasons. Neither are in a strong position to be able to teach the actual skills which their students most need, and which, in our view should be the distinctive expertise of professional tutors.

Those students who had done this basic CQSW course would see themselves as offering a friendly and largely practical service in which the client's definition of a problem would be given more weight than is usually the case currently. Such social workers would constitute the majority of fieldworkers in any social services department. In addition, there would be a range of specialist social work training courses for those who wanted to go on to acquire special expertise in particular areas of social work, and these specialist areas would be represented in social services departments and other statutory and voluntary agencies. Specialist courses could be offered in each of the traditional social work skills – casework/therapeutic counselling, group work and community work. Welfare rights, residential social work and social work research might be other areas for specialist courses. In addition, other bases for specialization might well include youth work, psychiatric social work, work with the deaf and educational social work. These could possibly be run as shorter courses or be organized on an in-service training model.

In order for such further specialist training to be worthwhile for social workers, attention would have to be given to the structure of career opportunities, particularly in social service departments. At present, it is usual for social workers to practise in the field for only a few years before they are promoted and cease to carry a caseload. Seniority is thus defined in managerial, not professional terms. Seniority in fields other than social work is usually based on the exercise of professional skill. For example, in law, medicine, academic study, architecture and psychoanalysis, there is an institutionalized requirement for a continuing engagement by each professional in the most difficult kinds of primary work. Some different professional structure will therefore be needed, whereby advancement can take place to positions of professional as well as managerial seniority, to consultant as well as senior and directorial roles. This would also bring about some change in the ethos of social work, giving a greater solidity and confidence to the knowledge-base from which the work is handled.

The relationship between the specialist workers and the basic grade social worker would vary. One imagines that the specialist caseworker would get most of her referrals from basic grade social workers, while group and community workers, for instance, would be able to take more initiative in starting groups and community projects and activities. The welfare rights expert would often be used as a consultant by social workers, but might in addition take up particular cases which were thought to demand extended professional work. A specialist in social work research would probably be based in the research and development section, but should, in our view, be a key person in developing the capacity of social work teams for analysing their work, and collecting information to be used in generating pressure for change.

The development of a more defined and authentic professional knowledge would also give rise to wider roles for social workers with special skill, not only in advising generic social workers, but in advising others not professionally qualified who are working in community services. One current ambition for professional social work is to have it take over, in time, the whole field of social service provision, by steadily training a higher proportion of social workers and devising 'sub-professional' qualifications for their assistants. We think this is undesirable and impracticable, and we support, on the contrary, the wider involvement of community resources and voluntary activity in social care. Potentially such a strategy could surely enhance rather than diminish the role of the professionally trained, since what they should have to offer to community groups, foster-parents adult fosterers, or residential institutions, for example, is a helping capacity based on their recognized knowledge and skill. Such advisory services are quite compatible with a more democratic and self-active ideal of community provision.

We have tried to identify some of the major material and organizational constraints impeding the practice of social work at the present time. We hold that a sociological analysis of social work should clarify such constraints, and enable the problems facing social workers to be related to the historical development of the social services. While such analysis does not of itself solve any problems, it should enable more realistic and soundly based judgements to be made about future policy. Sociological approaches to social work have recently come under increasing criticism, notably from the Central Council for Education and Training in Social Work (Wright, 1977, 7), and have been blamed for the undermining of established beliefs and for introducing unduly political attitudes into training schools and among practising social workers. We consider such criticism to be misconceived. Only, in our view, through a more discriminating and sociologically based understanding of social work can the state of crisis and confusion that endemically faces social workers be resolved.

References

(all works cited are published in London unless otherwise stated)

Anderson, P. 1965: Origins of the present crisis. In Anderson, P. and Blackburn, R., *Towards socialism*, Fontana.
1968: Components of the national culture. *New Left Review* 50 (July–August).
1974a: *Passages from antiquity to feudalism*. New Left Books.
1974b: *Lineages of the absolutist state*. New Left Books.
Appleby, A. B. 1975: Agrarian capitalism or seigneurial reaction? *American Historical Review* 80.
Aschrott, P. F. 1902: *The English poor law system, past and present*, 2nd edn. by H. Preston Thomas. Knight.
Aydelotte, F. 1913: *Elizabethan rogues and vagabonds*. Oxford University Press.
BASW Working Party Report 1977: *The social work task*. Pamphlet no. 361, Birmingham.
Badcock, C. R. 1975: *Levi-Strauss: structuralism and sociological theory*. Hutchinson.
Bailey, R. and Brake, M. (eds) 1975: *Radical Social Work*. Arnold.
Bailward, W. A. 1907: The Charity Organisation Society. *Quarterly Review* 206, 57–76.
Bains (chairman) 1972: *The new local authorities: management and structure*. Report of a study group appointed jointly by the Secretary of State for the Environment and local authority associations to examine management principles and structures in local government at both elected member and officer levels.
Ball, N. 1963: *Her Majesty's Inspectorate, 1839–1849*. Edinburgh: Oliver & Boyd.
Bannatyne, K. V. 1902: The place and training of volunteers in charitable work. *Charity Organisation Review* (June).
Baruch, G. and Treacher, A. 1978: *Psychiatry observed*. Routledge.
Baugh, D. A. 1975: The cost of poor relief in southeast England, 1790–1834. *Economic History Review* 28.
Beales, H. L. 1931: The New Poor Law. *History* 15.

1945: *The making of social policy.* Oxford University Press.

1948: The passing of the Poor Law. *Political Quarterly* 9.

Beattie, J. M. 1974: Pattern of crime in England, 1660–1800. *Past and Present* 62.

Beier, A. L. 1974: Vagrants and the social order in Elizabethan England. *Past and Present* 64.

1976: Rejoinder. *Past and Present* 71.

Bell, P. 1972: *Social reform and social structure in Victorian England: a handlist of university theses.* Leicester: Victorian Studies Centre.

Bennet, W. J. E. 1846: *Crime and education: the duty of the state therein.* Cleeve.

Berger, J. 1967: *A fortunate man: the story of a country doctor.* Allen Lane.

Bessell, B. 1976: Quality not quantity is our greatest need. *Community Care* 6 (October).

Beveridge Report 1942: Social insurance and allied services. HMSO, Cmd. 6404.

Beveridge, W. H. 1948: *Voluntary action: a report on methods of social advance.* Allen and Unwin.

Bibby, P. 1976: Can colleges educate and train social workers? *Probation Journal* 23, 2–7.

Birch, R. C. 1974: *The shaping of the welfare state.* Longman.

Blaug, M. 1963: The myth of the old poor law and the making of the new. *Journal of Economic History* 23, reprinted Smout (1974), ch. 6.

1964: The Poor Law Report re-examined. *Journal of Economic History* 24.

Blencoe, R. 1832: Memoir (selections). *History of Childhood Quarterly* 2.

Bloch, M. 1940: *Feudal society.* 2 vols, Routledge (1965).

Bochel, D. 1976: *Probation and after-care: its development in England and Wales.* Edinburgh and London: Scottish Academic Press.

Bosanquet, B. (ed.) 1895: *Aspects of the social problem.* Macmillan.

Bosanquet, B. 1901: Meaning of social work. *International Journal of Ethics* 11.

1907: *The social criterion,* Blackwood.

1916: The philosophy of casework. *Charity Organisation Review* 39.

Bosanquet, H. (neé Dendy) 1893: The industrial residuum. *Economic Journal* 111.

1896: *Rich and poor.* Macmillan.

1897: Psychology of social progress. *International Journal of Ethics* 7.

1902: *The strength of the people.* Macmillan.

1906: *The Family*. Macmillan.

1914: *Social work in London*. Murray.

Bossy, J. 1977: Holiness and society. *Past and Present* 75.

Bowlby, J. **1952:** *Maternal care and mental health*. World Health Organization.

Braithwaite, W. J. 1957: *Lloyd George's ambulance wagon: being the memoirs of W. J. Braithwaite, 1911–12* (ed.) with an introduction by Sir H. Bunbury KCB and with a commentary by Richard Titmuss. Methuen.

Brill, M. 1972: The local authority social worker. In Jones K. (ed.), *The yearbook of social policy in Britain, 1971*, Routledge.

Bruce, M. 1961: *The coming of the welfare state*. Batsford.

1973: *The rise of the welfare state: English social policy, 1601–1971*. Weidenfeld.

Busfield, J. 1974: Family ideology and family pathology. In Armistead N. (ed.), *Reconstructing social psychology*, Penguin.

CCETSW 1975: *A new form of training: the Certificate in Social Service*. CCETSW paper 9·1.

1976: *The Certificate in Social Service: a guide to planning*. CCETSW paper 9·2.

1977: *Guidelines for courses leading to the certificate of qualification in social work CQSW*. CCETSW paper 15·1.

Cannan, C. 1972: Social workers: training and professionalism. In Pateman T. (ed.), *Countercourse – a handbook for course criticism*, Penguin.

Carter, D. and Barter, J. 1972: Climbing off the Fence. *Social Work Today*, 3, 10.

Crossman, R. H. S. 1976: The role of the volunteer in the modern social services. In Halsey A. H. (ed.), *Traditions of social policy*, Oxford: Blackwell.

Chamberlain, J. 1895: Old-age pensions and friendly societies. *National Review* 24, 592–615.

Chamblis, W. J. 1964: Sociological analysis of the law of vagrancy. *Social Problems* 12.

Charity Organization Society 1898: 'First report of the Committee on training'. *Occasional Paper*, 11, 2nd series.

Checkland, S. G. and E. O. A. (eds) 1974: *The Poor Law Report of 1834*. Penguin.

Clark, P. and Slack, P. 1976: *English towns in transition, 1500–1700*. Oxford University Press.

Clarke, J. 1971: An analysis of crisis management by mental welfare officers *British Journal of Social Work* 1(1).

1975: *The three R's — repression, rescue and rehabilitation.* Centre for Contemporary Cultural Studies, stencilled occasional paper.

1976: Personal troubles, professional problems or political contradictions? *Probe* 7, published by NAPO Members Action Group.

1979: Social democratic delinquents and Fabian families: a background to the 1969 Children and Young Persons Act. In Fitzgerald, M. *et al.* (eds)., *Permissiveness and control,* 1979, Macmillan.

Cockburn, C. 1977: *The local state: management of cities and people.* Pluto Press.

Cohen, S. 1975: It's all right for you to talk. In Bailey and Brake (1975).

Collins, R. 1972: A conflict theory of sexual stratification. In Dreitzel H. P. (ed.) *Family marriage and the struggle of the sexes,* Macmillan.

Cooper, D. 1971: *The death of the family.* Allen Lane.

Cormack, U. 1964: The last fifty years. In New Barnett Papers, *The family in modern society,* Oxford.

1968: The welfare state — the formative years, 1905–9, in Lochhead, A. V. S. (ed.), *A reader in social administration,* Constable.

Corner, E. P. 1959: *Morals and the social worker.* Report of the Conference, September 1959, Association of Social Workers.

Corrigan, P. 1976: The welfare state as an arena of class struggle. *Marxism Today* (March).

1977a: Feudal relics or capitalist monuments? *Sociology* 11.

1977b: State formation and moral regulation in 19th-Century Britain. Unpublished DPhil (Durham).

1978: *State formation.* Macmillan.

1979: *State servants.* Forthcoming.

Corrigan, P. and Gillespie, V. 1974: *Class struggle, social literacy and idle time: the provision of public libraries.* Brighton: Labour History Monographs (1977).

Corrigan, P. and Leonard, P. 1978: *Social work practice under capitalism: a marxist approach.* Macmillan.

Corrigan, P, Ramsay, H. and Sayer, D. 1977: *The state as a relation of production.* Paper to British Sociological Association Conference.

1978: *Socialist construction and marxist theory.* Macmillan.

Cox, C. B. and Boyson, R. (eds) 1977: *Black paper.* Temple Smith.

Cullen, A. J. 1975: *The statistical movement in early Victorian England.* Hassocks: Harvester Press.

Curtis (chairman) 1946: *Report of the care of children committee.* HMSO, Cmd. 6922.

Davis, K. 1938: Mental hygiene and the class structure. *Psychiatry* 1.

Deutscher, I. 1954: *The prophet armed: Trotsky 1879–1921.* Oxford University Press.

De Schweinitz, K. 1947: *England's road to social security 1349–1947.* Philadelphia: University of Pennsylvania.

Dicey, A. V. 1867: The balance of classes. In *Essays on Reform.*
  1905: *Lectures on the relation between law and public opinion in England during the nineteenth century.* Macmillan.
  1914: *Introduction to the second edition of Lectures.* ... Re-issued as a PaperMac, Macmillan (1962).

Digby, A. 1975: The labour market and the continuity of social policy after 1834. *Economic History Review* 28.
  1976: The rural poor law. In Fraser (1976), ch. 7.

Ditton, J. 1976: Perks, pilferage and the fiddle: the historical structure of invisible wages. *Theory and Society* 4.

Donnison, D. 1978: 'Research for policy'. In Bulmer, M. (ed.), *Social Policy Research*, MacMillan.

Eden, F. M. 1797: *The state of the poor.* ... 3 vols, reprinted Cass (1976).

Ewins, D. 1974: The origins of the compulsory commitment provisions of the mental health act, 1959. MA dissertation, University of Sheffield.

Elton, G. R. 1953a: *The Tudor Revolution in government.* Cambridge University Press.
  1953b: An early Tudor poor law. *Economic History Review* 6.
  1972: *Policy and police: the enforcement of the Reformation in the age of Thomas Cromwell.* Cambridge University Press.
  1973: *Reform and renewal: Thomas Cromwell and the Commonweal.* Cambridge University Press.

Englander, D. 1977: *The diary of Fred Knee.* Society for the Study of Labour History, Aids to Research no. 3.

Evans, E. J. 1978: *Social policy 1830–1914: individualism, collectivism and the origins of the welfare state.* Routledge.

Finer, S. E. 1952: *Life and times of Sir Edwin Chadwick.* Methuen.

Finer, (chairman) 1974: *Report of the committee on one-parent families.* Cmnd. 5629–I, 2 vols.

Finlayson, G. B. A. M. 1969: *England in the eighteen thirties: decade of reform.* Arnold.

Fish, S. 1528: *The supplication of beggars.* Reprinted Primary Publications (1970).

Fletcher, J. 1851 : *Education: national, voluntary and free*. Ridgeway.

Flinn, M. W. 1961 : The Poor Employment Act, 1918. *Economic History Review* 14.

  1971 : Policy of 'public works'. *New Society*, 18 November.

  1976 : Medical services. In Fraser (1976), ch. 2.

Forder, A. (ed.) 1971 : *Penelope Hall's social services of modern Britain*. Routledge.

Foster, J. 1966 : Nineteenth-century towns: a class dimension. In Dyos, H. J., *Study of urban history*, Arnold, reprinted Smout (1974), ch. 8.

  1974 : *Class struggle and the industrial revolution*. Weidenfeld, reprinted Methuen (1977).

Fraser, D. 1973 : *Evolution of the British welfare state*. Macmillan.

Fraser, D. (ed.) 1976 : *The New Poor Law in the nineteenth century*. Macmillan.

Galper, J. H. 1975 : *The politics of the social services*. New Jersey: Prentice Hall.

Gardiner, R. K. and Judd, H. O. 1959 : *The development of social administration*. Oxford University Press.

George, D. 1931 : *England in transition: life and work in the eighteenth century*. Revised edn, Penguin (1953).

Geras, N. 1972 : Althusser's marxism: an assessment and an account. *New Left Review* 71 (January–February).

Gettleman, M. E. 1974 : The whig interpretation of social welfare history. *Smith College Studies in Social Work* 44 149–57.

Gilbert, A. D. 1976 : *Religion and society in industrial England: church, chapel and social change, 1740–1914*. Longmans.

Gilbert, B. B. 1965 : The British National Insurance Act of 1911 and the commercial insurance lobby. *Journal of British Studies* 4, 127–48.

  1966 : *The evolution of national insurance in Great Britain: origins of the welfare state*. Michael Joseph.

Goldthorpe, J. 1964 : The development of social policy in England 1800–1914. *Transactions of the Fifth World Congress of Sociology* 4.

Goldthorpe, J. E. and Lockwood, D. 1963 : Affluence and the British class structure. *Sociological Review* 2 (July).

Gosden, P. H. J. H. 1961 : *The Friendly Societies in England, 1815–75*. Manchester University Press.

  1973 : *Self-help: voluntary associations in the nineteenth century*. Batsford.

Gould, J. *et al.* 1977 : *The attack on higher education: marxism and radical penetration*. Institute for the Study of Conflict.

Gow, H. J. 1900: Methods of training II. *Charity Organisation Review* 8, 109–11.

Gowers, Sir E. 1948: *Plain Words*. HMSO.

Gray, R. Q. 1976: Bourgeois hegemony in Victorian Britain. In Bloomfield, J., *Papers on class, hegemony and party*, Lawrence and Wishart (1977).

1978: *State and society in nineteenth-century Britain*. Croom Helm.

Hair, P. E. H. 1968: Mortality from violence in Britain's coal mines 1800–1850. *Economic History Review* 21.

Halevy, E. 1919: A policy of social peace in England. In Halevy (1965).

1922: The present state of the social question in England. In Halevy (1965).

1923: *The liberal awakening, 1815–1830*. Benn (1949).

1965: *The era of tyrannies*, (ed.) R. K. Webb. Allen Lane.

Hall, S. Critcher, C. Jefferson, T. Clarke, J. and Roberts, B. 1978: *Policing the crisis*. Macmillan.

Hallam, R. 1974: The production of poverty. *Economy and Society* 3(4).

Halmos, P. 1965: *The faith of the counsellors*. Constable.

Hammen, O. J. 1972: Marx and the agrarian question. *American Historical Review* 77.

Handler, J. 1973: *The coercive social worker*. Chicago: Rand McNally.

Harris, J. S. 1955: *British government inspection*. Stevens.

Harris, J. 1977: *William Beveridge: a biography*. Oxford: Clarendon Press.

Harris, R. W. 1946: *National health insurance in Great Britain 1911–46*. Allen and Unwin.

Harrison, B. 1971: *Drink and the Victorians: the temperance question in England 1815–1872*. Faber.

Hay D. 1975a: Property, authority and the criminal law. In Hay (1975c).

1975b: Poaching and the game laws. ... In Hay (1975c).

1975c: *Albion's fatal tree: crime and society in eighteenth-century England*. Allen Lane.

Hay, J. R. 1975: *The origins of the liberal welfare reforms, 1906–1914*. Macmillan.

Hennock, E. P. 1968: Social security: a system emerges. *New Society* 7 March.

Henriques, U. 1967: Bastardy and the New Poor Law. *Past and Present* 37.

1968: How cruel was the Victorian poor law? *Historical Journal* 11.

Heraud, B. J. 1967: *Teaching of sociology in professional social work courses*. Unpublished paper given to Sociology Teachers section of the BSA.

Heywood, J. and Allen, B. 1971: *Financial help in social work*. Manchester University Press.

Heywood, J. 1964: *An introduction to teaching casework skills*. Routledge.

Hill, C. 1967: *Reformation to industrial revolution, 1530–1780*. Weidenfeld, reprinted Penguin (1969).

1972: *The world turned upside down*. Temple Smith.

Hilton, R. 1973: *Bondmen made free*. Temple Smith, reprinted Methuen (1977).

Hintze, O. 1897: The state in historical perspective. In Bendix, R., *State and society: a reader*, revised edn, California University Press.

1975: *Historical essays*. New York: Oxford University Press.

Hobsbawm, E. J. 1968: *Industry and empire, from 1750 to the present day*, Weidenfeld, Penguin (1969).

1975: *The age of capital, 1848–1875*. Weidenfeld.

Hobson, J. A. 1909: *The crisis of liberalism*. P. S. King.

Hoggart, R. 1957: *The uses of literacy*. Chatto.

Holgate, E. and Keidan, O. 1975: The personal social services. In Mays J., Forder A. and Keidan O. (eds), Penelope Hall's *Social Services of England and Wales*, revised edn, Routledge.

Holton, R. 1976: *British syndicalism 1900–14: myths realities*. Pluto.

Home Office 1965: *The child, the family and the young offender*. HMSO, Cmnd. 2742, Parliamentary Accounts & Papers, XXIX, 193–206.

1968: *Children in trouble*. White Paper, HMSO, Cmnd. 3601.

Hoskins, W. G. 1976: *The age of plunder: the England of Henry VIII, 1500–1547*. Longman.

Hunt, E. H. 1972: How mobile was labour in nineteenth-century Britain? *Exeter Papers in Economic History* 6.

1973: *Regional wage variation in Britain 1850–1914*, Oxford: Clarendon Press.

Hurstfield, J. 1973: *Freedom, corruption and government in Elizabethan England*. Cape.

Hurt, J. S. 1972: *Education in evolution*. Paladin.

Hutchins, B. L. 1913: *Conflicting ideals: two sides of woman's question*. T. Murphy.

Huzel, J. P. 1969: Malthus, the poor law and population in early nineteenth-century England. *Economic History Review* 22.

Ingleby Committee 1960: *Report of the committee on children and young persons.* HMSO, Cmnd. 1191.

Inglis, B. 1972: *Poverty and the industrial revolution.* Revised edn Panther.

Irvine, E. E. 1954: Research into problem families. *British Journal of Psychiatric Social Work* 9.

Johnson, R. 1970: Educational policy and social control in early Victorian England. *Past and Present* 49.

1976a: Notes on the schooling of the English working class 1780–1850. In Dale, R., *Schooling and Capitalism*, Routledge.

1976b: Barrington Moore, Perry Anderson and English social development. *Working Papers in Cultural Studies* 9.

Johnston, T. 1946: *History of the working classes in Scotland.* Reprinted, Wakefield: E.P. Publishing (1974).

Jones, C. 1976: The foundation of social work education. *Working Papers in Sociology* 11, University of Durham.

1977: An analysis of the development of social work and social work education 1869–1977. Submitted PhD thesis, University of Durham.

Jones, D. V. 1974: Crime, protest and community in nineteenth-century Wales. *Llafur* 1.

1976: The second Rebecca riots. *Llafur* 2.

1977: SSRC project: crime in Welsh communities in the nineteenth century. *Social History* 4.

Jones, H. (ed.) 1975: *Towards a new social work.* Routledge.

Jones, K. 1972: *A history of the mental health service.* Routledge.

Jordan, B. 1974: *Poor parents.* Routledge.

Jordan, W. J. O. 1976: *Freedom and the welfare state.* Routledge.

Jordan, W. K. 1959: *Philanthropy in England, 1480–1660.* Allen and Unwin.

Kay-Schuttleworth, J. P. 1853: *Public education.* Longman.

Keith-Lucas, A. 1953: The political theory implicit in social casework theory. *American Political Science Review* 47, 1076–91.

Kendall, K. 1950: New goals for social work education. *5th International Conference of Schools of Social Work.* Paris.

Kirkman Gray B. 1908: *Philanthropy and the state, or social politics.* Kirkman Gray, E. and Hutchins, B. L. King.

Kornreich, B. 1978: A critique of social work education. *Bulletin of Social Policy* 1.

Lafitte, R. 1974: The relief function. In Brow, M. J., *Social issues and the social services*, Knight.

Laing, R. D. 1971: *The politics of the family.* Tavistock.

Laski, H. J. 1931: *The limitations of the expert.* Fabian Tract 235.

Lee, J. M. 1974: Central capability. In Chapman, B. and Potter, A., *WJMM*, Manchester University Press, ch. 10.

Leonard, P. 1975: Towards a paradigm for radical practice. In Bailey and Brake (1975).

Leubuscher, C. 1946: Training for social service as a branch of university education. In Nuffield College *Training for Social Work*, Oxford University Press.

Levy, S. L. 1943: *Nassau W. Senior, 1790–1846.* Reprinted, Newton Abbot: David and Charles (1970).

Lewis, R. 1977: Artful dodgers of the world – unite? In Cox and Boyson (1977).

Lezonick, W. 1974: Karl Marx and enclosures in England. *Review of Radical Political Economics* 6.

Lindsay, J. 1975: *The Scottish poor law ... 1745–1845.* Ilfracombe: Stockwell.

Linebaugh, P. 1972: Eighteenth-century crime. *Bulletin of the Society for the Study of Labour History* 25.
   1975: The Tyburn riot. In Hay (1975c), ch. 2.
   1976: Karl Marx, the theft of wood and working-class composition. *Crime and Social Justice* 6.

Llewellyn, A. 1972: *The Decade of reform, the 1830s.* Newton Abbot: David and Charles.

Loades, D. M. 1974: *Politics and the nation, 1450–1660: obedience, resistance and public order.* Fontana.

Loch, C. S. 1890: *Charity Organization.* Swan Sonnenschein.
   1892: The confusion in medical charities *Nineteenth Century* (August), 298–310.
   1898: Poor relief in Scotland, 1791–1891. *Journal of the Royal Statistical Society* 61.
   1906: Introduction, *Annual Charities Register and Digest* (15th edn). Longmans.
   1910: *Charity and social life.* Macmillan.
   1923: *A great ideal and its champion.* Allen and Unwin.

Loch, C. S. (ed.) 1904: *Methods of social advance.* Macmillan.

Longmate, N. 1974: *The workhouse.* Temple Smith.

Lubenow, W. C. 1971: *The politics of government growth.* Newton Abbot: David and Charles.

McCloskey, D. 1973: New perspectives on the old poor law. *Explorations in Economic History* 10.

McCord, N. 1976: The poor law and philanthropy. In Fraser (1976).

McDougall, K. 1972: BASW: The British Association of Social

Workers. In Jones, K. (ed.), *The year book of social policy in Britain 1971*, Routledge.

McLennan, G. Molina, V. and Peters, R. 1977: Althusser's theory of ideology. In *Cultural Studies* 10 (1977), Birmingham.

MacDonald, D. F. 1976: *The state and the trade unions*. Macmillan.

Mandell, B. R. 1975: *Welfare in America: controlling the 'dangerous classes'* – *the handout as a form of social control*. Englewood Cliffs (New Jersey): Prentice Hall.

Mantoux, P. 1928: *The industrial revolution in the eighteenth century*. Reprinted Methuen (1964).

Marshall, T. H. 1946: Basic training for all types of social work. In Nuffield College *Training for Social Work*, Oxford University Press.

1963: Citizenship and social class. In *Sociology at the crossroads; and other essays*, Heinemann.

1965: *Social policy*. Revised edns (1967, 1970 and 1975) Hutchinson.

Martin, E. W. 1972: *Comparative development in social welfare*. Routledge.

Martin, I. 1971: *From workhouse to welfare*. Penguin.

Marx, K. 1842: Debates on the law of the theft of wood. *Collected Works* 1.

1858: *Grundrisse*. Penguin (1973).

1867: *Capital, I*. Moscow: Progress Publications (1967).

1871: *The civil war in France*. Peking: Foreign Languages P. (1970).

Masterman, L. 1939: *C. F. G. Masterman a biography*. Nicholson.

Mayer, H. 1959: Marx, Engels and the politics of the peasantry. *Etudes de Marxologie* 3.

Mayer, J. E. and Timms, N. 1970: *The client speaks*. Routledge.

Mayo M. 1975: Community development: a radical alternative? In Bailey and Brake (1975).

Mays, J. B. 1954: *Growing up in the city*. Liverpool University Press.

1959: *On the threshold of delinquency*. Liverpool University Press.

Mencher, S. 1961: The changing balance of status and contract in assistance policy. Reprinted in Gilbert, N. and Specht, H. (eds), *The emergences of social welfare and social work*, Itasca, Illinois: F. E. Peacock.

Mess, H. A. *et al.* 1948: *Voluntary social service since 1918*. Gertrude Williams (ed.). Routledge.

Midwinter, E. C. 1968: *Victorian social reform*. Longman.

Middleton, C. 1974: Sexual inequality and stratification theory. In Parkin, F. (ed.), *The social analysis of class structure*, Tavistock.

Middleton, N. 1971: *When family failed*. Gollancz.

Mills, J. S. 1840: On Coleridge. In his *On Bentham and Coleridge*, F. R. Leavis (1950), Chatto.

Mishra, R. 1975: Marx and welfare. *Sociological Review* 23.
  1977: *Society and social policy: theoretical perspective on welfare.* Macmillan.

Mitchell, J. 1974: *Psychoanalysis and feminism*, Allen Lane.

Mitchison, R. 1974: The making of the old Scottish poor law. *Past and Present* 63.

Moore, B. 1966: *Social origins of dictatorship and democracy*, Penguin (1969).

Morris, P. 1969: *Put away*. Routledge.

Munday, B. 1972: What is happening to social work students. *Social Work Today* 3(6).

Nairn, T. 1964: Anatomy of the Labour Party. *New Left Review* 27 (September–October).

Newman, G. 1975: Anti-French propaganda and British liberal nationalism. *Victorian Studies* 18.

Nicholls, G. 1898: *A history of the English poor law*, 3rd vol. by MacKay, T. revised edn, Willinck, H. G., 3 vols, King.

Olin Wright, E. 1976: Class boundaries in advanced capitalist societies. *New Left Review* 98.

Oswin, M. 1971: *The empty hours*. Allen Lane.

Owen, D. 1965: *English philanthropy 1660–1960*. Cambridge, Mass.: Harvard University Press.

Oxley, G. W. 1973: *Poor relief in England and Wales 1601–1834*. Newton Abbot: David and Charles.

Page, R. and Clark, G. A. 1977: *Who cares?* National Children's Bureau.

Parry, N. C. A. and Johnson, D. 1974: *Sexual divisions in lifestyle and leisure*. Paper given at the British Sociological Association Annual Conference (1974).

Parry, N. C. A. and J. 1974: The teachers and professionalism: the failure of an occupational strategy. In Flude, M. and Ahier, J., *Educability, schools and ideology*, Croom Helm.
  1976: *The rise of the medical profession: a study of collective social mobility*. Croom Helm.
  1977: Professionalism and unionism: aspects of class conflict in the national Health Service. *Sociological Review* 25, 4.

Parsons, T. 1943: The kinship system of the contemporary United States. In *Essays in Sociological Theory* (1964), Free Press of Glencoe.

Paul, W. 1917: *The state: its origin and function*. Glasgow: Socialist Labour.

Pearson, G. 1974: Prisons of love: the reification of the family in family therapy. In Armistead, N. (ed.), *Reconstructing social psychology*, Penguin.
1975: *The deviant imagination*. Macmillan.
1976: Making social workers. In Bailey and Brake (1975).
Philp, A. F. and Timms, N. 1957: *The problem of 'the problem family'*. Family Service Units.
Pinker, R. 1971: *Social theory and social policy*. Heinemann.
Piven, F. F. and Cloward, R. 1974: *Regulating and poor*. Revised edn, Tavistock.
Pollard, S. 1963: Factory discipline in the industrial revolution. *Economic History Review* 16.
1965: *The Genesis of modern management*. Penguin, (1971).
Pound, J. 1971: *Poverty and vagrancy in Tudor England*. Longman.
1976: Comment, *Past and Present* 71.
Ramsay, H. 1977: Cycles of control: worker participation in sociological and historical perspective. *Sociology* 11.
Reid, D. A. 1976: The decline of 'Saint Monday' 1766 to 1876. *Past and Present* 71.
Rex, J. 1961: *Key problems of sociological theory*. Routledge.
Rex, J. and Moore, R. 1967: *Race, community and conflict*. Oxford University Press.
Reynolds, S. and Woolley, B. T. 1911: *Seems so! a working-class view of politics*. Macmillan.
Richardson, J. 1974: *Local historians encyclopedia*. New Barnet: Historical Publications.
Roberts, D. 1960: *Victorian origins of the British welfare state*. Yale University Press.
Robertshaw, P. and Curtin, C. A. 1977: Legal definitions of the family: an historical and sociological exploration. *Sociological Review* 25.
Rodgers, B. N. and Stevenson, J. 1973: *A new Portrait of social work*. Heinemann.
Rogers, F. W. 1971: Gateshead and the Public Health Act of 1848. *Archeologia Aeliana* 49.
Rooff, M. 1972: *A hundred years of family welfare*. Michael Joseph.
Rose, H. and Jakubowicz, A. 1978: The rise and fall of welfare rights. *New Society*, 28 September.
Rose, M. 1970: The anti-poor law agitation. In Ward (1970), ch. 3.
1971: *The English poor law 1780–1930*. Newton Abbot: David and Charles.
1972: *The relief of poverty 1834–1914*. Macmillan.

Rowbottom, R., Hey, A. and Billis, D. 1974: *Social services departments*. Social Services Organization Research Unit, BIOSS, Heinemann.

Royal Commission on the Poor Laws 1834: *The poor law report.* Corrected edn, S. G. and E. O. A. Checkland, Penguin (1974).

Rutter, M. 1972: *Maternal deprivation reassessed*. Penguin.

Sabine, G. H. 1951: *A history of political theory*. George Harrap.

Sainty, J. C. (ed.) 1972: *Treasury officials, 1660–1870.*
1973: *Officials of the secretaries of state, 1660–1872.*
1974: *Officials of the Board of Trade, 1660–1870.*
1975: *Admiralty officials, 1660–1870.*

Samaha, J. 1974: *Law and order in historical perspective: the case of Elizabethan Essex*. Academic Press.

Satyamurti, C. 1978: *Continuity and change in the role of local authority social workers, 1970–72*. Unpublished PhD dissertation, University of London.

Saville, J. 1957: The welfare state: an historical approach. *New Reasoner* 3.
1969: Primitive accumulation and early industrialixation in Britain. *Socialist Register.*

Scott, W. 1969: Professional employees in a bureaucratic structure: social work. In Etzioni, A. (ed.), *The semi-professions and their organixation*, New York: Free Press.

Scull, A. T. 1975: *Museums of madness: the social organization of insanity in nineteenth-century England*. PhD dissertation, University of Princeton.

Searle, G. R. 1971: *The quest for national efficiency a study in British politics and political thought, 1899–1914*. Oxford: Blackwell.

Seebohm (Chairman) 1968: *Report of the committee on local authority and allied personal social services*. HMSO, Cmnd. 3703.

Seed, P. 1973: *The expansion of social work in Great Britain*. Routledge.

Semmel, B. 1960: *Imperialism and social reform: English social imperial thought 1895–1914*. Allen and Unwin.

Shepherd, M. A. 1977: Lunacy and labour. *Bulletin of the Society for the Study of Labour History* 34.

Silcock, T. H. 1950: Training social workers in universities. *Universities Quarterly* 4, 168–76.

Simmel, G. 1950: Superordination and subordination. In Wolff, K. H. (ed.), *The sociology of George Simmel*, Free Press of Glencoe.

Slack, P. 1974: Vagrants and vagrancy in England 1598–1664. *Economic History Review* 27.

Slater, G. 1930: *Poverty and the state*. Constable.

Smith, M. J. 1953: *Professional education for social work in Britain: an historical account*. Family Welfare Association.

Smout. T. C. 1969: *A history of the Scottish people 1560–1830*. Fontana.

Smout, T. C. and Flinn, M. W. 1974: *Essays in social history*. Oxford: Clarendon Press.

Stedman-Jones, G. 1971: *Outcast London*. Oxford: Clarendon Press.

Stein, H. D. 1968: Professions and universities. *Journal of Education for Social Work* 4, 53–65.

Stevenson, O. 1973: Claimant or client? a social worker's view of the Supplementary Benefits Commission. Allen and Unwin.

 1976: Some dilemmas in social work education. *Oxford Review of Education* 2, 149–55.

Stratton, J. Y. 1872: Methods of improving the labouring classes by altering the conditions of poor relief and providing them with a system of insurance through the post office. *Journal of the Royal Agricultural Society of England*, n.s. 8.

Strayer, J. R. 1977: *On the medieval origins of the modern state*. Princeton University Press.

Supple, B. 1974: Legislation and virtue: an essay on working class self-help and the state in the early nineteenth century. In *Historical perspectives: studies in English thought and society in honour of J. H. Plumb*, Europe Publications.

Sweezy, P. 1938: *Monopoly and competition in the English coal trade 1550–1850*. Harvard University Press.

E. T. (ed.) 1918: *Keeling letters and recollections*, with an introduction by H. G. Wells. Allen and Unwin.

Taylor, A. J. 1972: *Laissez-faire and state intervention in nineteenth-century Britain*. Macmillan.

 1975: *The standard of living in Britain in the industrial revolution*. Methuen.

Taylor, G. 1969: *The problems of poverty 1660–1834*. Longman.

Taylor, I., Walton, P. and Young, J. 1975: Critical criminology in Britain: review and prospects. In *Critical Criminology*, Routledge.

Taylor, J. S. 1969: The mythology of the Old Poor Law. *Economic History Review* 29.

 1972: The unreformed workhouse 1776–1834. In Martin (1972).

 1976: The impact of pauper settlement 1691–1834. *Past and Present* 73.

Thomas, K. 1971: *Religion and the decline of magic*, Weidenfeld, reprinted Penguin (1973).

Thompson, E. P. 1963: *The Making of the English working class.* Gollancz.

1965: Peculiarities of the English. *Socialist Register.*

1967: Time, work-discipline and industrial capitalism. *Past and Present* 38, reprinted Smout (1974) ch. 3.

1968: Postscript to Penguin edn of Thompson (1963).

1971: Moral economy of the English crowd in the eighteenth century. *Past and Present* 50.

1972: Eighteenth-century crime. *Bulletin of the Society for the Study of Labour History* 25.

1975: *Whigs and hunters.* Allen Lane.

1977: Common rights and enclosures. In his *Customs in Common*, Merlin Press.

Tilly, C. 1975: *The formation of national states in western Europe.* Princeton University Press.

Tillyard, E. M. W. 1943: *The Elizabethan world picture.* Penguin (1963).

Titmuss, R. M. 1958: The social division of welfare in *Essays on the welfare state*, 1st edn, ch. 2, Allen and Unwin.

1963: The irresponsible society. In *Essays on the welfare state*, 2nd edn, ch. 11, Allen and Unwin.

1968: *Commitment to welfare.* Allen and Unwin.

1971: *The gift relationship: from human blood to social policy.* Allen and Unwin.

Townsend, P. 1962: *The last refuge.* Routledge.

1963: *The family life of old people: an inquiry into east London.* Penguin.

1975: *Sociology and social policy.* Allen Lane.

Townshend, Mrs 1911: *The case against the COS.* Fabian Tract 158.

Treble, J. H. 1970: The attitudes of the Friendly Societies towards the movement in Great Britain for state pensions, 1878–1958. *International Review of Social History* 15, 266–99.

Tucker, G. L. S. 1975: The old poor law revisited. *Explorations in Economic History* 12.

Turner, J. 1977: Social work privateers. *New Society* 17 November.

Turner, R. H. 1969: The theme of contemporary social movements. *British Journal of Sociology* 20 (4 December).

Urwick, E. J. 1904: A school of sociology. In Loch (1904).

Walter, J. and Wrightson, K. 1976: Dearth and the social order in early Modern England. *Past and Present* 71.

Walton, R. G. 1975: *Women in social work.* Routledge.

Ward, J. T. 1970: *Popular movements, c. 1830–1850.* Macmillan.

Watkin, D. 1975: *Documents on health and social security: 1834 to the present day.* Methuen.

Webb, B. 1926: *My apprenticeship.* Longmans.

1948: *Our partnership.* Longmans.

Webb, S. 1890: *Reform of the poor law.* Longmans.

1890: The Reform of the Poor Law. *Contemporary Review* 58.

Webb, S. and Webb, B. 1909a: *The break-up of the poor law.* Longmans.

1909b: *The public organization of the labour market.* Longmans.

1910: *English poor law policy.* Longmans.

1911: *The prevention of destitution.* Longmans.

1929a: *English poor law history, part I.* Longmans.

1929b: *English poor law history, part II.* 2 vols, Longmans.

Weber, M. 1918: Politics as a calling. In his *From Max Weber,* Routledge (1948).

1920: *Lectures on economic history.* New York: Collier Macmillan (1961).

1972: The 'Rationalization' of education and training. In Cosin, B. R., *Education: structure and society,* Penguin.

White, R. J. 1957: *Waterloo to Peterloo.* Reprinted Penguin (1963).

Wilkins, L. 1967: *Social policy, action and research.* Tavistock.

Williams, R. 1958: *Culture and society: 1780–1950.* Chatto.

Winter, J. M. 1974: *Socialism and the challenge of war: ideas and politics in Britain 1912–1918.* Routledge.

Wilson, D. 1974: Uneasy bedfellows. *Social Work Today* 5, 9–12.

Wilson, E. 1977: *Women and the welfare state.* Tavistock.

Wilson, R. 1949: Aims and methods of a department of social studies. *Social Work* 6.

Wolfenden (chairman) 1978: *Report on the future of voluntary organizations.* Croom Helm.

Woodward, C. 1961: The COS and its place in history. *Social Work* 18.

Wootton, B. 1959a: Daddy knows best. *The Twentieth Century* 166, 248–61.

1959b: *Social science and social pathology.* Allen and Unwin.

Wright, R. 1977: *Expectations of the teaching of social workers in courses leading to the certificate of Qualification in Social Work.* Consultation document no. 3, CCETSW.

Young, A. F. and Ashton, E. T. 1956: *British social work in the nineteenth century.* Routledge.

Young, J. 1971: The role of the police as amplifiers of deviancy. In Cohens, S. (ed.), *Images of deviance,* Penguin.

Young, M. and Willmott, P. 1957: *Family and kinship in east London.* Routledge.

1973: *The symmetrical family.* Routledge.

Younghusband, E. 1947/51: *Report on the employment and training of social workers.* Edinburgh: T. A. Constable.

1964: *Social work and social change.* Allen and Unwin.

Younghusband (chairman) 1959: *Report of the working party on social workers in the local authority health and welfare services.* HMSO.

Younghusband, E. (ed.) 1965: *Social work with families: readings in social work,* Allen and Unwin.

1966: *New developments in casework: readings in social work.* Allen and Unwin.

1967: *Social work and social values.* Allen and Unwin.

Zweig, S. 1961: *The worker in an affluent society.* Heinemann.

Notes on contributors

John Clarke studied at the University of Aston and the Centre for Contemporary Cultural Studies, University of Birmingham. Currently he lectures in sociology at the North East London Polytechnic. He is co-author of *Policing the Crisis; Mugging, the State, and Law'n'Order* (Macmillan, 1978), and author of several articles.

Philip Corrigan studied in London and Durham and is a chartered librarian. He was SSRC Senior Research Fellow at Durham University, lecturer in sociology at North East London Polytechnic and is currently principal lecturer in complementary studies at the London College of Printing. He has edited various volumes and is co-author with Derek Sayer and Harvie Ramsay of *Socialist Construction and Marxist Theory*, and *For Mao* (Macmillan 1978 and 1979). He has written numerous articles and pamphlets.

Val Corrigan BA, ALA, is a librarian working on a post-graduate thesis on the New Poor Law. She has published work on the history of libraries and on the provincial press and radical movements in the early nineteenth century.

Chris Jones followed a four year social science degree which included CQSW at the Middlesex Polytechnic. He then went on to Durham University where he undertook his PhD research on the development of social work and social work education in Britain from the mid-nineteenth century until the present day. On completing his research he practised social work at the Bishop Auckland Family Service Unit before moving to Preston Polytechnic as a lecturer in social policy. He is currently a member of the editorial collective of the *Bulletin on Social Policy*, a broadsheet concerned with developing a socialist critique of social welfare.

José Parry graduated at Leeds University and has been a researcher at the Department of Applied Economics, Cambridge, the Hatfield Polytechnic and North East London Polytechic. She is currently employed on the Gulbenkian study of the economic situation of the visual artist at Goldsmiths' College.

Noel Parry studied at Regent Street Polytechnic (now the Polytechnic of Central London) and at the London School of Economics. He has lectured at the University of Leeds, the Hatfield Polytechnic and North East London Polytechnic. He is currently Head of Department of Sociology at the Polytechnic of North London. He has written with José Parry, *The Rise of the Medical Profession, a study of Collective Social Mobility* (Croom Helm, 1976) as well as making contributions to published volumes and periodicals. He has also undertaken several funded research projects for local government and the SSRC. Currently he is researching in the areas of leisure and public policy and employment in the National Health Service.

Michael Rustin read PPE at Oxford and was subsequently at the London School of Economics. He has taught since 1964 at North East London Polytechnic where he is currently Head of Department of Sociology. He has published several articles and is author of *Sociology as a Profession.* (SIP Papers no. 1, 1976.) He was a founder member of SIP and has served as its president.

Carole Satyamurti graduated from the University of London in 1960. Following graduate work in sociology in the United States, she taught in the Extra-Mural Studies Department of the University of Singapore. She then did a professional training in social work at the University of Birmingham. She has worked as a child-care officer and as a psychiatric social worker, and also worked for the Save The Children Fund in Uganda. In 1968 she joined the sociology department of what is now North East London Polytechnic where she is a principal lecturer. She recently completed a full-length study of local authority social workers, the fieldwork for which was carried out at the time of Seebohm reorganization.

Clive Unsworth holds a lectureship in law at University College, Cardiff, where his teaching includes the sociology of law. He completed a degree in law at Brasenose College, Oxford in 1974, and then studied for three years at the SSRC Centre for Socio-Legal Studies, Wolfson College, Oxford for the degree of D Phil. The research he commenced there, on the historical and social origins of the Mental Health Act, 1959, is still in progress.

Stephen Yeo teaches history at the University of Sussex. He has written *Religion and Voluntary Organizations in Crisis* (Croom Helm, 1976); 'A New Life; the Religion of Socialism in Britain 1883–1896' in *History Workshop* 4 (1977); 'On the Uses of Apathy' in *European Journal of Sociology* XV (1974); and many other articles. He edits a social history series for Croom Helm. Currently, he is working on Co-ops, Friendly Societies, Working Men's Clubs, Educational Associations and other such working-class forms.

Index